☆☆☆ Forbes

TRAVEL GUIDE

Formerly Mobil Travel Guide

SOUTHERN GREAT

LAKES

ACKNOWLEDGMENTS

We gratefully acknowledge the help of our representatives for their efficient and perceptive inspections of the lodgings listed. Forbes Travel Guide is also grateful to the talented writers who contributed to this book.

2

3 9082 11435 7950

ISBN: 9-780841-61427-7   Manufactured in the USA

10 9 8 7 6 5 4 3 2 1

TABLE OF CONTENTS

STAR ATTRACTIONS

If you've been a reader of Mobil Travel Guide, you will have heard that this historic brand partnered with another storied media name, Forbes, in 2009 to create a new entity, Forbes Travel Guide. For more than 50 years, Mobil Travel Guide assisted travelers in making smart decisions about where to stay and dine when traveling. With this new partnership, our mission has not changed: We're committed to the same rigorous inspections of hotels, restaurants and spas—the most comprehensive in the industry with more than 500 standards tested at each property we visit—to help you cut through the clutter and make easy and informed decisions on where to spend your time and travel budget. Our team of anonymous inspectors are constantly on the road, sleeping in hotels, eating in restaurants and making spa appointments, evaluating those exacting standards to determine a property's rating.

What kind of standards are we looking for when we visit a proprety? We're looking for more than just high-thread count sheets, pristine spa treatment rooms and white linen-topped tables. We look for service that's attentive, individualized and unforgettable. We note how long it takes to be greeted when you sit down at your table, or to be served when you order room service, or whether the hotel staff can confidently help you when you've forgotten that one essential item that will make or break your trip. Unlike other travel ratings entities, we visit the places we rate, testing hundreds of attributes to compile our ratings, and our ratings cannot be bought or influenced. The Forbes Five Star rating is the most prestigious achievement in hospitality—while we rate more than 8,000 properties in the U.S., Canada, Hong Kong, Macau and Beijing, for 2010, we have awarded Five Star designations to only 53 hotels, 21 restaurants and 18 spas. When you travel with Forbes, you can travel with confidence, knowing that you'll get the very best experience, no matter who you are.

We understand the importance of making the most of your time. That's why the most trusted name in travel is now Forbes Travel Guide.

STAR RATED HOTELS

Whether you're looking for the ultimate in luxury or the best value for your travel budget, we have a hotel recommendation for you. To help you pinpoint properties that meet your needs, Forbes Travel Guide classifies each lodging by type according to the following characteristics:

★★★★★These exceptional properties provide a memorable experience through virtually flawless service and the finest of amenities. Staff are intuitive, engaging and passionate, and eagerly deliver service above and beyond the guests' expectations. The hotel was designed with the guest's comfort in mind, with particular attention paid to craftsmanship and quality of product. A Five Star property is a destination unto itself.

★★★★These properties provide a distinctive setting, and a guest will find many interesting and inviting elements to enjoy throughout the property. Attention to detail is prominent throughout the property, from design concept to quality of products provided. Staff are accommodating and take pride in catering to the guest's specific needs throughout their stay.

★★★These well-appointed establishments have enhanced amenities that provide travelers with a strong sense of location, whether for style or function. They may have a distinguishing style and ambience in both the public spaces and guest rooms; or they may be more focused on functionality, providing guests with easy access to local events, meetings or tourism highlights.

★★The Two Star hotel is considered a clean, comfortable and reliable establishment that has expanded amenities, such as a full-service restaurant.

★The One Star lodging is a limited-service hotel or inn that is considered a clean, comfortable and reliable establishment.

For every property, we also provide pricing information. All prices quoted are accurate at the time of publication; however, prices cannot be guaranteed.

STAR RATED RESTAURANTS

Every restaurant in this book comes highly recommended as an outstanding dining experience.

★★★★★Forbes Five Star restaurants deliver a truly unique and distinctive dining experience. A Five Star restaurant consistently provides exceptional food, superlative service and elegant décor. An emphasis is placed on originality and personalized, attentive and discreet service. Every detail that surrounds the experience is attended to by a warm and gracious dining room team.

★★★★These are exciting restaurants with often well-known chefs that feature creative and complex foods and emphasize various culinary techniques and a focus on seasonality. A highly-trained dining room staff provides refined personal service and attention.

★★★Three Star restaurants offer skillfully-prepared food with a focus on a specific style or cuisine. The dining room staff provides warm and professional service in a comfortable atmosphere. The décor is well-coordinated with quality fixtures and decorative items, and promotes a comfortable ambience.

★★The Two Star restaurant serves fresh food in a clean setting with efficient service. Value is considered in this category, as is family friendliness.

★The One Star restaurant provides a distinctive experience through culinary specialty, local flair or individual atmosphere.

Because menu prices can fluctuate, we list a pricing range rather than specific prices. The pricing ranges are per diner, and assume that you order an appetizer or dessert, an entrée and one drink.

STAR RATED SPAS

Forbes Travel Guide's spa ratings are based on objective evaluations of more than 450 attributes. About half of these criteria assess basic expectations, such as staff courtesy, the technical proficiency and skill of the employees and whether the facility is clean and maintained properly. Several standards address issues that impact a guest's physical comfort and convenience, as well as the staff's ability to impart a sense of personalized service. Additional criteria measure the spa's ability to create a completely calming ambience.

★★★★★Stepping foot in a Five Star spa will result in an exceptional experience with no detail overlooked. These properties wow their guests with extraordinary design and facilities, and uncompromising service. Expert staff cater to your every whim and pamper you with the most advanced treatments and skin care lines available. These spas often offer exclusive treatments and may emphasize local elements.

★★★★Four Star spas provide a wonderful experience in an inviting and serene environment. A sense of personalized service is evident from the moment you check in and receive your robe and slippers. The guest's comfort is always of utmost concern to the well-trained staff.

★★★These spas offer well-appointed facilities with a full complement of staff to ensure that guests' needs are met. The spa facilities include clean and appealing treatment rooms, changing areas and a welcoming reception desk.

ILLINOIS

WHERE DO YOU START IN ILLINOIS? WITH AN URBAN ADVENTURE BENEATH TOWERING SKY-scrapers in Chicago? Or by ambling the charming streets of the state's touristy towns? No matter which road you follow, you'll find an ideal getaway.

If you do start in Chicago, you'll be busy. With its famed architecture, legendary blues and jazz scenes and world-renowned museums like the Art Institute and the John G. Shedd Aquarium, Chicago is celebrated for its thriving cultural scene almost as much as its culinary classics: hot dogs and deep-dish pizzas.

When you're in Chicago, you'll want to experience the city like native Chicagoans do. That means catching a Cubs game at Wrigley Field, strolling Millennium Park, taking an architectural boat cruise on the Chicago River or twirling with the kids on Navy Pier's Ferris wheel.

If the only sights you're interested in seeing are designer labels, make Michigan Avenue your first stop. The mile-long stretch isn't named the "Magnificent Mile" for nothing. Highlighted by the seven-level Water Tower Place and big-name stores like Gucci, Chanel and Hugo Boss, the avenue is among the world's most cosmopolitan shopping districts. And if you really feel like splurging, check out the high-end boutiques on Oak Street, just a step away from Michigan Avenue.

Even die-hard urbanites need a break from the city. If you're starved for nature, take a breather at Utica's Starved Rock State Park, featuring sandstone canyons, gushing waterfalls and miles of hiking trails. Or stop at the 8,000-acre Pere Marquette State Park—Illinois' largest—known for its 20-mile scenic bike trail and towering limestone cliffs.

Love golf? Have fun at southern Illinois' Rend Lake. The 18,000-acre manmade reservoir in Wayne Fitzgerrell State Recreation Area is popular with fishermen and boaters, but the Rend Lake Golf Course is an even bigger draw. The 27-hole championship course is considered one of the best in the Midwest.

For a more historic look at Illinois, take the family to Springfield and tip your hat to the 16th president at the Abraham Lincoln Presidential Library and Museum. Or drive toward the Illinois-Iowa border to Galena, an old lead-mining town known for its historic 19th century architecture, gorgeous vistas and boating trips down the Mississippi and Galena rivers.

ALGONQUIN

See also Barrington, Crystal Lake
Before it was founded in 1834, this area was home to the Potawatomi Indians. With the introduction of the railroad in 1855, Algonquin grew and became a popular summer destination for Chicagoans.

WHERE TO EAT
★★PORT EDWARD
20 W. Algonquin Road, Algonquin, 847-658-5441; www.portedward.com
Seafood. Lunch, dinner, Sunday brunch. Children's menu. Bar. $16-35

ALTON

See also Collinsville, Père Marquette State Park

Located on the bluffs above the confluence of the Illinois, Mississippi and Missouri rivers, Alton is rich in history. In 1837 Elijah Lovejoy, the abolitionist editor, died here protecting his press from a proslavery mob. Young Abraham Lincoln dueled on a sandbar in the river and later debated Stephen Douglas in Alton in 1858. Alton was also the home of Robert Wadlow, the tallest man in history. The "Gentle Giant" is celebrated with a life-size nine-foot statue on College Avenue.

WHAT TO SEE
ALTON MUSEUM OF HISTORY AND ART

2809 College Ave., Alton, 618-462-2763; www.altonmuseum.com

Founded in 1971, the Museum is in Loomis Hall, the oldest building in Illinois. There are displays on local history and culture, including an exhibit on Alton's Robert Wadlow.

Wednesday-Saturday 10 a.m.-4 p.m., Sunday 1-4 p.m.

BRUSSELS FERRY

16211 State Highway 100 W., near Grafton, 618-786-3636

This ferry navigates the Illinois River where it meets the Mississippi River.

WHERE TO STAY
★★HOLIDAY INN

3800 Homer Adams Parkway, Grafton, 618-462-1220, 800-655-4669;
www.holiday-inn.com

137 rooms. Restaurant, bar. Business center. Fitness center. Pool. Pets accepted. $61-150

ANTIOCH

See also Gurnee, Waukegan

Founded prior to the Civil War, this village became a popular summer destination for Chicagoans in the 1890s. One famous summer resident was Al Capone. Most of the town was destroyed by fire in 1904, but it was rebuilt and has grown steadily since.

WHAT TO SEE
CHAIN O' LAKES AREA

This year-round recreational facility offers boating, fishing, ice fishing, cross-country skiing and snowmobiling.

WHERE TO STAY
★BEST WESTERN REGENCY INN

350 Highway 173, Antioch, 847-395-3606, 800-780-7234; www.comfortinn.com

68 rooms. Complimentary breakfast. Bar. Pool. Pets accepted. $61-150

ARLINGTON HEIGHTS

Chicago O'Hare Airport, Schaumburg, Wheeling

Twenty-five miles northwest of Chicago, Arlington Heights possesses numerous public parks, tree-lined neighborhoods and a thriving downtown with an eclectic mix of shops and restaurants. The village may be best known for Arlington Park, where the Arlington Million thoroughbred race is held annually in August.

WHAT TO SEE
ARLINGTON PARK

2200 W. Euclid, Arlington Park, 847-385-7500; www.arlingtonpark.com

From mid-May to mid-September, you can spend a day at the races here and bet on your favorite horse. Tours of the park and its 1 1/8-mile track are offered Saturday and Sunday; register at the Clubhouse Information Booth. Crafts for children in Arlington Craft Stable are offered most weekends.

KEMPER LAKES GOLF CLUB

24000 N. Old McHenry Road, Kideer, 847-320-3450; www.kemperlakesgolf.com

A regular host of PGA events in the Chicago area is Kemper Lakes, which was the site of the 1989 PGA Championship as well as several Champions Tour and LPGA events. Located in Long Grove, northwest of the city, the course plays 7,217 yards long, a challenging length for almost any golfer. The greens fee may be steep, but with the course's twilight rates you can save a bundle. Its state-of-the-art global positioning system helps players judge the yardage to a given hole from any golf cart.

LONG GROVE CONFECTIONARY COMPANY

333 Lexington Drive, Buffalo Grove, 800-373-3102, 888-459-3100; www.longgrove.com

Take a tour of this family-owned confectionery, which produces more than 300 sweet treats. Learn how the chocolates are made, sample the products and then purchase discounted goodies from the outlet store.

Store: Monday-Saturday 9:30 a.m.-5:30 p.m., Sunday 11 a.m.-4 p.m. Tours: Monday-Thursday 9 a.m., 11 a.m., noon, 1 p.m., other times by appointment; reservations are required.

WHERE TO EAT
★★★LE TITI DE PARIS

1015 W. Dundee Road, Arlington Heights, 847-506-0222; www.letitideparis.com

The wine list at this French restaurant has more than 800 selections. chefs Pierre Pollin and Michael Maddox serve innovative cuisine with nearly impeccable service. Save room for one of the creatively presented desserts.

French. Dinner. Closed Monday. Reservations recommended. Outdoor seating. Bar. $36-85

★★PALM COURT

1912 N. Arlington Heights Road, Arlington Heights, 847-870-7770; www.palmcourt.net

American. Lunch (Monday-Friday), dinner. Reservations recommended. Children's menu. Bar. $16-35

AURORA

See also DeKalb, Geneva, Joliet, Naperville, St. Charles

Potawatomi chief Waubonsie and his tribe inhabited this area on the Fox River when pioneers arrived from the East in the 1830s. Waterpower and fertile lands attracted more settlers. Today, the city prospers because of its location along a high-tech -corridor.

WHAT TO SEE
AURORA ART & HISTORY CENTER

20 E. Downer Place, Aurora, 630-906-0650; www.aurorahistoricalsociety.org

In the restored Ginsberg building, this museum contains displays of 19th-century life, a collection of mastodon bones, a history center and research library and public art displays.

Wednesday-Sunday noon-4 p.m.

BLACKBERRY FARM'S PIONEER VILLAGE

100 S. Barnes Road, Aurora, 630-892-1550; www.foxvalleyparkdistrict.org

This rural spot has an 1840s-1920s living history museum and working farm. Exhibits include a children's animal farm, discovery barn and train. There are also craft demonstrations, wagon and pony rides and a farm play area.

Early April-August, Monday-Friday 9:30 a.m.-3:30 p.m.; September-early October, Friday-Sunday.

CHICAGO PREMIUM OUTLETS

1650 Premium Outlets Blvd., Aurora, 630-585-2200; www.premiumoutlets.com/chicago

This outlet mall has approximately 120 stores, including staples like Gap and Nike, as well as upscale brands like Versace and Giorgio Armani.

Monday-Saturday 10 a.m.-9 p.m., Sunday 10 a.m.-6 p.m.

PARAMOUNT ARTS CENTRE

23 E. Galena Blvd., Aurora, 630-896-6666; www.paramountarts.com

This theater was built in 1931 to compete with the opulent movie palaces of the area. It has been restored to its original appearance and stages a variety of productions throughout the year.

Tours: Monday-Friday. Reservations recommended.

SCHINGOETHE CENTER FOR NATIVE AMERICAN CULTURES

347 S. Gladstone Ave., Aurora, 630-892-6431; www.aurora.edu/museum

At Aurora University, this private collection contains thousands of Native American artifacts, including jewelry, textiles, pottery and baskets.

Tuesday-Friday 10 a.m.-4 p.m., Sunday 1-4 p.m. (during the academic year). Closed August.

SCITECH-SCIENCE HANDS-ON MUSEUM

18 W. Benton, Aurora, 630-859-3434; www.scitech.mus.il.us

Housed in a historic post office building, this interactive center provides more than 150 hands-on learning exhibits using motion, light, sound and science principles.

June-August, Monday-Saturday 10 a.m.-5 p.m., Sunday noon-5 p.m.; September-May, Monday-Tuesday 10 a.m.-2 p.m., Wednesday, Friday-Sunday, until 5 p.m., Thursday until 8 p.m., Sunday noon-5 p.m.

WHERE TO STAY
★COMFORT INN
111 N. Broadway, Aurora, 630-896-2800; www.comfortinn.com
95 rooms. Complimentary breakfast. Business center. Fitness center. Pool. $151-250

WHERE TO EAT
★★WALTER PAYTON'S ROUNDHOUSE
205 N. Broadway Ave., Aurora, 630-264-2739; www.walterpaytonsroundhouse.com
American. Lunch, dinner. Reservations recommended. Outdoor seating. Children's menu. Bar. $16-35

BELLEVILLE
See also Collinsville
Named Belleville by its early French settlers, this city is now populated by people of German descent. Belleville is the headquarters of Scott Air Force Base.

WHERE TO STAY
★HAMPTON INN
150 Ludwig Drive, Fairview Heights, 618-397-9705, 800-426-7866;
www.hamptoninn.com
62 rooms. Complimentary breakfast. Pool. $61-150

★★RAMADA INN
6900 N. Illinois, Fairview Heights, 618-632-4747, 800-272-6232;
www.ramadafairviewheights.com
158 rooms. Restaurant, bar. Fitness center. Pool. Pets accepted. $61-150

WHERE TO EAT
★★FISCHER'S
2100 W. Main St., Belleville, 618-233-1131; www.fischersrestaurant.com
American. Breakfast, lunch, dinner. Children's menu. Bar. $16-35

BLOOMINGTON
See also Peoria
The Illinois Republican Party was formed here in 1856 at the Anti-Nebraska convention, where Abraham Lincoln made the famous "lost speech" spelling out the principles that helped win him the presidency. Bloomington was also the home of Adlai E. Stevenson, vice president under Grover Cleveland. His grandson, Illinois Governor Adlai E. Stevenson II, U.S. Ambassador to the United Nations and twice a Democratic candidate for president, is buried here. The founding of Illinois Wesleyan University and the selection of North Bloomington (now its twin city of Normal) as the site for Illinois State University helped determine the town's economic future.

WHAT TO SEE
ILLINOIS STATE UNIVERSITY
220 N. Main St., Normal, 309-438-7000; www.ilstu.edu
The first state university in Illinois founded in 1857 now has 22,000 students.
Also on campus is the Adlai E. Stevenson Memorial Room (309-438-5669),
which houses personal memorabilia, photographs.
Monday-Friday.

MILLER PARK ZOO
1020 S. Morris, Bloomington, 309-434-2250; www.millerparkzoo.org
This zoo has big cats, river otters in natural settings, sea lions, a tropical rain
forest and a children's zoo. Other activities include swimming, fishing, boating, picnicking, tennis and miniature golf. Band concerts are held in season.
Daily 9:30 a.m.-4:30 p.m.

SPECIAL EVENT
ILLINOIS SHAKESPEARE FESTIVAL
Ewing Manor, Normal, Emerson and Towanda streets, 309-438-8974;
www.thefestival.org
This festival includes Shakespearean performances preceded by Elizabethan-
era music and entertainment.
June-early August.

WHERE TO STAY
★BEST WESTERN UNIVERSITY INN
6 Traders Circle, Normal, 309-454-4070, 800-780-7234; www.bestwestern.com
101 rooms. Complimentary breakfast. Fitness center. Pool. Pets accepted.
$61-150

★★★THE CHATEAU HOTEL AND CONFERENCE CENTER
1601 Jumer Drive, Bloomington, 309-662-2020, 866-690-4006; www.chateauhotel.biz
This hotel is located near Illinois State University and has an indoor pool, sauna
and whirlpool. Dining is made easy with an onsite restaurant and lounge.
180 rooms. Restaurant, bar. Fitness center. Pool. Pets accepted. $61-150

★EASTLAND SUITES LODGE
1801 Eastland Drive, Bloomington, 309-662-0000, 800-537-8483;
www.eastlandsuitesbloomington.com
112 rooms. Complimentary breakfast. Fitness center. Pool. Pets accepted.
$61-150

★HAMPTON INN
604 1/2 IAA Drive, Bloomington, 309-662-2800; www.hamptoninn.com
129 rooms. Complimentary breakfast. Pool. Pets accepted. $61-150

★★HOLIDAY INN
8 Traders Circle, Normal, 309-452-8300, 800-465-4329; www.holiday-inn.com
160 rooms. Restaurant, bar. Complimentary breakfast. Business center. Fitness center. Pool. Pets accepted. $61-150

WHERE TO EAT
★★CENTRAL STATION CAFE
220 E. Front St., Bloomington, 309-828-2323; www.centralstation.cc
American. Lunch, dinner. Closed Sunday-Monday. Reservations recommended. Bar. $16-35

CARBONDALE
See also Marion
Carbondale is surrounded by lakes and rivers, including Crab Orchard and Little Grassy Lakes and the Big Muddy River. Railroad yards, Southern Illinois University and surrounding coal fields give this community a unique personality.

WHAT TO SEE
BALD KNOB
3630 Bald Knob Road, Alto Pass, 618-893-2344
View three states from this high point in the Illinois Ozarks.

GIANT CITY STATE PARK
235 Giant City Road, Makanda, 618-457-4836; www.dnr.state.il.us
The park has picturesque rock formations and a prehistoric "stone fort" on 4,055 acres. Fishing, hunting, hiking and riding trails are available as well as picnicking, concession, lodge and dining room. Camping is permitted. Daily.

GOLCONDA MARINA AND SMITHLAND POOL
R.R. 2, Golconda, 618-683-5875; www.golcondamarina.com
This marina is the gateway to Smithland Pool, a 23,000-acre recreational area off the Ohio River.

WHERE TO STAY
★BEST INN
1345 E. Main St., Carbondale, 618-529-4801, 800-237-8466;
www.americasbestinn.com
82 rooms. Complimentary breakfast. Pool. $61-150

★★★MANSION OF GOLCONDA
222 Columbus St., Golconda, 618-683-4400
4 rooms. Built in 1894, this gabled 21-room Victorian mansion is a full-service inn included on the National Historic Register. $61-150

★SUPER 8
1180 E. Main St., Carbondale, 618-457-8822, 800-800-8000; www.super8.com
63 rooms. Complimentary breakfast. Pets accepted. $61-150

WHERE TO EAT
★★MANSION OF GOLCONDA
515 Columbus, Golconda; 618-683-4400
American. Lunch, dinner. Closed Monday. $16-35

★TRES HOMBRES
119 N. Washington St., Carbondale, 618-457-3308
Mexican. Lunch, dinner. Bar. $15 and under

CHAMPAIGN/URBANA
See also Arcola
Champaign and Urbana, separately incorporated, are united as the home of
the University of Illinois. Champaign started as West Urbana when the Illinois Central Railroad ran its line two miles west of Urbana, the county seat.
Defying annexation by Urbana in 1855, the new community was incorporated in 1860 as Champaign and prospered as a trade center. Today, the two
communities are geographically one; Champaign continues as a commercial
and industrial center, with the larger part of the university falling within the
boundaries of Urbana.

WHAT TO SEE
LAKE OF THE WOODS COUNTY PRESERVE
109 S. Lake of the Woods Road, Mahomet, 217-586-3360
This preserve offers swimming, boating rentals, fishing and golf. The Early
American Museum and botanical gardens is located here.
June-August, daily; September-early October, Saturday-Sunday. Daily.

ORPHEUM CHILDREN'S SCIENCE MUSEUM
346 N. Neil St., Champaign/Urbana, 217-352-5895; www.m-crossroads.org
Located in the historic Orpheum Theatre, this museum has hands-on exhibits
for kids.
Wednesday-Sunday 1-6 p.m., Tuesday 9 a.m.-6 p.m.

UNIVERSITY OF ILLINOIS
919 W. Illinois St., Champaign/Urbana, 217-333-4666; www.uiuc.edu
Founded in 1867, the University of Illinois now has a student population
of more than 42,000 students. Included among the 200 major buildings on
campus is the main library, which is the third-largest academic library in
the United States. Also on campus is the Krannert Art Museum, which has
a collection of 8,000 works including European and American paintings and
decorative arts, as well as Asian art and African art.

WHERE TO STAY
★BEST WESTERN PARADISE INN
709 N. Dunlap St., Savoy, 217-356-1824, 800-780-7234; www.bestwestern.com
62 rooms. Complimentary breakfast. Pool. Pets accepted. $61-150

★COMFORT INN
305 W. Marketview Drive, Urbana, 217-352-4055, 800-228-5150; www.comfortinn.com
67 rooms. Complimentary breakfast. Pool. $61-150

★EASTLAND SUITES

1907 N. Cunningham Ave., Urbana, 217-367-8331, 800-253-8331;
www.eastlandsuitesurbana.com

127 rooms. Complimentary breakfast. Bar. Fitness center. Pool. Pets accepted. $61-150

★★HISTORIC LINCOLN HOTEL

209 S. Broadway, Urbana, 217-384-8800; www.historiclincolnhotel.com

130 rooms. Restaurant, bar. Pool. Pets accepted. $61-150

★LA QUINTA INN

1900 Center Drive, Champaign, 217-356-4000, 800-509-5507; www.laquinta.com

122 rooms. Complimentary breakfast. Pool. Pets accepted. $61-150

WHERE TO EAT
★NED KELLY'S

1601 N. Cunningham Ave., Urbana, 217-344-8201

Steak. Lunch, dinner. Children's menu. Bar. $16-35

★★TIMPONE'S

710 S. Goodwin Ave., Urbana, 217-344-7619; www.timpones-urbana.com

Italian, American. Lunch, dinner. Closed Sunday. Reservations recommended. Bar. $16-35

CHARLESTON

See also Arcola, Mattoon

One of the great Lincoln-Douglas debates was held here on September 18, 1858. As an itinerate lawyer riding the circuit, Abraham Lincoln practiced law in the area. His father, Thomas Lincoln, and stepmother once lived in a cabin eight miles south of Charleston.

WHAT TO SEE
COLES COUNTY COURTHOUSE

651 Jackson Ave., Charleston, 217-348-0501

This courthouse sits on Charleston Square, where Lincoln practiced law in an earlier courthouse and where the Charleston Riot took place. The Riot involved 300 men in armed conflict during the Civil War.

FOX RIDGE STATE PARK

18175 State Park Road, Charleston, 217-345-6416; www.dnr.state.il.us

This is a rugged area of 1,500 acres including Ridge Lake and is maintained by the Illinois Natural History Survey.

LINCOLN LOG CABIN STATE HISTORIC SITE

400 S. Lincoln Highway Road, Lerna, 217-345-1845

This 86-acre site contains the Thomas Lincoln Log Cabin, reconstructed on the original foundation that Abraham Lincoln's father built in 1840. A reconstructed farm surrounds the cabin. In nearby Shiloh Cemetery are the graves of Thomas Lincoln and Sarah Bush Lincoln, the president's father and stepmother. Interpretive program offered as well as picnicking. May-October, Wednesday-Sunday.

WHERE TO STAY
★★BEST WESTERN WORTHINGTON INN
920 W. Lincoln Ave., Charleston, 217-348-8161, 800-528-8161; www.bestwestern.com
67 rooms. Complimentary breakfast. Restaurant. Pool. Pets accepted. $61-150

WHERE TO EAT
★★ALLIES AMERICAN GRILLE
200 Lee St. East, Charleston, 304-345-6500, 800-228-9290;
www.charlestonmarriott.com
American. Breakfast, lunch, dinner, late-night. Reservations recommended. Children's menu. $16-35

★★ATHLETIC CLUB GRILL
300 Court St., Charleston, 304-347-8700, 800-362-2779;
www.embassysuitescharlestonwv.com
American. Lunch, dinner. Children's menu. Bar. $16-35

CHICAGO
See also Chicago O'Hare Airport, Evanston, Highland Park
Rudyard Kipling wrote of Chicago, "I have struck a city, a real city and they call it Chicago." The city is thriving, with a vibrant downtown, growing population, booming industry and world-class dining and entertainment. Wicked winter weather aside, the Windy City is one of the country's top tourist destinations.

Chicago's past is distinctive, built on adversity and contradiction. Its worst tragedy, the Great Chicago Fire of 1871, was the basis for its physical and cultural renaissance. In the heart of one of the poorest neighborhoods, two young women of means, Jane Addams and Ellen Gates Starr, created Hull House, a social-service institution that has been copied throughout the world. A city of neat frame cottages and bulky stone mansions, it produced the Chicago School of Architecture, whose innovative style was carried on by Frank Lloyd Wright and Ludwig Mies van der Rohe. Even its most famous crooks provide a study in contrasts: Al Capone was one of Prohibition's most famous gangsters, while Samuel Insull was a financial finagler whose stock manipulations left thousands of small investors penniless in the late 1920s.

In 1803, the fledging U.S. government took possession of the area and sent a small military contingent from Detroit to select the site for a fort. Fort Dearborn was built at a strategic spot on the mouth of the Chicago River; on the opposite bank, a settlement slowly grew. There was little activity until Chicago was selected as the terminal site of the proposed Illinois and Michigan Canal. This started a land boom that carries on today.

Chicagoans are proud of their world-famous symphony orchestra, Lyric Opera and numerous and diverse dance companies. Chicago's theater community is vibrant, with more than 100 theaters. The collections at the Art Institute of Chicago, Museum of Contemporary Art and galleries in the River North area are among the best in the country. The 1996 expansion of Lake

Shore Drive made it possible to create the Museum Campus. This 57-acre extension of Burnham Park provides an easier and more scenic route to the Adler Planetarium, Field Museum and Shedd Aquarium, and surrounds them with one continuous park featuring terraced gardens and broad walkways. No visit to Chicago is complete without touring Millennium Park. This downtown park area includes the Harris Theater for Music and Dance, the 50-foot-high water-spewing towers of the Crown Fountain, the Frank Gehry-designed band shell and bridge, and the Cloud Gate sculpture, which locals lovingly call "the bean."

WHAT TO SEE AND DO
ADLER PLANETARIUM AND ASTRONOMY MUSEUM
1300 S. Lake Shore Drive, Chicago, 312-322-0300; www.adlerplanetarium.org
One of the oldest observatories in the country, the Adler Planetarium offers a high-tech look at the night sky. Exhibits commemorate the Space Race of the 1960s, as well as new techniques to learn more about the Milky Way. If you want a bargain, go on Monday or Tuesday between September and December, when admission is free.
Monday-Friday 9:30 a.m.-4:30 p.m., Saturday-Sunday 10 a.m.-4:30 p.m.; June-August, daily until 6 p.m.

AMERICAN GIRL PLACE
835 N. Michigan Ave., Chicago, 877-247-5223; www.americangirlplace.com
When strolling around downtown Chicago, you're bound to see legions of girls toting red shopping bags from American Girl Place. Dolls are the major draw here, but the store also sells clothing and accessories for them (and their owners), as well as doll furniture and toys. American Girl Place also features a café (reservations recommended); various special events and a Broadway-style show.
Sunday 9 a.m.-7 p.m., Monday-Thursday 10 a.m.-7 p.m., Friday 10 a.m.-9 p.m., Saturday 9 a.m.-9 p.m.

APOLLO THEATRE
2540 N. Lincoln Ave., Chicago, 773-935-6100; www.apollochicago.com
An intimate theater in Chicago's Lincoln Park neighborhood, the Apollo has been home to both famous and infamous productions over the years. Built in 1978, the theater saw many productions by the Steppenwolf Theater Company, as well as native Chicagoan Jim Belushi starring in David Mamet's *Sexual Perversity in Chicago*.
Show times vary.

ART INSTITUTE OF CHICAGO
111 S. Michigan Ave., Chicago, 312-443-3600; www.artic.edu
Adjacent to Millennium Park on South Michigan Avenue, this 1879 Beaux Arts building, originally part of the Columbian Exposition, houses more than 300,000 works of art within its 10 curatorial departments. The museum has what is considered the finest and most comprehensive modern and contemporary art collection in the world, one of the largest arms collections in America and one of the two finest collections of Japanese woodblock prints. Highlights include Georges Seurat's *A Sunday on La Grande Jatte*

1884, Grant Wood's *American Gothic*, Edward Hopper's *Nighthawks* and 33 Monet paintings. A new Renzo Piano-designed modern wing is now open to the public.
Free Tuesday. Monday-Wednesday, Friday 10:30 a.m.-5 p.m., Thursday 10:30 a.m.-8 p.m., Saturday-Sunday 10 a.m.-5 p.m.

AUDITORIUM BUILDING

430 S. Michigan Ave., Chicago
This landmark structure built in 1889 was designed by Chicago School architects Louis Sullivan and Dankmar Adler. The interior is noted for its intricate system of iron framing, ornamentation and near-perfect acoustics. It now houses Roosevelt University.

AUDITORIUM THEATRE

50 E. Congress Parkway, Chicago, 312-922-2110; www.auditoriumtheatre.org
The Auditorium Theatre building, designed by architects Louis Sullivan and Dankmar Adler, underwent a facelift in 2003, getting a new state-of-the-art stage and orchestra pit. The stage was returned to its original height as designed in the 1880s. The Joffrey Ballet opened the new stage, and the historic building begins yet another era.

BRIAR STREET THEATRE

3133 N. Halsted St., Chicago, 773-348-4000; www.blueman.com
The Briar Street Theatre has been the Chicago home of the national sensation *Blue Man Group*, which incorporates everyday objects like metal drums and pipes into a musical experience rife with color and comedy. It's easily accessible by CTA rapid transit, and tickets are less pricey than at many other theaters in the city.

CADILLAC PALACE THEATRE

151 W. Randolph St., Chicago, 312-977-1700; www.broadwayinchicago.com
This theater is a Chicago landmark whose design was inspired by the decadence of the palace at Versailles. It originally played first-run movies during the 1920s and 1930s and was converted to a live theater in the 1950s.

BROOKFIELD ZOO

8400 W. 31st St., Brookfield, 708-485-0263, 800-201-0784; www.brookfieldzoo.org
Located just 14 miles west of downtown Chicago, the Brookfield Zoo is a world-class 216-acre facility that houses more than 2,800 animals. Long known for its progressive approach to wildlife, the zoo was the first in the country to install animals in near-natural habitats instead of in cages. Children get special attention here: A 2-acre, 300-animal Family Play Zoo enables kids and their families to interact with the animals. The zoo also features botanical gardens, a dolphin show, several restaurants, a store, roving naturalists and ongoing special programming.
June-August, daily 9:30 a.m.-6 p.m.; April-Memorial Day and Labor Day-October, Monday-Friday 10 a.m.-5 p.m., Saturday-Sunday 10 a.m.-6 p.m.; November-March, daily 10 a.m.-5 p.m.

ARCHITECTURE RIVER CRUISE

Dock location on southeast corner of Michigan Avenue Bridge and Wacker Drive, Chicago, 312-922-3432; www.architecture.org

This 1½-hour tour covers the north and south branches of the Chicago River, with views of the city's celebrated riverfront architecture; historic 19th-century railroad bridges and warehouses, 20th-century bridge houses and magnificent Loop skyscrapers.

Reservations required. May-September, daily; October, Tuesday, Thursday, Saturday-Sunday.

CHICAGO ARCHITECTURE FOUNDATION TOURS

224 S. Michigan Ave., Chicago, 312-922-3432; www.architecture.org

This not-for-profit organization conducts one of the city's most popular tours, a 90-minute Architecture River Cruise that passes more than 50 architecturally significant sights on the Chicago River and Lake Michigan. Other offerings include walking tours of the Loop's historic skyscrapers, Art Deco buildings, the Theater District, modern skyscrapers and Loop sculpture, or individual city neighborhoods like Old Town, River North and Sheffield Historic District. You can purchase tickets and meet for tours at one of two tour centers on Michigan Avenue.

CHICAGO CULTURAL CENTER

78 E. Washington St., Chicago, 312-744-6630; www.ci.chi.il.us/tourism/culturalcenter

The Chicago Cultural Center is housed in a landmark Michigan Avenue building (formerly a library) that features Tiffany glass domes, mosaics and marble walls and stairs. The center itself often offers exhibitions of groundbreaking art as well as performances by renowned poets and musicians. On weekdays during the summer, you can catch "Lunchbreak," a program designed to offer good music in a great setting during the lunch hour.

Monday-Thursday 10 a.m.-7 p.m., Friday until 6 p.m., Saturday until 5 p.m., Sunday 11 a.m.-5 p.m. Archives closed Sunday.

CHICAGO FIRE ACADEMY

558 W. DeKoven St., Chicago, 312-747-7238; www.chicago.com

This academy is built on the site where the Great Chicago Fire of 1871 is believed to have started. Legend has it that a cow in Mrs. O'Leary's barn knocked over a lantern and began the fire, but recent investigations suggest this story may be fictitious. The fire academy pays tribute to the city's firefighters.

CHICAGO HISTORY MUSEUM

1601 N. Clark St., Chicago, 312-642-4600; www.chicagohistory.org

The society has rotating exhibits that focus on the history and development of Chicago. There are selected aspects of Illinois and U.S. history on display, including galleries devoted to costumes, decorative arts and architecture. There are pioneer craft demonstrations and a hands-on gallery.

Free Monday. Daily.

CHICAGO SYMPHONY ORCHESTRA (CSO)

220 S. Michigan Ave., Chicago, 312-294-3333; www.cso.org
Long considered one of the great orchestras of the world, the CSO has been a fixture on the Chicago cultural scene for more than 100 years. While the big-name shows may sell out in advance, it is often possible to get day-of-show or single-seat tickets at the box office, especially for weeknights or Friday and Saturday afternoons, at a reasonable price.

CHICAGO TEMPLE

77 W. Washington St., Chicago, 312-236-4548; www.chicagotemple.org
Built in 1923, this is considered the first Methodist Episcopal Church. At 568 feet from street level to the tip of its Gothic tower, this is the highest church spire in the world.
Tours. Monday-Saturday 2 p.m., Sunday after 8:30 a.m. and 11 a.m. services. Free flu shots, free screenings of blood pressure and diabetes.

CHICAGO THEATRE

175 N. State St., Chicago, 312-443-6300; www.thechicagotheatre.com
The Chicago Theatre may be best known for its flashy, classic marquee sign, but visitors to the theater may be more impressed by its French baroque design. The extravagant and ornate interior features bronze light fixtures with Steuben glass shades, crystal chandeliers, polished marble and soaring murals hand-painted on the auditorium's ceiling. Opened in 1921 as the city's first movie palace, the theater now hosts live performances by musicians, comedians and actors. The theater's original Wurlitzer pipe organ has been restored and still produces a lush, powerful sound.

CHICAGO TRIBUNE TOWER

435 N. Michigan Ave., Chicago, 312-222-3994; www.tribune.com
This 36-story tower, headquarters the Tribune Company, is a moderne building with a Gothic-detailed base and crown. It does exactly what publisher Joseph Medill intended: It "thames" the Chicago River. Bits and pieces of historic structures from around the world are embedded in the exterior walls of the lower floors.

CHINATOWN

Cermak Road and Wentworth Avenue, Chicago, 312-326-5320;
www.chicagochinatown.org
Chicago's Chinatown is a vibrant and lively cultural center that makes for a fascinating visit. Located south of the Loop at Cermak and Wentworth, Chinatown's boundary is marked by a tiled gateway. Within a 10-block radius are 10,000 community members, more than 40 restaurants, 20 gift shops, herbal and tea stores and bakeries. Neighborhood festivals include Chinese New Year, the Dragon Boat Festival and the mid-autumn Moon Festival.

CIVIC OPERA BUILDING

20 N. Wacker Drive, Chicago, 312-332-2244
On the lower levels under 45 floors of commercial office space, is the Art Deco, 3,400-seat Civic Opera House, home of the Lyric Opera of Chica-

go *(312-419-0033)*, which performs some of the biggest shows in operatic theater. Each season begins with a new 12-person repertory cast chosen in March and given additional professional training to make Chicago's performances among the finest anywhere.

DUSABLE MUSEUM OF AFRICAN-AMERICAN HISTORY

740 E. 56th Place, Chicago, 773-947-0600; www.dusablemuseum.org
This museum houses African and African-American art objects along with displays of black history in Africa and the United States. There is an extensive collection of paintings, sculptures, artifacts, books and photographs. Tuesday-Sunday, January-May. Free Sunday.

FIELD MUSEUM

1400 S. Lake Shore Drive, Chicago, 312-922-9410; www.fmnh.org
This more than 100-year-old natural history museum made headlines in 2000 when it unveiled Sue, the largest and most complete tyrannosaurus Rex skeleton. Sue joined a fine collection of artifacts from civilizations in Egypt and Mesopotamia and a vast assortment of taxidermy.
Daily 9 a.m.-5 p.m. Discounted admission in January-February, mid-September-late December on Monday-Tuesday.

FORD CENTER FOR THE PERFORMING ARTS ORIENTAL THEATRE

24 W. Randolph St., Chicago, 312-977-1700; www.broadwayinchicago.com
The Oriental Theatre was originally a movie house that doubled as an entertainment venue for musicians like Duke Ellington during the early 20th century. The theater closed its doors to moviegoers in the 1980s but came back with a flourish. Reopening in 1998, it was converted into a place to see live shows. The theater is currently hosting an unprecedented run of the musical *Wicked*, which will wrap up in 2009.

GARFIELD PARK CONSERVATORY

300 N. Central Park Ave., Chicago, 312-746-5100; www.garfield-conservatory.org
The park has outdoor formal gardens while the Conservatory has eight houses and propagating houses on more than 5 acres. There are four major shows annually at Horticultural Hall and Show House.
Friday-Wednesday 9 a.m.-5 p.m., Thursday until 8 p.m.

GOODMAN THEATRE

170 N. Dearborn St., Chicago, 312-443-3800; www.goodman-theatre.org
The Goodman Theatre can be considered a breeding ground for up-and-coming actors and productions. A good example is its production of Eugene O'Neill's *A Long Day's Journey into Night*, which took star Brian Dennehy with it to Broadway and captured several Tony Awards. Tickets can be pricey but not as expensive as a Broadway show, and there are discounts for students and groups.

GRACELAND CEMETERY TOUR

4001 N. Clark St., Chicago, 773-525-1105; www.gracelandcemetery.org
Walking through Graceland Cemetery on the city's north side is like taking a

step back into Chicago's early history. Not only will you recognize the names of the movers and shakers who put Chicago on the map, but there are also memorials to the people who helped build it. Highlights include Louis Sullivan's tomb for Carrie Eliza Getty, a landmark described as the beginning of modern architecture in America; Daniel Burnham's island resting place in the middle of the lake; and Mies van der Rohe's elegantly understated grave marker. Daily 8 a.m.-4:30 p.m.

GRANT PARK

337 E. Randolph St., Chicago, 312-742-7648; www.chicagoparkdistrict.com
Grant Park was built on a landfill created by debris from the Great Chicago Fire of 1871. Now it's one of the great landmarks of the city, with Buckingham Fountain as its centerpiece. The fountain was given to the city by Kate Buckingham in 1927 in honor of her brother. Every minute, 133 jets spray approximately 14,000 gallons of water as high as 150 feet. Every hour on the hour, there is a 20-minute water display (accompanied at dusk by lights and music). Each year, the Taste of Chicago is held here, as are many picnics and smaller festivals. Recently, the park hosted Lollapalooza, the huge three-day outdoor music festival, and a rally for President Barack Obama on the night he won the 2008 presidential election. You can enjoy concerts at the Petrillo Music Shell or relax on the lawn on summer evenings to watch outdoor movies during the yearly Chicago Outdoor Film Festival. Daily 6 a.m.-11 p.m.

GREEN MILL

4802 N. Broadway St., Chicago, 773-878-5552; www.greenmilljazz.com
The oldest jazz club in America, the Green Mill is located in the still-dicey Uptown neighborhood. With a vintage sign out front and a gorgeous carved bar inside, this is a former speakeasy of the Capone gang. The jazz, however, is strictly contemporary, showcasing some of the most acclaimed musicians working today. On weeknights, you might find swing or a big band; on weekend nights, several acts pack in crowds; and on Sundays, you can experience the Poetry Slam (the nation's first, hosted by Marc Smith, the godfather of poetry slams), where area poets test their mettle against audience reaction. Daily.

HOLY NAME CATHEDRAL

735 N. State St., Chicago, 312-787-8040; www.holynamecathedral.org
The home to the Chicago archdiocese and Francis Cardinal George, Holy Name is a good example of Gothic Revival architecture in Chicago. Thousands of parishioners attend services at Holy Name each week, many of them to hear the cardinal say Mass on Sunday morning. The church is also affiliated with the Francis Xavier Warde School.

JANE ADDAMS HULL-HOUSE MUSEUM

800 S. Halsted St., The Campus of the University of Illinois at Chicago, 312-413-5353; www.uic.edu/jaddams/hull/hull house.html
Two original Hull-House buildings, the restored Hull Mansion built in 1856 and dining hall built in 1905, formed the nucleus of the 13-building settle-

ment complex founded in 1889 by Jane Addams and Ellen Gates Starr, social welfare pioneers. There are exhibits and presentations on the history of Hull House, the surrounding neighborhood, ethnic groups and women's history. Tuesday-Friday 10 a.m.-4 p.m., Sunday noon-4 p.m.

JOHN HANCOCK CENTER
875 N. Michigan Ave., Chicago, 312-751-3680, 888-875-8439;
www.hancock-observatory.com
The John Hancock Center, standing at 1,127 feet and 100 floors, is the world's 13th-tallest building. Since completion in 1969, this innovative office and residential building has won awards for its distinctive exterior "X" bracing, which eliminated the need for inner support beams and increased usable space. The 94th-floor observatory features an open-air skywalk, a history wall chronicling Chicago's growth, multilingual sky tours and a 360-degree view that spans 80 miles and four states. Visitors can dine or have a drink at the 95th-floor Signature Room.
Daily 9 a.m.-11 p.m.

LAKE MICHIGAN
312-742-7529, Chicago; www.chicagoparkdistrict.com
Chicago's lakefront reflects the vision of architect Daniel Burnham, whose 1909 plan for Chicago specified that the shoreline remain publicly owned and enjoyed by all. It is also one of the things that makes this city unique. After all, how many major cities have beaches (31 in total) within the city limits? In addition, the lakefront sports 18 miles of bicycle, jogging and in-line skating paths, skating rinks, tennis courts, field houses, theaters and more, all easily accessible and open to the public.
Lakefront daily, sunrise-11 p.m.

LINCOLN PARK
2400 N. Stockton Drive, Chicago, 312-742-7529; www.chicagoparkdistrict.com
The largest in Chicago, Lincoln Park stretches almost the entire length of the north end of the city along the lake. It contains statues of Lincoln, Hans Christian Andersen, Shakespeare and others. There is a nine-hole golf course, driving range, miniature golf and bike and jogging paths and, of course, protected beaches. In the park is Lincoln Park Conservatory (2391 N. Stockton Drive, 312-742-7736) which has formal and rock gardens and an extensive collection of orchids. (daily 9 a.m.-5 p.m.) The Lincoln Park Zoo (2200 N. Cannon Drive, 312-742-2000) may be small (just 35 acres), but it's a leader in education and conservation.
Free. Daily; hours vary by season.

THE MAGNIFICENT MILE
625 N. Michigan Ave., Chicago, 312-642-3570; www.themagnificentmile.com
Although it's often compared to Rodeo Drive in Beverly Hills and Fifth Avenue in New York because of the quality and quantity of its stores, Michigan Avenue has a vibe all its own. Known as the Magnificent Mile, this one-mile, flower-lined stretch between Oak Street and the Chicago River boasts 3.1-million square feet of retail space, 460 stores, 275 restaurants, 51 hotels,

numerous art galleries and two museums, all set among some of Chicago's most architecturally significant buildings.

MERCHANDISE MART

222 Merchandise Mart Plaza, Chicago, 312-527-4141; www.merchandisemart.com
The world's largest commercial building, the Merchandise Mart was built in 1930 and now houses restaurants, shopping and the city's top interior design showrooms.
Weekdays 9 a.m.-5 p.m.

MICHIGAN AVENUE BRIDGE

At the Chicago River between Michigan and Wabash avenues, Chicago
This well-known Chicago landmark offers stunning views of the city as it crosses the Chicago River. The bridge was completed in 1920, designed by Edward Burnnett and based on the Alexander III Bridge over the Seine River in Paris. Four 40-foot limestone bridge houses (two on either end) were added in 1928. Each contains a sculptured relief depicting historic Chicago events.

MILLENNIUM PARK

Michigan Avenue and Randolph Street, Chicago, 312-742-1168;
www.millenniumpark.org
The city's newest and most popular attraction, this 24½-acre park is a center of world-class art, music, architecture and landscape design. Don't miss the 50-foot-high Crown Fountain, the Frank Gehry-designed Pritzker Pavillion or the giant reflective silver Cloud Gate sculpture.
Daily 6 a.m.-11 p.m.

MONADNOCK BUILDING

53 W. Jackson Blvd., Chicago, 312-922-1890; www.monadnockbuilding.com
This Burnham and Root structure is the highest wall-bearing building in Chicago, and at the time of its construction (1889-1891), it was the tallest and largest office building in the world. It is now considered one of the master works of the Chicago School of Architecture.

MUSEUM OF CONTEMPORARY ART

220 E. Chicago Ave., Chicago, 312-280-2660; www.mcachicago.org
Just half a block east of Michigan Avenue lies the Museum of Contemporary Art, one of the nation's largest facilities dedicated to post-1945 works. With a large rotating permanent collection and a reputation for cutting-edge exhibits, the museum showcases some of the finest artists working today. The museum has been in its current building since 1995, and positions itself as a cultural center. The terraced sculpture garden with views of Lake Michigan serves as a peaceful urban sanctuary.
Free Tuesday. Tuesday-Sunday.

MUSEUM OF SCIENCE AND INDUSTRY

5700 S. Lake Shore Drive, 773-684-1414, 800-468-6674; www.msichicago.org
This museum includes a free tour of a German U-boat captured during World War II, a re-creation of a coal mine and a model train layout that encapsulates

almost the entire country. The museum also includes an exhibit on genetics and the improvements made to medicine through the Human Genome Project, as well as several rooms dedicated to the telling of time, with more than 500 unique instruments.

Daily; hours vary by season. Free admission varies by season; see Web site for details.

MUSIC BOX THEATRE

3733 N. Southport Ave., Chicago, 773-871-6604; www.musicboxtheatre.com

This circa-1929 neighborhood art house attracts a loyal following not just because it's one of the few places in town devoted to independent, foreign, cult, documentary and classic films, but because the Music Box is one of the last surviving old-time movie palaces. The theater is also home to screenings for the Chicago International Film Festival, held for three weeks each October.

Daily.

NAVY PIER

600 E. Grand Ave., Chicago, 312-595-7437; www.navypier.com

Known as one of the city's top venues for families, Navy Pier is an old naval station renovated during the 1990s and converted into an urban playground. It's most visible attraction, the 150-foot-high Ferris wheel, offers spectacular views of the lake and skyline and is modeled after the world's first, which was built in Chicago in 1893. Take advantage of the city's free trolley service from downtown hotels and other locations. Also here is the Chicago Children's Museum.

Daily 10 a.m.-8 p.m.

THE NOTEBAERT NATURE MUSEUM

2430 N. Cannon Drive, Chicago, 773-755-5100; www.naturemuseum.org

Hands-on exploration of nature is the mission of the Notebaert Nature Museum, built in 1999 as an offshoot of the Chicago Academy of Sciences. Visitors can connect with the natural world via indoor exhibits and outdoor adventures. Permanent exhibits include a 28-foot-high butterfly haven, a city science interactive display and a wilderness walk, and a children's gallery designed for kids ages 3-8.

Free Thursday. Monday-Friday 9 a.m.-4:30 p.m., Saturday-Sunday 10 a.m.-5 p.m.

OLD CHICAGO WATER TOWER AND PUMPING STATION

806 N. Michigan Ave., Near North Side, Chicago, 312-742-0808

These castle-like Gothic Revival buildings survived the Great Chicago Fire of 1871. Today, they house a visitor center and City Gallery, presenting photography exhibits with a Chicago theme, and are also the home of the acclaimed Lookingglass Theatre Company.

Monday-Saturday 10 a.m.-6:30 p.m., Sunday 10 a.m.-5 p.m.

THE OPRAH WINFREY SHOW

1058 W. Washington Blvd., Chicago, 312-591-9222; www.oprah.com

One of the most coveted tickets in town is for *The Oprah Winfrey Show*, taped at Harpo Studios in Chicago's West Loop. The show generally tapes only on Tuesday, Wednesday and Thursday from September through early December and from January to June. The only way to get tickets is to call the studio's Audience Department in advance. Security for the show is tight, and you must be over 18 to attend (although teens ages 16 and 17 can attend with a parent or legal guardian if they bring a copy of their birth certificate for check-in).

POLISH MUSEUM OF AMERICA

984 N. Milwaukee Ave., Chicago, 773-384-3352; www.prcua.org
The museum has one of the best collections of Polish music and literature outside of Warsaw, catering to Chicago's large Polish population. There are exhibits on Polish culture, folklore and immigration. Founded in 1935, the museum is used by many Polish scholars to complete research on projects they produce.
Friday-Wednesday 11 a.m.-4 p.m.

PRAIRIE AVENUE HISTORIC DISTRICT

1800 S. Prairie Ave., Chicago, 312-326-1480; www.glessnerhouse.org
This is the area where millionaires lived during the 1800s. The Clarke House (circa 1835), the oldest house in the city, has been restored and now stands at a site near its original location. The Glessner House, 1800 S. Prairie Ave., is owned and maintained by the Chicago Architecture Foundation and was designed by architect Henry Hobson Richardson. Two-hour guided tours of both houses are offered Wednesday-Sunday. Other houses on the cobblestone street are the Kimball House (1890), 1801 S. Prairie Ave., a replica of a French chateau; Coleman House (circa 1885), 1811 S. Prairie Ave.; and Keith House (circa 1870), 1900 S. Prairie Ave. Architectural tours are available. Free Wednesday.

RICHARD J. DALEY CENTER AND PLAZA

50 W. Washington Blvd., Chicago, 312-603-7980; www.daleycenter.com
This 31-story, 648-foot-tall building houses county and city courts and administrative offices. In the plaza is the Chicago Picasso sculpture; across Washington Street is Miro's Chicago sculpture.

RIVER NORTH GALLERY DISTRICT

With the highest concentration of art galleries outside of Manhattan, Chicago's River North Gallery District, just a short walk from Michigan Avenue and the Loop, offers world-class art in a stylish setting of renovated warehouses and upscale restaurants. Find the majority of galleries on Superior and Franklin streets. If you happen to be in town on the second Friday of the month, wander over to an opening-night reception (5-7 p.m.) for a glass of wine and a glimpse of up-and-coming artists.
Tuesday-Saturday.

ROOKERY

209 S. LaSalle St., Chicago, 312-325-8950; www.usbank.com
This is the oldest surviving steel-skeleton skyscraper in the world. Designed

by Burnham & Root in 1886, the remarkable glass-encased lobby was remodeled in 1905 by Frank Lloyd Wright.

ROYAL GEORGE THEATRE

1641 N. Halsted St., Chicago, 312-988-9000; www.theroyalgeorgetheatre.com

Located in Chicago's Lincoln Park neighborhood, this theater features seats that are sparse in number but well spaced, creating a relaxing theater experience. It has hosted such shows as Tony Kushner's acclaimed *Angels in America* and the review *Forever Plaid*.

Show times vary.

WILLIS TOWER

233 S. Wacker Drive, Chicago, 312-875-9696; www.thesearstower.com,

www.theskydeck.com

It's fitting that the town that gave birth to the skyscraper should lay claim to North America's tallest building. Built in 1974 by Skidmore, Owings & Merrill, the 110-story Willis Tower (previously known as the Sears Tower) soars ¼ mile (1,450 feet) above the city, making it one of the most prominent buildings in the skyline. The building was constructed of black anodized aluminum in nine bundled square tubes, an innovation that provides both wind protection and the necessary support for its extraordinary height. The 103rd-floor observatory offers panoramic views of the city; on a clear day, you can easily see 35 miles away. During the height of the tourist season expect long waits, and expect locals to still refer to it as the Sears Tower.

May-September, daily 10 a.m.-10 p.m.; October-April, daily 10 a.m.-8 p.m.

THE SECOND CITY

1616 N. Wells St., Chicago, 312-664-4032; www.secondcity.com

Opened in 1959 by a group of University of Chicago students, this comedy troupe has launched the careers of many successful comics, including John Belushi, Bill Murray, Steve Carrell, Stephen Colbert and Mike Myers. Resident troupes perform original comedy revues nightly on two stages: The Second City Mainstage, which seats 340, and The Second City e.t.c., which seats 180. The Second City also operates a comedy training center, with student productions held at Donny's Skybox Studio Theatre.

SHEDD AQUARIUM

1200 S. Lake Shore Drive, Chicago, 312-939-2438; www.sheddnet.org

This aquarium features more than 8,000 freshwater and marine animals displayed in 200 naturalistic habitats while divers hand-feed fish, sharks, eels and turtles several times daily in the 90,000-gallon Caribbean Reef exhibit. The beluga whale breeding program has been particularly successful, with calves born in 2006 and 2007. In the summer, the aquarium hosts live jazz performances.

Free Monday-Tuesday (September-February only). Summer, daily 9 a.m.-6 p.m.; winter, daily 9 a.m.-5 p.m.

SOLDIER FIELD

1410 S. Museum Campus Drive, Chicago, 312-235-7000; www.soldierfield.net

Soldier Field opened in 1924 as Municipal Grant Park Stadium. The first game played saw Notre Dame defeat Northwestern 13 to 6. The Chicago Bears didn't play home games at the stadium until 1971, when they moved from baseball's Wrigley Field. In 2003, the stadium underwent a massive renovation that maintained its look from the outside, but provided a modern venue inside.

STEPPENWOLF THEATRE COMPANY

1650 N. Halsted St., Chicago, 312-335-1650; www.steppenwolf.org

One of the most acclaimed theater groups in the country, Steppenwolf not only helped put Chicago theater on the map, but also gave many famous actors, including John Malkovich, Joan Allen and Gary Sinise their start. Steppenwolf quickly became known for its risky choices and edgy performances, an approach critics aptly termed rock-and-roll theater. Today, the company has its own state-of-the-art building in the Lincoln Park neighborhood. Performances are almost uniformly excellent, with stunning sets, strong acting and plenty of original material.

SYMPHONY CENTER

220 S. Michigan Ave., Chicago, 312-294-3000; www.cso.org

The historic Symphony Center is the home of the Chicago Symphony Orchestra and the stage for the Civic Orchestra of Chicago, chamber music groups, diverse musical attractions and children's programs. The center includes Buntrock Hall, a ballroom, rehearsal space and restaurant.

THEATRE BUILDING CHICAGO

1225 W. Belmont Ave., Chicago, 773-327-5252; www.theatrebuildingchicago.org

The Theatre Building serves as the impromptu home for traveling companies to show their wares. More often than not, these shows are a little more "off the beaten path" and do not include names or plays that may be recognizable, but this does not take away from the enjoyment of the experience. Shows are generally cheaper than at other area theaters, but some may not be for the entire family.

UNITED CENTER

1901 W. Madison St., Chicago, 312-455-4500; www.unitedcenter.com

Affectionately known as the house that Michael built, the United Center replaced the cavernous Chicago Stadium in the mid-1990s as the home of Chicago Bulls. It's also home to the Blackhawks, Chicago's hockey team, and numerous concerts and special events are held here.

UNIVERSITY OF CHICAGO

5801 S. Ellis Ave., Chicago, 773-702-8374; www.uchicago.edu

On this campus, Enrico Fermi produced the first sustained nuclear reaction. The University of Chicago has also had one of the highest numbers of Nobel Prize winners of any institution. The campus includes the Oriental Institute, which has an outstanding collection of archaeological material; Robie

House, designed by Frank Lloyd Wright in 1909 and the ultimate example of a Prairie house (daily 10 a.m.-3 p.m.); and Rockefeller Memorial Chapel, designed by Bertram Grosvenor Goodhue Associates and noted for its Gothic construction, vaulted ceiling, 8,600-pipe organ and 72-bell carillon.

VICTORY GARDENS THEATER
2257 N. Lincoln Ave., Chicago, 773-549-5788; www.victorygardens.org
Although it often produces plays by lesser-known authors, the Victory Gardens did win the Regional Theatre Tony Award in 2001. Some better-known playwrights and plays have been produced here as well, such as Neil Simon's *Lost in Yonkers.*

WRIGLEY BUILDING
410 N. Michigan Ave., Chicago, 312-923-8080; www.wrigley.com
Perched on the north bank of the Chicago River on Michigan Avenue, the sparkling white Wrigley Building has been one of Chicago's most recognized skyscrapers since its completion in 1924 by architects Graham, Anderson, Probst and White. The building's triangular shape is patterned after the Giralda Tower in Seville, Spain, and its ornamental design is an adaptation of French Renaissance style. The building is actually two towers linked by an open walkway at street level and two enclosed walkways on the third and 14th floors. Today, the building remains the headquarters of the Wrigley family of chewing gum fame.

WRIGLEY FIELD
1060 W. Addison St., Chicago, 773-404-2827; www.cubs.com
America's second-oldest Major League ballpark is also one of its most unique, located within a vibrant city neighborhood where residents often watch games from their roof decks. While the Cubs' long-term losing streak is a perpetual heartbreak, it never keeps people away from the ballpark—games are consistently sold out.

SPECIAL EVENTS
57TH STREET ART FAIR
57th St., Chicago, 773-493-3247; www.57thstreetartfair.org
Every year, the 57th Street Art Fair takes over a city block between Kenwood and Dorchester to showcase more than 300 artists from around the country. Early June.

AIR AND WATER SHOW
1600 N. Lake Shore Drive, Chicago, 312-744-2400; www.egov.cityofchicago.org
The nation's largest two-day air shows is a free event that attracts more than 2 million people every August. There are daredevil pilots, parachute teams and jets flying in formation, as well as a waterskiing and boat-jumping component. Mid-August.

ART CHICAGO/ARTROPOLIS
Merchandise Mart, Chicago, 312-527-3701; www.artchicago.com
This fair attracts hundreds of dealers from around the globe. Before the show

opens, serious collectors can attend the Vernissage party to preview the art before the general public is admitted the following day.
Mid-May.

CHICAGO BLUES FEST
Grant Park, 331 E. Randolph St., Chicago, 312-744-2400; www.egov.cityofchicago.org
In a city virtually synonymous with the blues, Chicago's annual Blues Fest features local stars as well as national names. This free outdoor festival attracts more than 600,000 visitors over its four-day run.
Early-mid-June.

CHICAGO INTERNATIONAL FILM FESTIVAL
Various theaters, Chicago, 312-683-0121
This is the oldest international film festival in North America. For three weeks each October, Chicago is introduced to some of the best cinema from the United States and around the world. Over the years, the festival has helped introduce innovative filmmakers like Martin Scorsese and John Carpenter.
October.

CHICAGO JAZZ FEST
Grant Park, 331 E. Randolph St., Chicago, 312-744-2400; www.egov.cityofchicago.org
This event has become a giant outdoor jazz cafe with more than 300,000 people in attendance. Lesser-known and local artists perform during the day on the small stage, but world-class jazz musicians take over the main stage at the Petrillo Music Shell after 5 p.m.
Labor Day weekend.

CHICAGO OUTDOOR FILM FESTIVAL
Grant Park, 331 E. Randolph St., Chicago, 312-744-2400; www.egov.cityofchicago.org
Once a week in July and August, free movies are shown in Grant Park, from *Casablanca* and *Vertigo* to new classics like *Ferris Bueller's Day Off*.
Mid-July-late August.

GRANT PARK JULY 3 CONCERT
Petrillo Music Shell, 235 S. Columbus Drive, Chicago, 312-744-3370;
www.grandparkmusicfestival.com
The lakefront blazes with cannon flashes and fireworks as the Grant Park Symphony welcomes Independence Day with Tchaikovsky's *1812 Overture*.
July 3.

ST. PATRICK'S DAY PARADE
1340 W. Washington Blvd., 312-942-9188; www.chicagostpatsparade.com
Chicago's St. Patrick's Day parade is famous around the world, not because of its size or its spirit, but because on the day of the parade, the city dyes the Chicago River green, a tradition started during the early 1960s. The parade features dozens of bands, Irish step dancers, floats and representatives of unions and local organizations and politicians.
Weekend closest to St. Patrick's Day.

TASTE OF CHICAGO

Grant Park, Chicago, 312-744-2400; www.egov.cityofchicago.org

What began in 1980 as a way to sample cuisines from some of the city's best-known restaurants has become an all-out food fest that attracts more than 3½ million visitors a year. This 10-day event features booths from more than 50 area vendors, free live music by big-name headliners and amusement park rides.

Late June-early July.

VENETIAN NIGHT

Monroe Harbor, 100 S. Lake Shore Drive, Chicago, 773-267-9131

This Chicago tradition has a Venetian-themed aquatic parade and fireworks.
Late July.

WHERE TO STAY
★★★AFFINIA

166 E. Superior St., Chicago, 312-787-6000; www.affinia.com

Close to Michigan Avenue and Chicago's top shopping, this contemporary hotel recently underwent a complete renovation, primarily to make room for upgraded beds in each of the guest rooms. To top those thick, fluffy mattresses, the hotel offers a pillow menu with everything available from goose down to foam. Other thoughtful touches include a full range of complimentary toiletries (contact lens solution, toothpaste, hairspray) to replace anything you weren't allowed to bring through airport security in your carry-on. Even pets are pampered here with everything from sitter services to pet psychics.

215 rooms. Restaurant, bar. Business center. Pool. Spa. Pets accepted.
$151-250

★★★THE ALLERTON HOTEL—MICHIGAN AVENUE

701 N. Michigan Ave., Streeterville, 312-440-1500, 877-701-8111;
www.theallertonhotel.com

During the Roaring Twenties, the Allerton was one of the first high rises to pop up on the Chicago skyline. Now a designated landmark, the Michigan Avenue hotel retains some classic elements (such as its exterior sign that reads "Tip Top Tap"—the name of the popular cocktail lounge that closed in 1961) while adding some contemporary accents. The hotel had a makeover in May 2008 and the rooms are now in tip-top shape. The sophisticated spaces are done up in traditional navy blue and white, while modern touches, such as trendy patterned throw pillows, white upholstered headboards and iPod docking stations, are sprinkled throughout. Beware of the rooms labeled "Classic"—that's code for "tiny."

443 rooms. Restaurant, bar. Fitness center. Business center. $151-2500

★★★THE AMBASSADOR EAST HOTEL

1301 N. State Parkway, Gold Coast, 312-787-7200, 888-506-3471;
www.theambassadoreasthotel.com

Many celebs have checked into this Gold Coast hotel, including Vince Vaughn, Richard Gere and Frank Sinatra (who has a celebrity suite named after him). One reason for its popularity is its location. The hotel sits among residential buildings in a tony neighborhood, plus it's near the jogging trail and volleyball courts of Oak Street Beach. Another reason may be the famed Pump Room restaurant, where Old Hollywood stars flocked to its fabled Booth One, a table that only the most exclusive diners could snag. Robert Wagner and Natalie Wood toasted their wedding in that booth, as did Lauren Bacall and Humphrey Bogart when they got hitched. Frequent guest Judy Garland even paid tribute to the hot spot in her song *Chicago*: "Chicago, we'll meet at the Pump Room, Ambassador East." If you meet at the Pump Room today, you'll feast on contemporary American cuisine from executive chef Nick Sutton.

285 rooms. Restaurant, bar. Fitness center. Business center. $151-250

★★★AMALFI HOTEL CHICAGO

20 W. Kinzie St., River North, 312-395-9000, 877-262-5341; www.amalfihotelchicago.com

When you check into the Amalfi, you first sit for a consultation with your "Experience Designer" (or concierge) to discuss your stay. Then an "Impressionist" (doorman) brings your luggage up to your contemporary "Space" (room). This River North boutique hotel may be a bit pretentious, but it has the goods to back it up. You'll sleep well on the pillow-top mattresses and Egyptian cotton linens, and enjoy the multi-head showers and Aveda bath products. An in-room CD collection, the hotel's DVD library and the gratis breakfast on every floor make it feel like home. (Then the "Comfort Stylist" (housekeeper) knocks on the door and reminds you where you are.)

215 rooms. Restaurant, bar. Complimentary breakfast. Business center. Fitness center. Pets accepted. $251-350

★BEST WESTERN HAWTHORNE TERRACE

3434 N. Broadway, Lakeview, 773-244-3434, 888-860-3400; www.hawthorneterrace.com

If you are more into the Cubs than Chanel, try this Lakeview hotel for a more neighborhood experience. Located about a half-mile from Wrigley Field, the hotel copies the Friendly Confines' ivy exterior, but the vines cover a charming brick, canopied building rather than a ballpark. The rooms aren't as quaint, but the place tries to make up for it with a free breakfast buffet as well as in-room kitchenettes. Business travelers will appreciate the free wireless Internet.

59 rooms. Complimentary breakfast. Fitness center. $61-150

★★★THE BLACKSTONE

636 S. Michigan Ave., Loop, 312-447-0955, 800-468-3571; www.blackstonerenaissance.com

If there's anything to that whole law of attraction business, that's reason enough to stay at The Blackstone. This 1910 Beaux-Arts hotel, listed on the National Register of Historic Places, has hosted presidents, royalty, sports icons and celebrities (including Rudolph Valentino, Joan Crawford, Spencer Tracy, Katharine Hepburn, Tennessee Williams, Truman Capote and Carl Sandburg). If you are not one to name names, though, the handsome renovation completed in the spring of 2008 will still convince you. Preserving the old-fashioned elegance and architectural integrity, Sage Hospitality Resources bought the long-dormant property, stripped it, then gave it a modern edge. The finished product features a grand gilded lobby with opulent designer details and extravagant extras like a video-generated computer art piece or the constantly changing lakefront landscape; a curated collection of more than 1,400 pieces of original art by Chicago artists is displayed on the walls. The guest rooms weren't forgotten either, tastefully adorned with black, white and red décor, rainshowers, Aveda bath amenities, Eames furniture, flat-screen TVs (and TVs integrated into the bathroom mirrors in upgraded rooms). Locals crowd the restaurant, Mercat a la Planxa, for delicious Catalan-inspired food and drinks.

332 rooms. Restaurant, bar. Business center. Fitness center. $251-350

★★★CHICAGO MARRIOTT AT MEDICAL DISTRICT/UIC

625 S. Ashland Ave., Chicago, 312-491-1234, 800-228-9290;
www.marriottchicago.com

This comfortable hotel has a business center, a car rental desk and airline desk. You'll be within five miles of a large number of the city's best sights, but you won't have to stay amid the congestion of the major tourist areas. Enjoy a fireside dinner at Rook's Corner and then a nightcap at Rook's Lounge, both located in the hotel.

113 rooms. Restaurant, bar. Business center. Fitness center. Pool. $151-250

★★★CONRAD CHICAGO

521 N. Rush St., River North, 312-645-1500; www.conradhotels.com

Architecture buffs will want to check into the Conrad, located in the landmark McGraw-Hill Building. Be sure to take a look at the façade's sculpted zodiac panels, which make the Art Deco structure stand out. Although it's situated above shops such as A|X Armani Exchange and Nordstrom, this Magnificent Mile hotel can help you find some quiet. You'll discover tranquility in your room by lounging on 500 thread-count Pratesi linens while watching the 42-inch plasma TV, playing the Bose entertainment system or listening to your iPod on the room's docking station. A better escape is the rooftop Terrace at Conrad. It may only be five stories up, but it's still a swanky place where you can enjoy a cocktail and tapas underneath the Chicago sky while gazing at the skyscrapers.

311 rooms. Restaurant, bar. Business center. Fitness center. Pets accepted. $251-350

★★COURTYARD BY MARRIOTT

30 E. Hubbard St., River North, 312-329-2500, 800-321-2211; www.marriott.com

The hotel's environs are typical of the steady Marriott brand with neutral rooms and snug beds. The no-frills room won't break the bank and, since it's just outside the flurry of the Magnificent Mile, it's close enough to the action. Bliss-seekers can relax in nearby spas such as Kiva or the Tiffani Kim Institute and shoppers are only three blocks away from ritzy boutiques. Caffeine fiends don't have to look any further than the hotel lobby for their Starbucks fix.

337 rooms. Restaurant, bar. Business center. Fitness center. Pool. $151-250

★★★DANA HOTEL

660 N. State St., River North, 888-301-3262; www.danahotelandspa.com

Dana is new to Chicago's boutique hotel scene, having opened in June 2008.

To compete with the bigwigs, Dana offers guests some extras, including luxurious all-natural treatments at the Spa (try the hydramemory facial to treat jet-lagged skin) and tasty bites from a floating sushi bar. The rooms are filled with light wood and natural tones for a Zen vibe, and the luxe bathrooms feature Italian rain showers roomy enough for two. To unwind, dip into the stocked wine chiller in your room. Or if you want some scenery, visit the rooftop Vertigo Sky Lounge, which features a fire pit to keep you warm on those chilly Chicago nights.

216 rooms. Restaurant, bar. Fitness center. Spa. Pets accepted. $251-350

★★★THE DRAKE HOTEL CHICAGO

140 E. Walton Place, Gold Coast, 312-787-2200, 800-774-1500; www.thedrakehotel.com
The Drake is the hotel of choice for visiting politicians and dignitaries. Winston Churchill, Pope John Paul II and Princess Diana all roomed at the 1920 landmark hotel, ideally located at the beginning of North Michigan Avenue. But this old star could use some polish to regain its luster. While the public spaces still preserve the splendor of the past and some rooms got updated in early 2008, other guest rooms haven't yet gotten their makeovers. Avoid disappointment by asking for a newly renovated room (with gold and white linens and a flat-screen TV).

535 rooms. Restaurant, bar. Fitness center. Business center. $251-350

★★★EMBASSY SUITES

600 N. State St., River North, 312-943-3800, 800-362-2779;
www.embassysuiteschicago.com
A less sophisticated alternative to its nearby sister inn in Streeterville, this outpost screams "hotel chain" with old-style comforters in mauves and blues and the obligatory generic framed landscapes in the bedrooms. What this place lacks in style, it makes up for in roominess. The spacious suites include a separate living room with a sofa, not to mention microwave, coffeemaker and fridge. If you don't feel like chowing down on a frozen dinner, stop off for a complimentary aperitif at the daily manager's reception (5:30-7:30 p.m.) before heading to the hotel's Osteria Via Stato & Enoteca for some Italian eats.

367 rooms. Restaurant, bar. Complimentary breakfast. Business center. Fitness center. Pool. $151-250

★★★EMBASSY SUITES DOWNTOWN/LAKEFRONT

511 N. Columbus Drive, Streeterville, 312-836-5900, 888-903-8884;
www.chicagoembassy.com
Traveling families can spread out here and make it a home away from home. The two-room suites have a separate living room with a sofa bed and dining table, a microwave, a coffeemaker and a fridge. After a March 2008 renovation, the bland beige-hued suites got an upgrade with two flat-panel TVs per room and local artwork on the walls to add some Chicago flavor. If sticking close to your new home makes you stir-crazy, head to the atrium lounge, order a cocktail from the nearby bar and enjoy the soothing sound of the 70-foot cascading water wall. Or you can just wait until the free daily manager's reception to tipple and munch on some appetizers. Also be sure to take advantage of the complimentary made-to-order breakfast before rounding up

the kids and trekking over to nearby Navy Pier—you'll need the energy.
455 rooms. Restaurant, bar. Complimentary breakfast. Fitness center. Pool.
Business center. $151-250

★FAIRFIELD INN

216 E. Ontario St., Streeterville, 312-787-3777, 800-228-2800; www.fairfieldsuites.com
The Fairfield, just steps from Michigan Avenue and a half mile from Oak Street
Beach, is simply decorated and modestly sized, which suits us just fine—the
proximity to the Mag Mile is all we need to convince us to stay here. If you are
looking for incentives, check out the packages: One for anyone who loves to
shop includes a $50 gift card, plus a free breakfast and valet parking.
159 rooms. Complimentary breakfast. Fitness center. Business center. $61-150

★★★THE FAIRMONT CHICAGO, MILLENNIUM PARK

200 N. Columbus Drive, Loop, 312-565-8000, 866-540-4408; www.fairmont.com
The Fairmont wrapped up renovations in June 2008, and with them came a
change from traditional chintzes and furniture to Mid-Century modern neu-
trals and striped wallpaper. While the hotel is still in transition (you may spot
those classic florals in some of the hallways and common areas), rooms are
an updated retreat with flat-screen TVs and remodeled bathrooms with natural stone tile and rainshowers. Locals head to the new mySpa for treatments.
The spa is all about the details: It uses vegan nail polish and pipes your iPod's
music into the treatment room, with nary a stripe in sight.
687 rooms. Restaurant, bar. Fitness center. Pets accepted. $151-250

★★★★★FOUR SEASONS HOTEL CHICAGO

120 E. Delaware Place, Gold Coast, 312-280-8800; www.fourseasons.com/chicagofs
With its prime Mag Mile location and attractive, contemporary rooms, this
luxe hotel is a top choice for visiting celebrities and those who appreciate the
peace and quiet the polished staff practically guarantees. A recent renovation
took the formerly traditional English country décor and transformed it by
adding French deco style, with flowery prints replaced with rich chocolate,
deep blue and shimmery silver hues, and new leather window seats in many
rooms overlooking Lake Michigan and the Gold Coast. The lobby, grand
ballroom, restaurants and the larger suites and apartments received updates
in early 2009. Two things that haven't changed: the wonderful, personal
service, and the location. It's situated just above Bloomingdale's and other
stores such as Gucci, Williams-Sonoma and Michael Kors in the 900 North
Michigan building.
343 rooms. Restaurant, bar. Fitness center. Spa. Pool. Business center. $351
and up

★★HAMPTON INN CHICAGO AND SUITES

33 W. Illinois St., River North, 312-832-0330, 800-426-7866;
www.hamptoninnchicago.com
Business travelers and Internet junkies will be at home at Hampton Inn. Each
room comes with a portable wooden laptop desk, so you can work or surf the
Web from the comfort of your bed. If you have to burn the midnight oil to get
that big report done, the hotel offers free coffee 24 hours a day at a beverage
station and you'll have a gratis hot breakfast waiting for you in the morning.

Traveling for pleasure? Go for a meal at Ruth's Chris Steak House, lounge at nightspot Ballo, laze on the sundeck or check out the Frank Lloyd Wright-inspired lobby. The hotel brags that the rooms also are influenced by the architect's signature style, but really, Wright probably would have shrugged at the standard tan-and-cream-hued suites.

230 rooms. Restaurant, bar. Complimentary breakfast. Business center. Fitness center. Pool. $61-150

★★★HARD ROCK HOTEL CHICAGO

230 N. Michigan Ave., Loop, 312-345-1000, 866-966-5166;
www.hardrockhotelchicago.com

Located in the landmark Carbide and Carbon Building, the Hard Rock gives some edge to the Art Deco skyscraper. Step into the lobby, which was recently renovated for a classic vibe. Be sure to tour the hotel's display cases, which show off noted musicians' outfits, instruments and other rock 'n' roll memorabilia. But the hotel is more sleek than kitschy. Its modern silver-gray rooms offer Aveda toiletries, pillow-top beds and laptop safes, and they keep to the music theme with bathroom murals of icons such as Bowie and the Beatles. Get the rock-star treatment by staying in the Extreme Suite, a 950-foot-space penthouse that's on its own floor with private elevator access.

381 rooms. Restaurant, bar. Business center. Fitness center. Spa. Pets accepted. $151-250

★★★HILTON CHICAGO

720 S. Michigan Ave., South Loop, 312-922-4400; www.hilton.com

Overlooking Grant Park, Lake Michigan and Millennium Park, this South Loop hotel is all about grandeur. The sumptuous Renaissance-style Great Hall is decorated in white with towering columns and gold accents to go along with intricate ceiling work. The theme tries to carry to the guest rooms with gold-trimmed wood dressers and cabinets and gold-tinged ornate duvets, but it doesn't translate as well in a smaller space. Still, the location across from Grant Park is superb, and if you're in town for St. Patrick's Day, onsite Kitty O'Shea's is the place to be.

1,544 rooms. Restaurant, bar. Business center. Fitness center. Pool. Pets accepted. $151-250

★★★HILTON SUITES CHICAGO/MAGNIFICENT MILE

198 E. Delaware Place, Gold Coast, 312-664-1100; www.hilton.com

This all-suite hotel is in the heart of downtown, making it a convenient choice for business travelers and families alike. The classic navy and maroon suites come with a separate living room complete with a flat-screen TV, mini-fridge and pullout sofa. But who would want to veg on the couch when you can head to the nearby Hancock Tower and peer out from the 94th-floor observatory or—even better—zip up to the 95th-floor Signature Lounge to relax with a sidecar and a vista of downtown? Go ahead and order another round or two; your hotel is within stumbling distance anyway.

345 rooms. Restaurant. Fitness center. Pool. Business center. Pets accepted. $151-250

★★HOMEWOOD SUITES CHICAGO DOWNTOWN

40 E. Grand Ave., River North, 312-644-2222; www.homewoodsuiteschicago.com

Families will appreciate the roomy suites here, but the bedrooms have a cookie-cutter feel thanks to unimaginative tan décor, and although the living rooms are somewhat brighter with a red and gold sleeper sofa and chair, they're still generic. Yet the reason to come here is the full kitchen. It offers plenty of cupboard space, plates and accessories, a microwave, a fridge, a dishwasher and more. If you're not in the mood to cook, there's a free daily breakfast buffet and complimentary receptions Monday through Thursday from 5 to 7 p.m. featuring a light meal and drinks.

233 rooms. Business center. Fitness center. Pool. $61-150

★★★HOTEL ALLEGRO

171 W. Randolph St., Loop, 312-236-0123, 800-643-1500; www.allegrochicago.com

An early 2008 renovation has transformed Hotel Allegro into a posh retreat. The stylish blue and gray rooms have sleek geometric-patterned walls, 37-inch flat-screen TVs, animal-print bathrobes, Aveda toiletries and alarm clocks with iPod docking stations. Savor the soothing ambiance by indulging in an in-room spa treatment—go for the Calm Mind massage, which will fill the room with scents of lavender. If you can pry yourself out of your room, head to the gratis wine hour in the lobby. For sustenance, grab dinner at 312 Chicago for some delicious Italian eats, and then sip a pomegranate Mojito from Encore Liquid Lounge before catching a play at the Cadillac Palace Theatre next door.

483 rooms. Restaurant, bar. Business center. Fitness center. Spa. Pets accepted. $251-350

★★★HOTEL BLAKE

500 S. Dearborn St., Chicago, 312-663-3200; www.hotelblake.com

Hotel Blake stands out from the ostentatious old-fashioned Chicago hotels, offering instead a more stylish option in Printers Row. The contemporary, spacious rooms feature floor-to-ceiling windows, earth tones with splashes of red, and black and white photos of barren tree limbs, which are a nice alternative to the forgettable landscapes that usually hang on hotel walls. For dinner, head to the hotel's equally sophisticated Custom House restaurant, where you'll find delicious Mediterranean-influenced artisanal meat dishes (though at press time there was a rumor that this restaurant was going to be reconcepted).

162 rooms. Restaurant, bar. Business center. Fitness center. Spa. $151-250

★★★HOTEL BURNHAM

1 W. Washington St., Loop, 312-782-1111, 877-294-9712; www.burnhamhotel.com

The landmark Hotel Burnham, the first precursor to modern skyscrapers, retains touches of its past life, with mosaic floors, marble ceilings and walls, and ornamental metal grills on the elevators and stairwells. The rooms, well, not so much: Decked out in navy and gold, they take on a nautical look, with the sunburst mirror and gold emblem on the deep-blue headboard mimicking a ship's wheel. Located across from the former Marshall Field's department store (now Macy's), the hotel is nestled in the middle of the Theater District. Before you catch a show, stop in the Atwood Café, an upscale American restaurant with an inviting jewel-tone dining room that resembles an old Parisian brasserie. Perks for pets are as swanky as those for you: Animals get beds made of hypoallergenic fleece and cedar chips with an optional turn-down service. If you left Fido at home and are feeling lonely, the hotel will lend you a goldfish to keep you company.

122 rooms. Restaurant, bar. Fitness center. Pets accepted. $151-250

★★★HOTEL INDIGO

1244 N. Dearborn St., Gold Coast, 312-787-4980, 866-521-6950;
www.goldcoastchicagohotel.com

If you want something beyond a cookie-cutter hotel room bathed in banal beige, retreat to Hotel Indigo. The guest rooms are more like calming beach houses than typical hotel spaces. Hardwood floors, whitewashed furniture, teak benches, and navy and indigo blue dominate the rooms along with lime green accents, and vibrant wall-size photo murals of blueberries, irises and sky-blue cable-knit sweaters transform the space. Certain touches make it clear that it's not just another day at the beach: spa-style showerheads, sleek Melitta coffee-makers, Aveda toiletries and personal trainers at the fitness center.

165 rooms. Restaurant, bar. Fitness center. Spa. Business center. Pets accepted. $251-350

★★★HOTEL INTERCONTINENTAL CHICAGO

505 N. Michigan Ave., Chicago, 312-944-4100; www.chicago.intercontinental.com

Originally the 1929 Medinah Athletic Club, Hotel InterContinental still maintains some of its old-time glory. Its 12th floor Art Deco Junior Olympic pool is where Olympic swimmer and *Tarzan* actor Johnny Weissmuller frequently escaped from the jungle to do some laps. The hotel now has a state-of-the-art three-story fitness center, one of the largest hotel gyms in the city. If you don't want to be quite that healthy, swing by ENO, where you can order wine flights accompanied by artisanal cheese or luscious chocolate. The rooms in the Main Building are plain-Jane with cream duvets, maroon throw pillows, and maroon-and-gold striped curtains. If you like Old World décor, you'll appreciate the historic tower's rooms, which use the same color palette, but replace mahogany headboards with carved ones and basic bedding with fancy patterned covers.

790 rooms. Restaurant, bar. Fitness center. Pool. Business center. Pets accepted. $251-350

★★★HOTEL MONACO CHICAGO

225 N. Wabash Ave., Chicago, 312-960-8500, 888-775-9223;
www.monaco-chicago.com

It's om sweet om at the Hotel Monaco. Although the rooms feature whimsical Art Deco-inspired décor, with thick pistachio and butter cream striped walls, they are actually Zen dens. Each room comes with a meditation station, a large window with fluffy pillows meant for reflection. You can flip on the in-room yoga program and use the provided accessories to practice your sun salutation. If that doesn't work, take a bath with L'Occitane products. Then slip into the pillow bed and put the Relaxation Station on the TV, which will fill the room with soothing sounds and images. The height-advantaged will get restful sleep, when they stay in the Tall Rooms, which feature 9-foot-long, king-size beds. But if you don't do low-key, book the Rock and Roll Suite, which rolls out the zebra-print carpet with plush red velvet couches, a jukebox, guitar and amp.

192 rooms. Restaurant, bar. Fitness center. Business center. $151-250

★★★HOTEL SAX

333 N. Dearborn St., River North, 312-245-0333; www.hotelsaxchicago.com

Techies will blog about the high-end game room here, which is open to all guests and includes five Xbox 360 stations with wireless controllers, five Zune MP3 players preloaded with music and movies, and two laptops with Internet access. But gossip bloggers will write about the hotel's visiting celebs, such as Lindsay Lohan, who accompanies Samantha Ronson when she DJs at the red-hued Crimson Lounge before retiring upstairs into a suite at the mid-century cool Marina City complex. It's no wonder the hotel, which sits next to the House of Blues, draws such high-profile guests. The too-hip-to-handle slate-gray guest rooms are wallpapered with damask prints superimposed with fake shadows of candelabras, and textures abound with leather paisley headboards, suede throw pillows and chestnut furniture.

353 rooms. Bar. Business center. Fitness center. $251-350

★★★HYATT REGENCY MCCORMICK PLACE

2233 S. Martin Luther King Drive, Chicago, 312-567-1234, 800-633-7313;
www.hyattregencymccormickplace.com

Connected by an enclosed walkway to three exposition buildings, this hotel is a favorite of visiting conventioneers. Guest rooms here are spacious and well furnished.

800 rooms. Restaurant, bar. Complimentary breakfast. Business center. Fitness center. Pool. Spa. $151-250

★★★JAMES HOTEL

55 E. Ontario St., River North, 312-337-1000, 877-526-3755; www.jameshotels.com

The James attracts more stars than an awards show swag-bag giveaway: Jessica Simpson, Jennifer Hudson, Jeremy Piven and Jack Johnson have all checked into the hotel. The draw could be David Burke's Primehouse, which is known for its dry-aged steaks and whimsical desserts such as cheesecake lollipops. Or it could be popular nightspot J Bar. You also can't discount the attractive rooms: Dashes of brown, red or black give the all-white, contemporary design a mod slant, and features like vinyl headboards make this one chic spot. Forget your standard mini-bar. Each room here comes outfitted with a large bar of high-end liquors.

297 rooms. Restaurant, bar. Fitness center. Business center. Pets accepted. $151-250

★★★MARRIOTT CHICAGO DOWNTOWN

540 N. Michigan Ave., River North, 312-836-0100, 800-228-9290; www.marriott.com

As its name implies, this Marriott is conveniently situated on the Magnificent Mile. But the harried shoppers below won't faze you when you've melted underneath the plush down comforter in your bold blue- and gold-colored room (courtesy of upgrades in spring 2006) for a nap. If you can't get any Z's, take a dip in the hotel pool, or give in and join the crowds at nearby Oak

Street Beach. Those who are all work-and-no-play should head to the onsite Starbucks to get some java and free WiFi. Self-check out kiosks also will help business travelers on tight schedules.

1,198 rooms. Restaurant, bar. Business center. Fitness center. Pool. $151-250

★★OLD TOWN CHICAGO BED AND BREAKFAST

1442 N. North Park Ave., Chicago, 312-440-9268; www.oldtownchicago.com

Guests staying in this modern, four-room bed and breakfast housed in an Art Deco mansion have access to amenities such as a complimentary washer and dryer, a private bathroom and walk-in closet. There is also a communal kitchen where guests can do their own cooking.

Four rooms. Complimentary breakfast. Business center. Fitness center. $151-250

★★★OMNI CHICAGO HOTEL

676 N. Michigan Ave., River North, 312-944-6664, 888-444-6664; www.omnihotels.com

If the name sounds familiar, it's because Oprah puts up many of her show's guests at this all-suite hotel. The beige and cream suites offer roomy digs and plasma TVs. Kids get milk and cookies every night. Ask for a free Get Fit Kit ($50 deposit is required), which includes a mat and weights so that you can work out in your hotel room while the little ones play. Afterward, head up to one of the two rooftop decks where you can catch some sun in warm weather.

347 rooms. Restaurant, bar. Business center. Fitness center. Spa. Pool. Pets accepted. $251-350

★★★PALMER HOUSE HILTON

17 E. Monroe St., Loop, 312-726-7500; www.hilton.com

Named after business mogul Potter Palmer, the historic Palmer House is one of the longest continuously running hotels in the U.S., and also the first to be equipped with electric lights and telephones in each room. A 2008 renovation aimed to return the massive hotel to its roots, and thankfully it included more than just lights and phones; a health club and spa, standard elsewhere, are finally forthcoming. The rooms are now bathed in lavender, brown and sage, shades that mimic the lobby's original terrazzo flooring and opulent Beaux-Arts ceiling, but the décor is updated with monogrammed pillows, swirly and striped linens, and ebony headboards. Executive level rooms didn't get the modern makeover—they have a French Empire style with flowery pastels and ornate gold mirrors—but you'll get your own private concierge and a buffet of goodies such as the Palmer House brownies, which is appropriate since Bertha Palmer invented the chocolaty creation and the Palmer House debuted it at the 1893 World's Fair.

1,639 rooms. Restaurant, bar. Business center. Fitness center. Pool. Pets accepted. $151-250

★★★PARK HYATT CHICAGO

800 N. Michigan Ave., Gold Coast, 312-335-1234, 800-233-1234;
www.parkchicago.hyatt.com

The luxe Park Hyatt showers guests with butlers, personal safes with laptop rechargers and storage for wardrobes (who can travel without that?). The chic décor is simple and understated with cherry wood-filled guest rooms, gold and mocha accents and leather chairs. Make sure to bathe in the oversized tub; as you soak you can slide open the wall to reveal the bedroom and views of the skyline or Lake Michigan. For more relaxation, pamper yourself at the onsite medispa Tiffani Kim Institute with a customized facial. If you're the sporty type, borrow one of the hotel's free bicycles and do some sightseeing while pedaling along Chicago's many bike paths. Afterward, complete the experience with dinner at NoMI, an excellent contemporary French-Asian restaurant overlooking Michigan Avenue.

198 rooms. Restaurant, bar. Fitness center. Spa. Pool. Business center. Pets accepted. $351 and up

★★★★★THE PENINSULA CHICAGO

108 E. Superior St., Gold Coast, 312-337-2888, 866-288-8889;
www.chicago.peninsula.com

Stars like Ellen DeGeneres, Chris Rock and Brad Pitt and Angelina Jolie visit The Peninsula for its luxurious rooms and spa, but don't overlook it as a dining destination. The hotel is known for its highly acclaimed Shanghai Terrace and Avenues restaurants. There are also the afternoon teas, which offer exotic blends, including those made especially for The Peninsula, as well as a lavish chocolate buffet on Fridays and Saturdays. Even without the food options, The Peninsula stands out. The Peninsula Spa by ESPA offers a full menu of services and a relaxation lounge where you can lounge under a comforter in a sectioned-off area and relax uninterrupted after your treatment. Luxurious guest rooms are bright with light wood and muted earth tones, and the marble bathrooms have roomy tubs where you can watch TV while you soak. A bedside control panel allows you to shut off the light and signal that you don't want to be disturbed, all without having to leave the comfort of your 300-thread-count sheets.

339 rooms. Restaurant, bar. Fitness center. Spa. Pool. Business center. Pets accepted. $351 and up

★★★RENAISSANCE CHICAGO HOTEL

1 W. Wacker Drive, Chicago, 312-372-7200, 888-236-2427;
www.renaissancehotels.com

This Loop high-rise is an urban sanctuary. Comfortable rooms have views of the city. Additional amenities include 24-hour room service, expanded club-level rooms, a fitness club and pool, a lobby bar and a 24-hour FedEx Kinkos business center.

553 rooms. Restaurant, bar. Business center. Fitness center. Pool. Pets accepted. $251-350

★★★★THE RITZ-CARLTON CHICAGO, A FOUR SEASONS HOTEL

160 E. Pearson St., Gold Coast, 312-266-1000, 800-621-6906;
www.fourseasons.com/chicagorc

When you're at the Ritz, which rests atop shopping mecca Water Tower Place, the city view from the large-windowed rooms is hard to beat. The spacious accommodations were just given a makeover, and floral-patterned duvets and dark wood furniture were replaced with crisp white linens and a soothing grey color palette. If you don't want to leave, send up for the spa's in-room signature aromatherapy massage or have a customized fragranced bath drawn for you in your marble bathroom. After your treatment and soothing bath, you might want to rest your heavy head on the down pillow and bury yourself underneath the down blanket. But force yourself to grab a cocktail in the Greenhouse, where you won't have to sacrifice the view or being comfortable, as you can enjoy the lakefront panorama from sofas and comfortable chairs.

434 rooms. Restaurant, bar. Fitness center. Spa. Pool. Business center. Pets accepted. $351 and up

★★★SHERATON CHICAGO HOTEL AND TOWERS

301 E. North Water St., Loop, 312-464-1000, 800-325-3535; www.sheratonchicago.com
Overlooking the Chicago River, the Sheraton chain's flagship branch touts itself as the "premier convention and business hotel in the Midwest." In fact, its enormous size makes it seem more like a convention center than a luxury hotel. But the simply decorated cream and beige rooms with beds resting against wood-paneled walls are inviting, especially when you add in the calming views of the water. For a change of scenery, visit the surprisingly hip Chi Bar, where you can kick back in a cocoa-colored leather chair with a Chicago Sunset martini and forget about the conventioneers flitting around the rest of the hotel.

1,209 rooms. Restaurant, bar. Business center. Fitness center. Pool. Pets accepted. $151-250

★★★SOFITEL CHICAGO WATER TOWER

20 E. Chestnut St., Gold Coast, 312-324-4000; www.sofitel.comm
You can't miss the stylish Sofitel—look for the triangle-shaped building near downtown. The glass and steel structure looks like it leapt out from the pages of an interior design magazine and into the Gold Coast. The rooms aren't too shabby, either. They are a tad small but airy, thanks to light wood furniture, cream walls, bedding and mirrored closet doors. The bathrooms are roomier, with separate showers and tubs. This hotel goes Francophile all the way, with Café des Architectes, a French restaurant, and Le Bar, which has floor-to-ceiling glass walls and is the perfect place for a wine flight and a cheese plate.

415 rooms. Restaurant, bar. Fitness center. Business center. Pets accepted. $251-350

★★★THE SUTTON PLACE HOTEL—CHICAGO

21 E. Bellevue Place, Gold Coast, 312-266-2100, 866-378-8866; www.suttonplace.com
White is the shade of choice for the linens in the rooms here, while the drapes, carpeting and wallpaper are beige, replacing the old gloomy gray that used to dominate the rooms. The only vibrant color you'll see is a smattering of purple and bold blue in a stray chair or pillow. On the bright side, you can escape to MEXX Kitchen & Bar at The Whiskey to unwind with some authentic Mexican fare; try the shrimp tacos and wash them down with a margarita or two, which will put some color in your cheeks if your room is without.

246 rooms. Restaurant, bar. Business center. Fitness center. Pets accepted. $251-350

★★★SWISSÔTEL CHICAGO

323 E. Wacker Drive, Loop, 312-565-0565, 800-637-9477; www.swissotelchicago.com

After renovations in April 2008, the Swissôtel Chicago—the sole stateside outpost of the Swiss hotel chain—is more appealing to business travelers. Upgrades included larger desks, ergonomic chairs, tech docking stations to use various media devices simultaneously and 37-inch split-screen plasma TVs. And the hotel recently added more meeting space. But families will be at home here, too. Kid-friendly suites have child-sized beds, toys, a play area and books. Parents can hunker down within the heather gray and ivory striped walls and rest in a white bed with an oversized fabric headboard. Whether you're there for business or pleasure, be sure to take a dip in the 45-foot indoor pool. It's on the 42nd floor and offers a nice view of Lake Michigan, as well as a wall that features a beautiful tiled mural of the Chicago skyline.

661 rooms. Restaurant, bar. Business center. Fitness center. Pool. $251-350

★★THE TREMONT CHICAGO

100 E. Chestnut St., Gold Coast, 312-751-1900, 800-625-5144;
www.tremontchicago.com

The pale hues, dark wood and floral textiles in the small rooms aim for a romantic vibe, but they make this European-style hotel seem dated rather than for dating. The rooms also provide a strange juxtaposition to the hotel's restaurant, the decidedly unflowery Mike Ditka's Restaurant, owned by the legendary Bears coach. The two-floor steakhouse replaces the faux romanticism with a cigar lounge and a live Sinatra-esque singer. Odd pairings aside, the Tremont's best perk is its location; it's a half block away from Michigan Avenue, right near the Hancock Center and Water Tower Place shopping paradise.

130 rooms. Restaurant, bar. $151-250

★★★★TRUMP INTERNATIONAL HOTEL & TOWER CHICAGO

401 N. Wabash Ave., River North, 312-588-8000, 877-458-7867;
www.trumpchicagohotel.com

The Donald put his stamp on the Chicago skyline with his stainless-steel and iridescent glass hotel, which towers over the city at 92 stories. And he continues the splendor inside the tower. The modern, slate-gray rooms have floor-to-ceiling windows that give a gorgeous vista of the city, custom-designed furniture warms up the spaces, and chefs will come to your room to cook up a meal in your state-of-the-art kitchen. The lap-of-luxury treatment doesn't end there. You can get purifying massages using ruby and diamond-infused oils at the spa. If you don't opt for the in-room chef, go to the restaurant Sixteen, which has a seasonally driven menu. Afterward, have a drink at the inviting Rebar, which offers a lovely view of the adjacent Chicago River.

339 rooms. Restaurant, bar. Business center. Fitness center. Spa. Pool. $351 and up

★★★W CHICAGO CITY CENTER

172 W. Adams St., Loop, 312-332-1200, 888-625-5144; www.whotels.com

Staying at the W is less about the rooms and amenities and more about the scene. Socialites and Loop workers crowd the bar for happy hour in the neo-gothic lobby, or the "Living Room," with long drapes at the entryways, and

art projected on a wall set to music. The onsite Ristorante We serves Tuscan-inspired cuisine, and rooms are stylish and comfortable with pillow-top beds and eggplant comforters. The downside: if you want to visit the excellent Bliss spa, you'll have to head to the W's Lakeshore location.
369 rooms. Restaurant, bar. Business center. Fitness center. Pets accepted. $251-350

★★★W CHICAGO - LAKESHORE

644 N. Lake Shore Drive, Streeterville; 312-943-9200; www.starwoodhotels.com
Business travelers who yawn at the usual tedious hotel environs will seek refuge at the W, which has a prime spot on Lake Shore Drive. After settling into your small, dimly lit but sophisticated room, which offers a mix of taupe and deep purples, head up to the hotel's eighth floor to pamper yourself with a treatment at Bliss, a cheerful spa that lives up to its name. There you can have a pedicure while you catch an episode of *Entourage* on your own personal TV. Afterward, return to your room, crawl under the goose-down duvet and watch a DVD from the lending library. Or go to the penthouse lounge, Whiskey Sky, where you sip a cocktail and admire the Lake Michigan views. Adjacent to Whiskey Sky is Altitude, a revolving banquet room that would be an impressive spot for a business meeting.
520 rooms. Restaurant, bar. Business center. Fitness center. Pool. Spa. Pets accepted. $251-350

★★★THE WESTIN CHICAGO NORTH SHORE

601 N. Milwaukee Ave., Wheeling, IL, 847-777-6500, 800-937-8461;
www.starwoodhotels.com
This north suburban Chicago Westin outpost is contemporary and sleek in design and amenities. Rooms have luxury bedding, flat-screen TVs and The fitness center features an indoor lap pool and a gym stocked with Reebok equipment. Local chef Rick Tramonto is the force behind the hotel's restaurants, which include a steakhouse and an Italian-themed eatery.
412 rooms. Restaurant, bar. Business center. Fitness center. Pool. Pets accepted. $151-250

★★★THE WESTIN CHICAGO RIVER NORTH

320 N. Dearborn St., Chicago, 312-744-1900, 877-866-9216; www.westinchicago.com
This hotel overlooks the Chicago River and offers a welcoming home for business or leisure travelers visiting the city. The Kamehachi Sushi Bar delights fish lovers, the Celebrity Cafe features all-day dining with a focus on American dishes, and the Hana Lounge entertains nightly with hors d'oeuvres and live music.
424 rooms. Pets accepted. Restaurant, bar. Business center. Fitness center. Complimentary breakfast. $251-350

★★★WESTIN MICHIGAN AVENUE

909 N. Michigan Ave., Gold Coast, 312-943-7200, 800-937-8461;
www.westin.com/michiganave
The Westin tries to offer a little something for everyone. Shopaholics will love the hotel for its location across from Water Tower Place. Kids will enjoy the Kids Club, whose membership comes with a drawstring bag with a world

map and make-your-own postcard kit upon check-in. Parents of newborns will appreciate getting their own drawstring bag filled with first-aid items, socket covers and a nightlight. Pets sleep soundly on their own beds. Joggers will lap up the Runner's World-approved maps of local running routes. And everyone will have a restful sleep on the hotel's legendary plush mattresses 752 rooms. Restaurant, bar. Business center. Fitness center. Pets accepted. $251-350

★★★THE WHITEHALL HOTEL
105 E. Delaware Place, Chicago, 312-944-6300, 800-948-4255;
www.thewhitehallhotel.com
Built in 1927 and extensively renovated since then, the independent Whitehall retains its stature as a small sanctuary with personal service and old-world charm. Rooms combine traditional décor and modern technology. The pan-Italian restaurant, Fornetto Mei, offers an excellent wine service, a bar and outdoor dining.
222 rooms. Restaurant, bar. Business center. Fitness center. Pets accepted. $151-250

★★★WYNDHAM CHICAGO DOWNTOWN HOTEL
633 N. St. Clair St., Chicago, 312-573-0300, 800-996-3426; www.wyndham.com
The lobby of this downtown hotel is inviting with fresh fruit, beautiful marble floors and an abundance of natural light streaming in from the many windows. Caliterra Bar & Grill offers a convenient dining option, serving California and Italian cuisine, with live jazz in the evenings. The comfortable guest rooms feature pillow-top mattresses, Herman Miller desk chairs and Golden Door bath products.
417 rooms. Restaurant, bar. Complimentary breakfast. Business center. Fitness center. Pool. $151-250

WHERE TO EAT
★★★★★ALINEA
1723 N. Halsted St., Chicago, 312-867-0110; www.alinearestaurant.com
Not only did Alinea's internationally respected chef Grant Achatz win the 2008 James Beard Outstanding Chef Award, he's also got a hell of a story to tell. In 2007, Achatz was diagnosed with tongue cancer, and doctors said he might lose his sense of taste forever. Thankfully, an aggressive treatment looks to have beaten the cancer, and Achatz's sense of taste was saved. So now he's back in the kitchen, creating some of the most wildly creative dishes in the country. Alinea, the Latin word for that funny little symbol (¶) indicating the need for a new paragraph—or a new train of thought—is at the forefront of the molecular gastronomy movement, which re-imagines familiar foods in stunningly innovative ways. Behind the restaurant's purposefully hidden entrance and up a floating glass-and-metal staircase, you'll be treated to breathtaking creations such as the black truffle explosion, featuring truffle-topped ravioli filled with truffle broth which "explodes" in your mouth. Another dish is duck served with mango and yogurt on a pillow of juniper air. The complex meals often require equally complicated instructions from the patient waitstaff, but trust us—you won't complain.
American. Dinner. Closed Monday-Tuesday; July 4. Reservations recom-

mended. $86 and up

★★★ARIA

The Fairmont Chicago, 200 N. Columbus Dr., Loop, 312-444-9494;
www.ariachicago.com

Technically, Aria is located inside the Fairmont hotel, just east of tony Michigan Avenue. But the fact that the restaurant has its own entrance symbolizes how chef Brad Parsons wants his eclectic spot to separate itself from the norm. The globally influenced restaurant boasts its own tandoori oven for naan bread, and a hip sushi bar draws a lively crowd of saketini sippers. Those who want a globe-spanning culinary experience will have a great time in the dramatic dining room, which is filled with orchids and Tibetan artwork. The menu ranges from shrimp and chicken pad thai to a perfectly prepared New York strip steak to Hong Kong barbecue duck and lobster chow mein. The menu is all over the map, but it works.
International. Breakfast, lunch, dinner. Bar. $36-85

★★★ARUN'S

4156 N. Kedzie Ave., Northwest Side, 773-539-1909; www.arunsthai.com

Thai cuisine in Chicago was once consigned to BYOB storefronts, but owner Arun Sampanthavivat's gorgeous restaurant, which he opened in 1985, brought his native land's food to the level of haute cuisine. The 2,500-square-foot, bi-level dining room—its every nook and cranny filled with gorgeous Thai art (much of it painted by the owner's brother)—is located in far-flung Albany Park. The almost museum-like surroundings complement a dining experience that brilliantly combines heat and sweetness. The constantly changing offerings are part of a 12-course tasting menu consisting of six appetizers, four entrées and two desserts, and preparations range from a beef curry in a spicy sauce to whole tamarind snapper. The personable service is always ready to accommodate any preferences or tolerance for spiciness, and a meticulous wine-pairing is available for the asking.
Thai. Dinner. Closed Monday. $86 and up

★★★ATWOOD CAFE

Hotel Burnham, 1 W. Washington St., Loop, 312-368-1900; www.atwoodcafe.com

You can't get much more centrally located than the Atwood Café, which sits in the heart of the action of Chicago's Loop and provides floor-to-ceiling views of bustling State Street. And you can't get much more comfortable than the food on the Atwood Café's menu, which presents new takes on classic American standbys. Chef Heather Terhune prepares dishes like a huge Comport Family Farm pork chop served with vanilla-honey peach jam, and a tender grilled filet mignon with truffle butter and port wine sauce. She also wins plaudits for her dessert menu, which includes perfectly made classics such as scrumptious dark-chocolate soufflé cake and warm roasted banana and white chocolate bread pudding. The expansive bar serves as an ideal place for a drink before heading to the nearby Theater District (we told you it was centrally located) for a show.
Contemporary American. Breakfast, lunch, dinner, Sunday brunch. $36-85

★★★AVEC
615 W. Randolph St., West Loop, 312-377-2002; www.avecrestaurant.com

Avec means "with" in French, which fits here because you're likely to end up dining with complete strangers at one of the communal tables. You won't mind, because the restaurant's Euro-Mediterranean fare and surprisingly reasonable prices put you in such a good mood that you're happy to talk with your neighbors about the amazing food in front of you. Co-owned by chef Paul Kahan (better known for Blackbird, Avec's sister restaurant next door), Avec offers delicious fare such as the popular chorizo-stuffed madjool dates wrapped in smoked bacon and topped with a piquillo pepper-tomato sauce, and the crispy focaccia with taleggio cheese, truffle oil and fresh herbs. The menu, which is divided into large and small plates, is always changing, which means this restaurant is worth a trip every time you're in town. The small room looks almost sauna-like with its fully paneled cedar walls and ceiling, and its back display of glass wine bottles is both colorful and whimsical. Speaking of bottles, Avec offers some 125 wines from France, Italy, Spain and Portugal; we recommend buying a bottle to share with the newfound friends you'll undoubtedly meet at your table.

Contemporary American, Mediterranean. Dinner. Bar. $36-85

★★★★AVENUES
The Peninsula Chicago, 108 E. Superior St., River North, 312-573-6695;
www.chicago.peninsula.com

Forget the plain name, and overlook the fact that the intimate Avenues is in a hotel (though the hotel is the Peninsula, one of the best in the city). You might have to tolerate a setting that's a little more staid than luxurious. Instead, try to focus on the food, as chef Curtis Duffy offers cuisine that manages to be both simple and extravagant. Duffy succeeded acclaimed toque Graham Elliot Bowles (who left to start his own eponymous River North restaurant). But Duffy, who was Grant Achatz's right-hand man at Alinea, has made Avenues all his own. He favors unusual pairings that work despite seeming contradictory: A grilled Wagyu steak comes with smoked coconut and African blue basil, and lamb is poached in tangerine oil with mint blossom. The best bet might be to take a seat at the bar in front of the open kitchen and watch Duffy work his magic.

Contemporary American. Dinner. Closed Sunday-Monday. Reservations recommended. Bar. $86 and up

★★★BICE
158 E. Ontario St., Chicago, 312-664-1474; www.bicechicago.com

A chain that grew out of Milan, Bice stays true to its Northern Italian roots. While the menu changes monthly, expect hits such as veal Milanese and beef carpaccio. For a cheaper, more casual version of the menu, try the next-door sibling, Bice Café, a lunchtime favorite of Michigan Avenue shoppers.

Italian. Lunch, dinner. Reservations recommended. Outdoor seating. Bar. $36-85

★★BIN 36
339 N. Dearborn St., River North, 312-755-9463; www.bin36.com

Most restaurants serve food and enhance the experience with wine. At the cavernous Bin 36, it's the other way around. You'll see that love of the grape from the many wine flights served with dinner to the wine store on the premises that will sell you that wine you really liked with your dinner. "Wine Director" Brian Duncan—he refuses to be called a sommelier—offers some 50 wines by the glass, and about 300 bottles to choose from. But despite the hullabaloo about vino, the menu is hardly an afterthought. Chef John Caputo's seafood-oriented fare includes a seared ahi tuna with herb-ricotta dumplings, and peppercorn-crusted blue marlin with mashed potatoes, onion rings and bordelaise sauce. Bin 36 offers three different dining areas, depending on your mood: the bar, the cheese bar or at a standard table in the dining room. The wine list in the downstairs trattoria, A Mano, which the owners opened in late 2007, focuses on small producers. Take a seat here on a Thursday after 5 p.m. for the $5 piz-zas, and then grab a gelato from the gelato and sorbet bar on our way out. A sophisticated environment with options galore? We'll drink to that.

Contemporary American. Breakfast, lunch, dinner. Bar. $36-85

★★★BISTRO CAMPAGNE
4518 N. Lincoln Ave., Lincoln Square, 773-271-6100; www.bistrocampagne.com

We know this Lincoln Square bistro isn't exactly centrally situated, but the classic French fare and immaculate wine list make the cozy neighborhood spot well worth the trip to the North Side. Acclaimed chef Michael Altenberg is a vocal sustainable-food advocate, so he uses local, organic ingredients to create dishes like his flawless pan-seared salmon with braised lentils and succulent steak piled high with delicious fries. We can't talk about Bistro Campagne—let alone visit here—without mentioning Altenberg's steamed mussels, served in a tasty Belgian ale. The restaurant itself has a rustic feel with Prairie-style design touches and dark wood trim, while the outdoor space provides a beautiful mosaic fountain and a quaint cottage for a se-cluded retreat.

French. Dinner, Sunday brunch. Bar. $36-85

★★★BLACKBIRD
619 W. Randolph St., West Loop, 312-715-0708; www.blackbirdrestaurant.com

In an almost sacrilegious move, Blackbird's main man Paul Kahan recently handed over the apron at this spot to Mike Sheerin, formerly of New York's famed WD-50. It's not just that Kahan, who was named the James Beard Foundation's Best Chef in the Midwest in 2004, surrendered control—it's also that Sheerin has brought a slight element of playfulness to Kahan's sol-id menu. Now, for instance, the short ribs come with sesame gnocchi and ground cherries and the "fried" chicken comes with smoked potato salad. Foodies love it just as much as they always have. As for the restaurant it-self, it's sleek and minimalist—but it's not exactly roomy. Tables are packed tightly together, but you won't mind overhearing a few conversations for food of this caliber.

Contemporary American. Lunch (Monday-Friday), dinner. Closed Sunday. Reservations recommended. $36-85

★★★BOB SAN
1805-07 W. Division, Chicago, 773-235-8888; www.bob-san.com

Bob San's owner Bob Bee has created a veritable sushi empire throughout

Chicago, giving the city fixtures like Sai Café, Sushi Naniwa and Hachi's Kitchen. But it's Wicker Park's bustling Bob San that's earned Bee his biggest buzz. The restaurant features lively lounge music, an open wooden-beam ceiling and playful fish-shaped lighting fixtures. But the focus here is the expansive menu, which features some 45 handcrafted rolls that include classics like the spider roll with soft-shell crab, avocado and cucumber. There are also a dozen entrées for non-sushi eaters, including a teriyaki New York strip steak. The tables are packed closely together, so if you're hoping for a romantic meal, try to get one of the tables by the window, close to the bar.
Japanese. Dinner. Bar. $36-85

★★BONGO ROOM
1470 N. Milwaukee Ave., Wicker Park, 773-489-0690; 1152 S. Wabash Ave., South Loop, 312-291-0100
If you're looking for an imaginative breakfast in a playful environment, you'd better head to the Bongo Room early. Even 30 minutes before the doors open, the sidewalk outside this Wicker Park standby is packed with hungover urbanites anxiously awaiting a table. The breakfast burrito filled with guacamole and fluffy scrambled eggs is a favorite, but most come here for the outrageously sweet concoctions that mix breakfast with dessert, such as Oreo cookie pancakes or chocolate tower French toast. The spot is a little less crowded when lunchtime rolls around, when the kitchen offers inventive fare like a tasty maple-and-mustard-roasted pork loin sandwich and a delectable baby spinach, golden beet and duck confit salad. If you can't stomach the interminable brunch wait, try the South Loop location, where it's slightly—note, we said slightly—less crowded.
Contemporary American. Breakfast, lunch, Saturday-Sunday brunch. $16-35

★★BRASSERIE JO
59 W. Hubbard St., River North, 312-595-0800; www.brasseriejo.com
High ceilings and Art Deco accents aren't the only archetypal French elements at this River North fixture. With whimsical French accordion music constantly playing in the background, chef/owner Jean Joho's bistro has been a Chicago favorite since it opened in 1996, drawing adoring crowds with a casual Alsatian menu that features classics such as coq au vin and a juicy cut of steak topped with a heaping mound of frites. The value-conscious, however, don't need to venture beyond the tartes flambées, delicious pizzas topped with everything from pears, blue cheese and walnuts to spinach, mushroom and Gruyère. A large beer and wine selection (including the restaurant's own Hopla brew) makes this the next best thing to being in Paris.
French. Dinner. Bar. $36-85

★★CAFÉ ABSINTHE
1954 W. North Ave., Chicago, 773-278-4488; www.cafeabsinthechicago.com
It's telling that the entrance to this Wicker Park fave is not on teeming North Avenue but in an alley around the corner. The off-the-beaten-path entry likely keeps the tippling masses from stumbling in and disrupting the restaurant's dimly lit, romantic atmosphere. Chef Jose Garcia's seasonal, American-oriented menu changes daily, but a recent incarnation featured Australian herb-marinated lamb with sautéed watercress and rosemary jus, and horseradish-encrusted salmon with garlic mashed potatoes and cabernet butter sauce. The

signature dessert is a dark chocolate lava cake infused with Grand Marnier liqueur in a prickly-pear sauce—a treat that's well worth a trip down any alley. American. Dinner. Reservations recommended. Bar. $16-35

★★CAFE BA-BA-REEBA!

2024 N. Halsted St., Chicago, 773-935-5000, 888-538-8823; www.cafebabareeba.com

Spanish, tapas. Lunch, dinner. Reservations recommended. Outdoor seating. Children's menu. Bar. $16-35

★★CAFE IBERICO

739 N. La Salle Drive, Chicago, 312-573-1510; www.cafe-iberico.com

Spanish, tapas. Lunch, dinner. Reservations recommended. Children's menu. Bar. $16-35

★★★CALITERRA

633 N. St. Clair St., Chicago, 312-274-4444; www.wyndham.com

Aptly named considering its Cal-Ital culinary concept (Tuscany meets Northern California), this handsome and somewhat hidden spot in the Wyndham Chicago hotel draws a well-heeled Gold Coast business and shopping crowd. Innovative seasonal fare emphasizes organic produce and meats. The noteworthy cheese cart and Italian-American wine list are additional highlights. California, Italian. Breakfast, lunch (Monday-Saturday), dinner. Reservations recommended. Children's menu. Bar. $36-85

★★★THE CAPITAL GRILLE

633 N. St. Clair St., Chicago, 312-337-9400; www.thecapitalgrille.com

This steakhouse chain deliberately cultivates the "old boys network" vibe. The clubby, masculine décor features dark woods and original oil paintings of fox hunts, cattle drives and the like. Sizable à la carte entrées like porterhouse steak, filet mignon and broiled fresh lobster, along with traditional sides that serve three, tempt the taste buds. Beef is dry-aged on the premises for 14 days and hand-cut daily.

Steak. Lunch, dinner. Reservations recommended. Bar. $36-85

★★★★★CHARLIE TROTTER'S

816 W. Armitage Ave., Chicago, 773-248-6228; www.charlietrotters.com

There's not much about internationally renowned chef Charlie Trotter that hasn't already been said. Awards? He has them in spades. Books? He's written them. TV shows? He stars in a cooking series. Which brings us back to Trotter's food, and for that he uses only naturally raised meats, line-caught fish and organic produce to craft his world-famous fare. The formal waitstaff speak in hushed tones when talking about Trotter's exactingly prepared menu, which includes dishes such as chilled trout with watercress and crayfish, and Crawford Farm lamb rack with chanterelle mushrooms and fermented black garlic. Housed in an unassuming brick building in the tony Lincoln Park neighborhood, the understated restaurant—there is no art on the walls, as Trotter believes any art should be on the plate—provides a tasteful environment for what is always a remarkable evening. For those who want to see the restaurant's inner workings firsthand, Trotter's offers a table in the kitchen that comes with its own custom-prepared menu.

Contemporary American. Dinner. Closed Sunday-Monday. $86 and up

★★★CHEZ JOEL

1119 W. Taylor St., Chicago, 312-226-6479; www.chezjoelbistro.com

Just a few minutes from the Loop, tiny Chez Joel dares to be French within the friendly confines of Little Italy. Classic bistro fare is seasoned with more adventurous specials and an appealing sandwich selection at lunch.

French. Lunch, dinner. Closed Monday. Reservations recommended. Outdoor seating. Bar. $36-85

★★★CHICAGO CHOP HOUSE

60 W. Ontario St., River North, 312-787-7100; www.chicagochophouse.com

It's hard to capture authenticity—some places have it, while other spots feel like a couple of marketing majors drummed up a concept. But the Chop House has authenticity to spare, from the classic green awnings on the Victorian façade to the 1,400 pictures of Chicago icons on the walls. Of course, old-school charm is irrelevant if the food doesn't work—but the reasonably priced steaks here are wet-aged and perfectly prepared. The menu is light on perks, so don't expect anything fancy. Just start out with the prosciutto-wrapped asparagus before going for the massive New York strip (or the 64-ounce porterhouse, if you're up to it). The award-winning wine list features more than 600 bottles, from Oregon pinot noirs to renowned French cabs. Just be sure to leave the baseball caps and T-shirts at home; the dress code, while relatively relaxed, encourages smart attire.

Steak. Dinner. Reservations recommended. Bar. $36-85

★COALFIRE

1321 W. Grand Ave., Chicago, 312-226-2625; www.coalfirechicago.com

Chicago's reputation is changing dramatically these days: No one talks about Al Capone anymore, the Cubs are actually a good team and the city's pizza fans aren't all heading out for deep dish. The unassuming, relatively new Coalfire is a big reason for this last shift. This restaurant bakes its pies in a coal-heated oven, which produces an eyebrow-singeing temperature of 800 degrees. This high heat produces a smoky, slightly charred crust that's both crispy and chewy, while the housemade tomato sauce has the perfect amount of sweetness. The surprisingly spartan list of toppings includes prosciutto, red peppers and anchovies, but regulars swear by the simple margherita, which is made up of sauce, fresh buffalo mozzarella, ricotta and freshly cut basil leaves.

Pizza. Lunch (Saturday-Sunday), dinner. Closed Monday. $16-35

★★COCO PAZZO

300 W. Hubbard St., Chicago, 312-836-0900; www.cocopazzochicago.com

This classy Italian restaurant is decorated in dark woods and rich fabrics. Located near several theaters, it's popular among the show going crowd. The plates are carefully prepared with exquisite attention given to detail.

Italian. Lunch, dinner. Outdoor seating. Bar. $16-35

★★COOBAH

3423 N. Southport Ave., Chicago, 773-528-2220; www.coobah.com

Latin American. Lunch, dinner, late-night, brunch. Reservations recommended. Outdoor seating. Children's menu. Bar. $16-35

★★★CROFTON ON WELLS
535 N. Wells St., River North, 312-755-1790; www.croftononwells.com

In a city that features such renowned chefs as Charlie Trotter and Grant Achatz, it's telling that Suzy Crofton's eponymous River North restaurant has survived—thrived, actually—since 1997. By leaving the foam and froth to others, Crofton has earned a truckload of awards for her elegant contemporary cuisine. The restaurant's muted gray-and-white décor mirrors Crofton's French-tinged cooking: elegant and thoughtful, without pretense. She puts as much thought into her appetizers—including the crab cake and sautée of wild mushrooms with bacon, cracked peppercorn and brioche—as she does on her Amish chicken and smoked pork belly topped with her famous smoked-apple chutney. Vegetarians aren't relegated to a cursory dish at the corner of the menu—Crofton puts out a separate vegetarian menu, as well as several vegan options.

Contemporary American. Dinner. Closed Sunday. Bar. $36-85

★★CRUST
2056 W. Division St., Chicago, 773-235-5511; www.crustchicago.com

With its stark white-brick walls and orange plastic chairs, Crust sure doesn't seem like it's at the forefront of a revolution. Yet the spot, helmed by Bistro Campagne's Michael Altenberg, has created the Midwest's first certified organic restaurant. Using organic flour and ingredients including fresh-pulled water buffalo mozzarella, Altenberg coaxes delicious pizzas (inexplicably called "wood-oven flatbreads" on the menu) from the tile-encrusted wood-burning oven. The surprisingly small menu features only 12 options, but the possibilities include such gourmet combinations as the Carbonara—topped with roasted slab bacon, peas and an egg sunny-side up—and the Mexicali blues—with provolone, mozzarella, roasted shrimp, cilantro and pico de gallo. Even some of the beer offerings are organic, letting you get soused as sustainably as possible.

Pizza. Lunch, dinner. $16-35

★★★CUSTOM HOUSE
500 S. Dearborn St., Loop, 312-523-0200; www.customhouse.cc

This elegantly low-key Printers Row spot has a Zen-like feel with its decorations of pebbles, twigs and rocks, but the menu is all meat, all the time (save for some seafood). Appetizers include Wagyu beef tartare with potato chips and farm fresh egg, and rich veal sweetbreads with glazed bacon and mushrooms. Be sure to save room for the entrées, which feature such perfectly crafted steaks as a tender flatiron cut with onion rings, and a tender bone in short rib with horseradish cream puffs. If you have a finicky vegetarian in your group, don't despair; the chef will indeed make a special meal for him or her, proving that the restaurant is indeed aptly named. (At press time, there was talk of this restaurant being recast as a tavern.)

Steak. Lunch, dinner. Reservations recommended. Bar. $36-85

★★★DAVID BURKE'S PRIMEHOUSE
The James Hotel, 616 N. Rush St., River North, 312-660-6000; www.davidburke.com

Sure, many Chicago restaurants claim to be serious about their steaks, but we're guessing not many of them go as far as David Burke's Primehouse, which boasts its own salt-tiled aging room, in which the owners dry-age their own beef. Even more impressive: David Burke owns a stud steer in Kentucky whose offspring produce the meat for his aged steaks. These are just two of the reasons this spot stands apart from the herd. The room is a veritable ode to all things bovine: The chairs are a deep brown leather and the tables are wrapped in red leather. The steaks are the main draw, from the "South Side" bone-in filet to the châteaubriand for two. There is a respectable number of non-steak options as well, including a seared Alaskan king salmon and a grilled ahi tuna mignon. They're not bad, but when else will you have a chance to trace the family tree of your prime rib?

Steak. Breakfast, lunch (Monday-Saturday), dinner, Sunday brunch. Bar. $36-85

★★DINE
733 W. Madison St., Chicago, 312-602-2100; www.dinerestaurant.com

Dine's residence at the Crown Plaza draws the hotel crowd, but come here for a reliably decent and quick lunch in a nostalgic atmosphere. The place is all about American classics with a modern twist: The décor is vintage diner contrasted by a modern, open kitchen; the menu features quintessential comfort food such as a contemporary angus beef meatloaf served with sour cream whipped potatoes and a roasted tomato gravy. If you're craving a little home cooking while you're away, this should hit the spot.

Contemporary American. Breakfast, lunch, dinner. $36-85

★★★★EVEREST
440 S. LaSalle St., Loop, 312-663-8920; www.everestrestaurant.com

It takes a certain bravado to name a restaurant after the tallest mountain in the world—the damning reviews practically write themselves. Thankfully, chef Jean Joho's Everest has scaled the culinary heights and remains perched at the top of Chicago's fine-dining realm. Appropriately located on the 40th floor of the Chicago Stock Exchange, its magnificent city views (framed by floor-to-ceiling drapes) are a perfect companion for Joho's highbrow Alsatian cuisine. Served by an exceedingly polite waitstaff clad in suits, the menu includes a filet of wild sturgeon wrapped and roasted in cured ham, and venison served with wild huckleberries and braised pear. It's safe to say that a night at Everest will leave you feeling, well, on top of the world.

French. Dinner. Closed Sunday-Monday. $86 and up

★★FOGO DE CHAO
661 N. La Salle St., Chicago, 312-932-9330; www.fogodechao.com

Brazilian, steak. Lunch, dinner. Reservations recommended. Children's menu. Bar. $36-85

★★★FRONTERA GRILL
445 N. Clark St., River North, 312-661-1434; www.rickbayless.com

If you can't quite spring for the upscale offerings of Topolobampo next door—or maybe you want to save your money for Rick Bayless' acclaimed margaritas (we don't blame you)—you won't feel cheated if you opt for Frontera Grill. The always-popular spot has a festive atmosphere with colorful walls and hanging papier-mâché animals, which provides a perfect environment to enjoy the PBS chef's housemade moles and freshly ground corn tortillas. The menu features such mouthwatering fare as Puerco Al Chipotle, a grilled pork loin in a red-bean chipotle sauce, and carne Asada a la Oaxaquena, a grilled Angus rib steak marinated in red chile and served with black beans and plantains. Be forewarned: The restaurant takes reservations only for a limited number of tables, which explains the lines that form well before the doors open for dinner.

Mexican, Southwestern. Lunch, dinner, Saturday brunch. Closed Sunday-Monday. Bar. $36-85

★★THE GAGE
24 S. Michigan Ave., Loop, 312-372-4243; www.thegagechicago.com

From the elk ragout poutine to the Bison tartare to the roast elk with butter poached apples and ricotta, the Gage's pub grub is anything but common. Even the good ol' fish and chips get dressed up—in newspaper. The fringe-hugging menu combined with the hopping happy hour singles scene drew Christian Bale in while he was on location in the Windy City shooting *The Dark Knight*. Lunchtime service can get bogged down with larger groups meeting for business. Go elsewhere for a quick bite.

Gastropub. Lunch, dinner, Saturday-Sunday brunch. Bar. $36-85

★★GEJA'S CAFE
340 W. Armitage Ave., Chicago, 773-281-9101; www.gejascafe.com

Fondue. Dinner. Reservations recommended. $36-85

★★★GENE & GEORGETTI
500 N. Franklin St., River North, 312-527-3718; www.geneandgeorgetti.com

Chicago's famed stockyards officially closed in 1971, but the city's carnivorous tradition is still going strong—and perhaps no stronger than at this timeless Italian steakhouse that's resided in the shadow of the El since 1941. From the pictures of Frank Sinatra and Bob Hope on the walls to the red vinyl chairs, G&G (as it's known) is old-school through and through. The waiters have as much character as the classic environs, and they're not exactly known for their geniality, but you'll forget their brusqueness the second you dig into the juicy wet-aged New York strip or the 18-ounce filet that stands some four inches tall.

Italian, Steak. Lunch, dinner. Closed Sunday. Bar. $36-85

★★★GIBSONS
1028 N. Rush St., Gold Coast, 312-266-8999; www.gibsonssteakhouse.com

Pinky rings and massive steaks are the hallmark of Gibsons, a Gold Coast fixture since 1989. The walls are adorned with pictures of celebs ranging from Muhammad Ali to Clint Eastwood, but the restaurant is just as well-known as the haunt of local powerbrokers who make their deals over Gibsons' fishbowl-sized martinis and then celebrate with a 24-ounce porterhouse. Big spenders go for the surf and turf, which features a huge Australian lobster tail served with a massive fillet. You could save room for dessert, but we're guessing you won't get too far into the famed macadamia turtle pie.

Steak. Lunch, dinner. Reservations recommended. Bar. $36-85

★★★GRAHAM ELLIOT
217 W. Huron St., River North, 312-624-9975; www.grahamelliot.com

You'll either love or loathe the kookiness at acclaimed chef Graham Elliot Bowles' River North restaurant. The "informalized" dining room features '80s pop tunes (think Flock of Seagulls and Billy Ocean), and the snack between courses is popcorn (Parmesan-dusted and truffled popcorn, but popcorn nonetheless). Clad in jeans and Chuck Taylors, servers bring Bowles' playful haute cuisine that's divided into hot and cold appetizers and land and sea entrées. Bowles seems to have a jones for cheap beer—his openers include a duck leg confit served with Maytag blue cheese and Budweiser beer foam, and an aged cheddar risotto, featuring Pabst-glazed onions and Cheez-It crackers. He tones it down a little for his entrées, as the grilled rack of pork features a massive loin tastefully infused with root-beer barbecue sauce, while the salmon BLT served with crispy bacon and fresh tomatoes is delicious—good enough, even, for us to endure the overly-loud Reagan-era jams.
Contemporary American. Dinner. Closed Sunday. $36-85

★★GREEK ISLANDS
200 S. Halsted St., Chicago, 312-782-9855; www.greekislands.net

Greek. Lunch, dinner. Reservations recommended. Outdoor seating. Children's menu. Bar. $16-35

★★★GREEN ZEBRA
1460 W. Chicago Ave., Chicago, 312-243-7100; www.greenzebrachicago.com

Vegetarians often feel like they get a raw deal at restaurants, with maybe a token eggplant dish tossed their way at the corner of the menu. Not so at Green Zebra, chef Shawn McClain's small-plates ode to non-carnivores. After all, even a filet fanatic would get hooked on slow-roasted shiitake mushrooms in a crispy potato with savoy cabbage, or grilled asparagus with Camembert beignets. The elegant, earth-toned décor is more upscale than granola; you're more likely to hear Joy Division than the Grateful Dead, and the service is efficient and refined. If you simply must eat meat, there are one or two non-vegetarian items on the menu—though considering the diverse and delicious plant-based options, why settle for chicken?
American, vegetarian. Dinner. Closed Monday. Reservations recommended. Bar. $16-35

★★★THE GRILL ON THE ALLEY
909 N. Michigan Ave., Chicago, 312-255-9009; www.thegrill.com

An offshoot of the Beverly Hills eatery known for its power lunches, the Grill offers a vast selection of larger-than-life portions, including broiled steaks, seafood, pastas and specials that may feature comfort food like chicken pot pie, meat loaf or braised short ribs. The restaurant is located on the ground level of the Westin Michigan Avenue, steps away from world-class shopping.
American. Breakfast, lunch, dinner, brunch. Reservations recommended. Outdoor seating. Children's menu. Bar. $36-85

★★HARRY CARAY'S
33 W. Kinzie St., Chicago, 312-828-0966; www.harrycarays.com

Steak. Lunch, dinner. Reservations recommended. Children's menu. Bar. $36-85

★★HEAVEN ON SEVEN ON RUSH

600 N. Michigan Ave., Chicago, 312-280-7774; www.heavenonseven.com
Cajun, Creole. Lunch, dinner. Bar. $16-35

★HEMA'S KITCHEN

2111 N. Clark St., Chicago, 773-338-1627; www.hemaskitchen.com
Indian. Lunch, dinner. $15 and under

★★★JAPONAIS

600 W. Chicago Ave., River West, 312-822-9600; www.japonaischicago.com
You'll need to cab it over to this gentrifying but not exactly glitzy part of town. But when you're enjoying Japanese-French fusion next to some of the city's most stylish foodies, you'll see why Japonais remains one of the hottest tables in town. Gently thumping lounge music and chic décor provide a perfect environment for the glammed-up crowd (Brad and Angelina dined here when she was filming *Wanted)* that can be found sipping on colorful drinks in the downstairs lounge and outdoor patio. If you're all about the food, you'll be just as pleased. The menu leans toward sushi but also includes a seven-spice Kobe rib eye and Le Quack Japonais, a smoked duck served with hoisin sauce and chutney (yes, that's neither Japanese nor French, but trust us, it's delicious). If you like to play with your food, order The Rock, in which thinly sliced New York strip steak is cooked on a hot rock at your table. Whatever you order, be sure to add a side of fries, which come with a spicy sauce that's always a crowd pleaser. Cap off the night with an after-dinner drink in the downstairs lounge, where in summer months, you can sip on a patio overlooking the river.
Japanese, French. Lunch (Monday-Friday), dinner. Bar. $36-85

★★★KEEFER'S

20 W. Kinzie., Chicago, 312-467-9525; www.keefersrestaurant.com
In busy River North, stylish Keefer's offers prime steaks, chops, seafood and some bistro dishes served in a handsome circular dining room with a contemporary Arts and Crafts feel. Steakhouse classics like lobster bisque, Caesar salad and creamed spinach, as well as some updated but not fussy alternatives, are also featured. There's also a pared-down lunch menu, and the adjacent Keefer's Kaffé offers a menu of soups, salads and simple sandwiches.
Steak, seafood. Lunch, dinner. Closed Sunday. Reservations recommended. Outdoor seating. Bar. $36-85

★★★KIKI'S BISTRO

900 N. Franklin St., Chicago, 312-335-5454; www.kikisbistro.com
Long before bistros were blossoming all over town, this little spot on an out-of-the-way corner in River North was charming diners with its traditional bistro fare and regional specials. A somewhat older crowd frequents cozy, casual Kiki's for its romantic, country inn ambience, with its reliable kitchen and free French. Lunch, dinner. Closed Sunday. Reservations recommended. Bar. $16-35

★★★★L2O
2300 N. Lincoln Park West, Chicago, 773-868-0002; www.l2orestaurant.com

L2O has big shoes to fill: The restaurant resides in the space formerly taken up by Ambria, a longtime Chicago favorite. But award-winning chef Laurent Gras is up to the challenge, offering a French-oriented seafood menu that's as sophisticated as the restaurant's beautiful décor, with the dining room separated by partitions of stainless-steel cables. The menu is divided into Raw, Warm and Main sections, with the four-course tasting option offering one of each, plus a dessert. The generous selections range from fluke with lemon vinegar, caviar and basil seeds to black bass in shellfish bouillon with saffron and Rhode Island mussels. Even the bread service is memorable, with offerings of bacon croissants, anchovy twists and demi-baguettes served with housemade butter. To get an idea of Gras's meticulous nature, seize the opportunity to take the optional tour of the painstakingly clean kitchen—and keep an eye out for his astounding array of spices.

French, Contemporary American. Dinner. Closed Tuesday. $86 and up

★★★LANDMARK
1633 N. Halsted St., Chicago, 312-587-1600; www.landmarkgrill.net

With its striking décor and boisterous crowd, you'd forgive the owners of Landmark (who also run nearby Perennial and Boka) if they concentrated a little less on the food. But chef Kurt Guzowski ensures the fare remains a priority at this massive Lincoln Park favorite, committing to the details on his wide-ranging menu. Appetizer options include smoked ravioli with braised pork belly, and Kobe beef sliders with truffles, foie gras and Moroccan ketchup. Entrées including a lobster club sandwich and grilled black pepper ribeye with blue cheese potato gratin. We recommend going earlier in the evening, because the place gets packed at night with a throng that's clearly not there for the food.

Contemporary American. Dinner. Closed Monday. $36-85

★★★LA SARDINE
111 N. Carpenter St., Chicago, 312-421-2800; www.lasardine.com

Perhaps a bit large for a bistro, La Sardine nevertheless delivers wonderful aromas, creature comforts and menu classics. This restaurant draws both hip and mature urbanites who come for the escargots, brandade, bouillabaisse, roast chicken and profiteroles. Those scents waft from an open kitchen and rotisserie. The impressive wine list includes some hard-to-find French selections.

French. Lunch, dinner. Closed Sunday. Reservations recommended. Bar. $16-35

★★LE BOUCHON
1958 N. Damen Ave., Chicago, 773-862-6600; www.lebouchonofchicago.com

There's a reason this tiny storefront bistro has been packing in a crowd of regulars for more than 15 years. The food is delicious, the prices are reasonable, the mood is convivial, and the feeling is somehow unmistakably Parisian. The menu reflects owner Jean-Claude Poilevey's French roots (he's a native of Burgundy); Le Bouchon features standbys such as a creamy housemade pâté, beef Bourguignon over mashed potatoes, and white-wine poached salmon with cucumber and tomato beurre blanc. The onion tart—a classic intermingling of crispy pastry and tangy caramelized onions—is a signature dish. The closely packed tables and noisy room aren't for everyone, but those who seek out Le Bouchon's authentic environs will likely be glad they made the effort.

French. Lunch, dinner. Closed Sunday. $16-35

★★LE COLONIAL
937 N. Rush St., Gold Coast, 312-255-0088; www.lecolonialchicago.com

Chicago's Rush Street is a loud, bombastic avenue, often filled with rowdy revelers and tipsy tourists. But that's not the only reason the restrained elegance of Le Colonial stands out here. With its slowly rotating ceiling fans and potted palm trees, Le Colonial serves French-Vietnamese fare in a space that vividly evokes the feel of French colonial Southeast Asia. The authentic Vietnamese fare starts with pho, the popular beef soup with rice noodles and flavorful slivers of ginger and chilies. Then it's on to entrées like Ca Chien Saigon, a seared snapper in a sweet, spicy sauce, and Bo Bitet Tom Nuong, a grilled filet mignon with shrimp and tomato rice pilaf. Afterward, enjoy a cocktail in a high-backed rattan chair, which is a pleasant way to savor the last drop of atmosphere before heading back out into the boisterous night.

French, Vietnamese. Lunch, dinner. Bar. $36-85

★★★★LES NOMADES
222 E. Ontario St., Streeterville, 312-649-9010; www.lesnomades.net

From its location in a former townhouse to the fresh flowers placed throughout the restaurant, Les Nomades is nothing but low-key elegance. And despite being a mere croissant's throw from nearby Michigan Avenue, the serene spot is secluded and intimate for those seeking a romantic getaway within the city. That's not to say the French haute cuisine is an afterthought, though. From rack of lamb in a delicate mushroom soubise to perfectly roasted venison loin with puréed parsnips, Les Nomades' prix fixe French fare is expertly prepared and perfectly fits the restaurant's elegant atmosphere. In keeping with the formal feel, jackets are required for men, and cell phones are strictly prohibited.

French. Dinner. Closed Sunday-Monday. $86 and up

★★★LOCKWOOD
17 E. Monroe St., The Palmer House, Chicago, 312-917-3404;
www.lockwoodrestaurant.com

Don't assume its Palmer House digs totally dictate Lockwood's vibe. With chef Phillip Foss blogging daily on his latest culinary innovations (think "Faux" Gras, not Foie) at www.phillipfoss.net and updated décor (including leather and mohair furniture), you may be pleasantly surprised by the contemporary flair. try prosciutto-wrapped wild boar tenderloin accompanied by parsnips, huckleberries, and bitter chocolate (yes, you read that right), and a butterscotch-poached pear with brown butter ice cream and spiced streusel cake. Both convey a healthy balance of classic and current.

Contemporary American. Breakfast, lunch, dinner. $36-85

★★★MARCHÉ

833 W. Randolph St., West Loop, 312-226-8399; www.marche-chicago.com

Marché is hardly what you call subtle: Its light-filled dining room is packed with flamboyant touches, from gargantuan red lampshades hanging from the high ceilings to large metal bookshelves teeming with antique cameras and globes. But there's some serious culinary work going on behind the Moulin Rouge décor—the open kitchen gives you the opportunity to see chef Matt Tobin prepare dishes like his adored duck à la Montmorency, which is grilled over apple and cherry wood. The classic French menu also features stand-bys like moules mariniere and a lamb shank with sour cream whipped pota-toes, while the dessert options include a decadent plat à trois chocolats and a sumptuous classic crème brûlée. Come hungry, and come early unless you enjoy a little rowdiness with your frites—this place gets boisterous as the night goes on.

French. Lunch (Monday-Friday), dinner. Bar. $36-85

★★MIA FRANCESCA

3311 N. Clark St., Chicago, 773-281-3310; www.miafrancesca.com

Italian. Lunch, dinner. Reservations recommended. Outdoor seating. Chil-dren's menu. Bar. $16-35

★★MIKE DITKA'S

100 E. Chestnut St., Chicago, 312-587-8989; www.mikeditkaschicago.com

American. Lunch, dinner. Reservations recommended. Outdoor seating. Children's menu. Bar. $36-85

★★★MIRAI SUSHI

2020 W. Division St., Chicago, 773-862-8500

Need to impress a sashimi aficionado? Head to Mirai, where the emphasis is solely on the fish. In-the-know sushi lovers flock here for the unagi trio, a roll with unagi, avocado and an unagi sauce. Chef/partner Jun Ichikawa also specializes in elegantly simple rolls, such as the tuna tuna salmon, which features poached salmon topped with tuna and drizzled with a light wasabi mayonnaise. Those who want something other than sushi won't be disap-pointed with offerings like the perfectly made teriyaki salmon or kani ebi korekke (shrimp and snow crab cakes). For a pre- (or post-) dinner cocktail, Mirai has a funky lounge upstairs.

Japanese. Dinner. Reservations recommended. Outdoor seating. Bar. $36-85

★★★MK

868 N. Franklin St., River North, 312-482-9179; www.mkchicago.com

Founder Michael Kornick is no longer preparing meals at his namesake res-taurant (that falls to chef Erick Simmons), but there's still a lot of substance beneath the style of this renowned loft-like spot with the brick walls and massive skylight. The chic lounge is a popular stop for a pre-dinner drink, while the spacious bi-level dining room provides a warm atmosphere for a classic contemporary American menu. Simmons doesn't exactly reinvent the wheel, but we're not complaining: His specialties include grilled veal porter-house with balsamic brown butter, and bison rib eye with a cabernet sauce.

The dessert menu offers standbys like crème brûlée and sorbet, but you'll be glad to step outside the box for the Cake & Shake, which features layers of buttermilk chocolate cake, chocolate mousse, bittersweet chocolate pavé and a vanilla malted milkshake. The buzz isn't as deafening as it was a few years ago, but scoring a table is ten times easier.
Contemporary American. Dinner. $36-85

★★★MON AMI GABI
2300 N. Lincoln Park West, Chicago, 773-348-8886; www.monamigabi.com
The charming setting in Lincoln Park's Belden-Stratford, a 1922 landmark building, is so French you may start speaking with an accent. Solid bistro fare, including a selection of steak preparations and fresh seafood, is a big draw, as are the cozy ambience and rolling wine cart. There is also a large outdoor seating area for warm evenings.
French. Dinner. Reservations recommended. Outdoor seating. Children's menu. Bar. $36-85

★★★MORTON'S, THE STEAKHOUSE
1050 N. State St., Chicago, 312-266-4820; www.mortons.com
This steakhouse chain, which originated in Chicago in 1978, appeals to serious meat lovers. With a selection of belt-busting dishes—like the house specialty, a 24-ounce porterhouse—as well as fresh fish, lobster, and chicken entrées, Morton's rarely disappoints. Here, main course selections are placed on a cart that is rolled to your table, where servers describe each item in detail.
Steak. Lunch, dinner. Reservations recommended. Bar. $36-85

★★★MOTO
945 W. Fulton Market, West Loop, 312-491-0058; www.motorestaurant.com
Moto's brilliant chef Homaro Cantu has repeatedly said he wants his customers to play with their food. But sometimes, when facing the concoction the renowned chef has created, the desire is to stare in awe rather than disrupt such a lavish creation. Cantu's whimsical dinners begin with an edible menu (vegetable inks on modified food starch) and go on to include 10 to 20 courses, which may include inverted pumpkin pie or instant risotto. Some of Cantu's more celebrated dishes have included veal breast served with rice and runner beans, and fish cooked in an insulated box at the table. As you might expect, the presentation is both outrageous and practical. The "toro, sturgeon caviar, and utensil study," for instance, features a piece of tuna dabbed with caviar, served on a custom-made utensil for which the stem has been hollowed out and filled with fresh thyme. Playful? Certainly. Sublime? Absolutely.
International. Dinner. Closed Sunday-Monday. Reservations recommended. Bar. $86 and up

★★★NACIONAL 27
325 W. Huron St., River North, 312-664-2727; www.nacional27.net
The "27" in the name refers to the number of Latin American countries, but it also reflects this stylish restaurant's culinary diversity. In a large, dramatic space, Nacional 27 offers Nuevo Latino dishes that blend flavors and influences from throughout Central and South America. Starters include ceviche sampling platters with shrimp, scallops, ahi tuna and cold-smoked Tasma-

nian salmon. The menu also offers tapas (such as miniature lamb tacos with avocado salsa and smoked chicken empanadas), a five-course tasting menu, and à la carte dishes including a delicious grilled marinated skirt steak. If the food itself doesn't get you dancing, the restaurant's resident DJ will get you on the floor with weekend salsa and merengue music. (Have a spiked apple cider to best bring out your dance moves.)

Latin American. Dinner. Closed Sunday. Bar. $36-85

★★★NAHA
500 N. Clark St., River North, 312-321-6242; www.naha-chicago.com

In-the-know Chicagoans didn't need proof that NAHA, the creation of cousins Carrie and Michael Nahabedian, offers excellent contemporary cuisine with a Mediterranean flair. But that validation came anyway in the form of a 2008 James Beard award. Carrie's meals are served in an elegant, tranquil setting and emphasize locally grown, organic fare such as wood-grilled rib eye with braised red shallots in an oxtail red-wine sauce, and honey-lacquered aged moulard duck breast with apricots and turnips. Not everything is such highbrow fare: The Angus hamburger served on a sea-salt crusted ciabatta bun with cured tomatoes wins raves as well, elevating the simple hamburger above its typical reputation. You have to get it for lunch, though. Otherwise, you're stuck ordering from the fantastic dinner menu.

Contemporary American. Lunch (Monday-Friday), dinner. Closed Sunday. Reservations recommended. Bar. $36-85

★★★NICK'S FISHMARKET
51 S. Clark St., Chicago, 312-621-0200; www.nicksfishmarketchicago.com

Although Nick's specializes in seafood, it acts in every other way like a steakhouse. Consider the dark, subterranean room with low ceilings, colorful celebrity pictures and traditional dishes like lobster bisque and lobster thermador. Appetizers feature shellfish, sashimi and caviar, followed by sole, salmon and lobster entrées. Also consider the Grill, its more laid-back, inexpensive eatery located upstairs.

Seafood. Lunch, dinner. Reservations recommended. $16-35

★★★N9NE
440 W. Randolph St., West Loop, 312-575-9900; www.n9negroup.com

With its subtly changing light scheme and cosmo-sipping, air-kissing crowd, the slick N9NE occasionally gets criticized for being more of a scene than a restaurant (albeit one with a hip club, Ghostbar, on the second floor). Whoever says that likely hasn't delved into the menu, which features huge, prime-aged steaks and chops, augmented with a Maine lobster tail or Alaskan crab legs for a reasonable $23. There's also a wide array of seafood options, including a miso-marinated cod with scallions and shiitake mushrooms. Bolstering the restaurant's argument is a caviar service, offering Russian caviar by the ounce. But would a steakhouse dedicated only to the see-and-be-seen crowd offer a $26 hamburger? They must be doing something right, as this spot begat the N9NE/Ghost Bar in Las Vegas and Dallas.

Steak. Lunch (Monday-Friday), dinner. Closed Sunday. $36-85

★★★NOMI
Park Hyatt Chicago, 800 N. Michigan Ave., Gold Coast, 312-239-4030;
www.nomirestaurant.com

When you first arrive at NoMI, you have to go through a glass-encased wine "cellar" and take several turns before entering the main dining room. It's almost as if they want to reward you for your efforts—and what a reward it is. The beautiful space, which offers stunning views of Michigan Avenue and the Water Tower across the street, matches executive chef Christophe David's cuisine: simple, unpretentious and elegant. Sushi makes up much of the menu, with à la carte pieces and larger plates of several rolls offered. David also presents entrées such as slow cooked salmon with mushrooms, yellow curry and coconut, and a duet of beef with petite ribeye and braised veal cheek. After your meal, the outdoor garden's gently pulsing lounge music, comfortable tables and spectacular view make a perfect environment for a relaxing after-dinner drink.

French, Asian. Breakfast, lunch (Sunday-Thursday), dinner, Sunday brunch. Reservations recommended. Bar. $36-85

★★★NORTH POND
2610 N. Cannon Drive, Chicago, 773-477-5845; www.northpondrestaurant.com

Talk about off the beaten path: North Pond is situated in the middle of a pastoral setting in Lincoln Park, surrounded by trees and blocks away from the neighborhood's occasionally lunkheaded bar scene. The restaurant's gorgeous Prairie-style building—originally built in 1912 as a lodge for ice-skaters—overlooks a small pond and provides a stunning view of the Chicago skyline. Almost as impeccable is chef Bruce Sherman's sustainable-minded fare, which emphasizes seasonal local items in specialties such as oil-poached Alaskan halibut with smoked caviar, and Dijon-crusted rib eye with roasted farro. Sherman puts the Web sites of local nonprofits on his menu, but with a meal this delicious—capped by the chocolate-cherry dessert that boasts a decadent chocolate panna cotta with bing cherries and red beet sorbet—you'll put up with a little political grandstanding.

Contemporary American. Lunch (June-September, Wednesday-Friday), dinner (closed Monday-Tuesday from January-April), Sunday brunch. $36-85

★★★ONE SIXTYBLUE
1400 W. Randolph St., West Loop, 312-850-0303; www.onesixtyblue.com

For many Chicagoans, One Sixtyblue is known only as the restaurant that features Michael Jordan as one of the owners. He's still known to occasionally drop in, which is enough to bring in a crowd hoping to shake hands with His Royal Airness. For everyone else, the French-Mediterranean cuisine—which perfectly matches the quiet, romantic atmosphere of this converted former pickle factory—is the reason to eat here. Starters include a pork belly carbonara, and entrées feature show-stoppers like pork loin with picked peach purée, and the flat iron steak with black-eyed peas and pickled okra. Even if you don't spot MJ, you'll be glad you stopped by—especially if you happen to catch one of the restaurant's many specials (at press time, Wednesday nights were all about fried chicken and champagne).

Contemporary American. Dinner. Closed Sunday. Bar. $36-85

★★★OPERA

1301 S. Wabash Ave., Chicago, 312-461-0161; www.opera-chicago.com

Helping to position the South Loop as a foodie destination, Opera updates Chinese fare by banning gummy sauces and upping the presentation appeal. Top picks include five-spice squid and slow-roasted pork shoulder. The lively, art-filled interior encourages lingering over cocktails.

Chinese. Dinner. Reservations recommended. Bar. $36-85

★ORANGE

3231 N. Clark St., Chicago, 773-549-4400; www.orangebrunch.com

American. Breakfast, lunch, brunch. Children's menu. $15 and under

★★OSTERIA VIA STATO

620 N. State St., Chicago, 312-642-8450; http://www.osteriaviastato.com

Italian. Lunch, dinner. Reservations recommended. Outdoor seating. Children's menu. Bar. $36-85

★★★OTOM

951 W. Fulton Market, West Loop, 312-491-5804; www.otomrestaurant.com

The lower-priced, less-formal sister of haute cuisine standby Moto, Otom is a lively mix of minimalist elegance and playful mod, with orange plastic chairs and orange tableside flowers contrasting with the exposed brick walls. Décor aside, Otom stands out for its cuisine: Salmon ceviche on crispy wontons makes a perfect light start to the meal, and chef Thomas Elliot Bowman crafts clever fare for his entrées. There's the "TV Dinner," which comprises chicken-fried duck confit, carrot and edamame pie, and the wildly popular fried beef cheek ravioli with saffron-parsnip purée. Despite its proximity to its more-famous sibling, Otom's moderate prices, unique atmosphere and excellent food make it a spot worthy of standing on its own.

Contemporary American. Dinner. Closed Sunday. $36-85

★★★THE PALM

323 E. Wacker Drive, Chicago, 312-616-1000; www.thepalm.com

The Palm, located inside the Swissotel, delivers on its promise of giant steaks and lobsters in a steakhouse atmosphere. Caricatures of famous people who have dined here are featured on the walls. Seasonal outdoor seating offers great views of Lake Michigan and Navy Pier.

American, Steak. Lunch, dinner. Reservations recommended. Outdoor seating. Bar. $36-85

★★★PANE CALDO

72 E. Walton St., Chicago, 312-649-0055; www.pane-caldo.com

This little spot off the Magnificent Mile is home to some of the best Italian food this side of Piedmont. It's easy to miss this tiny restaurant so look for the shoppers enjoying risotto Milanese. An extensive wine list complements the kitchen's lovely creations, made with organic meats and locally grown organic produce.

Italian. Lunch, dinner. Reservations recommended. Outdoor seating. Bar. $36-85

★PENNY'S NOODLE SHOP

3400 N. Sheffield Ave., Chicago, 773-281-8222; www.pennysnoodleshop.com

Thai. Lunch, dinner. Closed Monday. Outdoor seating. $15 and under

★★★PERENNIAL

1800 N. Lincoln Ave., Lincoln Park, 312-981-7070; www.perennialchicago.com

One thing has become clear with the recent opening of Perennial: Lincoln Park has a new hot spot. The masterminds behind Chicago fixtures Boka and Landmark have transformed this space—formerly an unimaginative chain bar/restaurant—into a must-visit scene. With its canvas ceiling, birch trees in the center of the room, and floor-to-ceiling windows, Perennial's décor is as inviting as the perpetually smiling staff and the thoughtful cuisine prepared by chef Ryan Poli. The menu features crispy duck breast with herb bread pudding, braised red cabbage, chestnuts and foie gras emulsion, and house-made linguini carbornara that's worth every fat gram. The adjacent lounge provides an elegant spot for a post-dinner drink—provided you can get a seat, that is.

Contemporary American. Dinner, Saturday-Sunday brunch. $36-85

★PIECE

1923 W. North Ave., Chicago, 773-772-4422; www.piecechicago.com

Housed in a 5,800-square-foot former garage, Piece eschews classic deep-dish Chicago pizza in favor of a delicious thin-crust variety that was invented at the famed Sally's Apizza in New Haven, Connecticut. Piece (which is co-owned by Cheap Trick guitarist Rick Nielsen, who lent one of his five-necked guitars to the restaurant) serves huge rectangular pizzas featuring toppings that are both standard (pepperoni, onions) and not-so-standard (mashed potatoes, clams). Some of the combinations might sound strange but they somehow meld perfectly with the pizza's crunchy thin crust and tangy tomato sauce. The pizzas aren't the only reason that the massive space is always packed with a randy crowd checking out the game (and each other): Piece's onsite, handcrafted brews won the World Beer Cup's Small Brewpub Award in 2006.

Pizza. Lunch, dinner. Bar. $15 and under

★PIZZERIA UNO

29 E. Ohio St., River North, 312-321-5125; www.unos.com

Despite the trendy thin-crust-pizza spots that have been popping up across Chicago lately, many still come to the city for chewy, gooey deep-dish pizza. There are many arguments about whose stuffed pizza is the best, but no matter who's doing the rating, Pizzeria Uno is almost always near the top. This standby—which actually served the world's first stuffed pizza, back in the 1940s—draws huge crowds, and it's not exactly spacious, so either arrive early (the restaurant doesn't take reservations) or be prepared for a long wait for a table (which will likely be cramped). But oh, how it's worth the wait: The cheese is melty, the tomato sauce is sweet but has a nice zip of garlic, and the crust is slightly crunchy. You'll quickly tune out the tourists that surround you as you dig in.

Pizza. Lunch, dinner. $16-35

★★★THE PUBLICAN

837 W. Fulton Market, West Loop, 312-733-9555; www.thepublicanrestaurant.com

At the Publican, the tastemakers behind Blackbird and Avec have turned their focus to pork, oysters and beer. The space resembles a swank German beer hall. If you want privacy, ask for one of the walnut booths, which have small salon doors. Dishes are served as soon as they are ready, so be prepared to share or steal as your boudin blanc may arrive prior to your date's massive porchetta or pork rinds. The frites with the sunny side egg may be tempting, but go for the addictive aioli instead. The family-style Sunday dinners are a great way to try the restaurant. One recent menu featured a salad with a pancetta, basil and a poached farm egg, mussels with pork confit, whole roasted pig, and butterscotch pudding for dessert.

Gastropub. Lunch, dinner, Sunday brunch. $36-85

★★★PUMP ROOM

1301 N. State Parkway, Chicago, 312-266-0360; www.pumproom.com

This revered Chicago classic combines grand hotel dining with contemporary French-American fare. The Pump Room remains popular with tourists and special-occasion celebrants. Booth One comes complete with a vintage telephone, and the bar could have been transported from the Thin Man set. Highlights include live music with a small dance floor and a Sunday champagne brunch.

American. Breakfast, lunch, dinner, Sunday brunch. Reservations recommended. Children's menu. Bar. $36-85

★★QUARTINO

626 N. State St., Chicago, 312-698-5000; www.quartinochicago.com

Italian. Lunch, dinner. Reservations recommended. Outdoor seating. Bar. $16-35

★★★RESTAURANT AT CONRAD

521 N. Rush St., Chicago, 312-377-0979; conradhotels1.hilton.com

Infusing its food with some of the upscale Hilton chain's international flair, chef Baasim Zafar draws inspiration for this menu from his travels. The result when you subtract the old standbys and add some social sustainability? Guilt-free meals like butter-poached Maine lobster or wild organic mushrooms—that have been carefully crafted to account for minimal carbon emissions. That's a welcome solution for both your travel-fueled appetite and carbon footprint.

American. Breakfast, lunch, dinner. $36-85

★★★RESTAURANT TAKASHI

1952 N. Damen Ave., Bucktown, 773-772-6170; www.takashichicago.com

It seemed like the pinnacle of chef Takashi Yagihashi's career: After putting together an award-winning résumé in Chicago and Detroit, he headed to Las Vegas to lead a restaurant in the Wynn Resort. Thankfully for Chicagoans, Yagihashi returned after 18 months to helm his namesake restaurant, a minimalist spot in Bucktown that expertly blends high-end American influences and French technique with the simplicity of Japanese fare. In a small, low-key room of gray walls accented with cherry wood, the menu offers hot and

cold small plates that feature fresh hamachi, salmon, tuna and other seafood. The more substantial large plates menu offers dishes such as roasted potato/prosciutto-crusted Atlantic salmon and a roasted New York strip with fresh wasabi and miso-glazed fingerling potatoes. In a neighborhood with more than a few so-so sushi spots, Takashi simultaneously expands the palate while refining the details of Japanese cuisine.
Contemporary American, Japanese. Dinner. Closed Monday. $36-85

★★★RL RESTAURANT
115 E. Chicago Ave., Chicago, 312-475-1100; www.rlrestaurant.ralphlauren.com
Located in Ralph Lauren's flagship Chicago store on Michigan Avenue, RL restaurant focuses its efforts on American classics. Menu items such as Crab Louie, Green Goddess salad or Steak Diane are updated, presented with flair and worthy of a splurge. The restaurant exudes the warmth and elegance of a city club, with herringbone hardwood floors and mahogany ceilings.
American. Lunch, dinner, Sunday brunch. Reservations recommended. Outdoor seating. Children's menu. Bar. $36-85

★★★RODAN
1530 N. Milwaukee Ave., Chicago, 773-276-7036; www.rodan.ws
A funky Wicker Parker spot, Rodan unites the foods of South America and Asia on its menu. Graze from gingered swordfish and shrimp rolls back West to adobo Cornish hen and fish tacos with mango salsa. Somewhere in between lie the tasty wasabi tempura fries. Go casual to Rodan, and go late-night if you're looking for a hip lounge. As the night progresses, audio and visual artists show digital images and mix music.
Pan-Asian, South American. Dinner, late-night. Reservations recommended. Bar. $16-35

★★ROSEBUD
1500 W. Taylor St., Chicago, 312-942-1117; www.rosebudrestaurants.com
Italian. Lunch, dinner. Reservations recommended. Outdoor seating. Bar. $16-35

★★★ROY'S
720 N. State St., Chicago, 312-787-7599; www.roysrestaurant.com
Don't expect luau fare at this sleek, contemporary Hawaiian restaurant. Lots of creative seafood dishes populate the menu, with several unusual fish varieties and French and Asian fusion dishes evident throughout. Menu selections are listed with suggested wine pairings.
Pacific-Rim/Pan-Asian. Dinner. Reservations recommended. Outdoor seating. Children's menu. Bar. $36-85

★★SAI CAFE
2010 N. Sheffield Ave., Chicago, 773-472-8080; www.saicafe.com
There are plenty of neighborhood sushi restaurants in Chicago, but few offer fish that's as fresh—and generously portioned—as this Lincoln Park standby. The menu offers several different entrées, but it's the sushi that packs people into the restaurant's three laid-back rooms. Any of the sushi creations will delight you, but the rainbow maki with tuna, yellowtail, salmon and avocado deli-

cately wrapped around rice and a crab stick is particularly fresh and delicious. Japanese, sushi. Dinner. Reservations recommended. Bar. $16-35

★★★SALPICON

1252 N. Wells St., Chicago, 312-988-7811; www.salpicon.com

Chef Priscilla Satkoff grew up in Mexico City and honors her native cuisine here with rich moles, tender-roasted meats and upscale twists like an ancho chile quail. The extensive wine list, managed by the chef's husband, has won numerous awards, but it's hard to get past the 50-some tequilas on offer to mix in margaritas.

Mexican. Lunch, dinner. Reservations recommended. Outdoor seating. Bar. $16-35

★★SANTORINI

800 W. Adams St., West Loop, 312-829-8820; www.santorinichicago.com

Chicago's Greektown is packed with restaurants that make a solid spana-kopita and serve a decent flaming saganaki. But the rustic Santorini stands apart from the crowd with its fresh seafood, white walls with dark wood trim, and bi-level dining room featuring a large fireplace. The spot serves excellent versions of Greek standards, like melt-in-your-mouth center-cut lamb chops and juicy chicken baked with vegetables and zesty feta cheese in phyllo dough. The true don't-miss entrées here are the grilled octopus (a house specialty) and whole fish such as tender red snapper, which can be fileted tableside and served in a tangy simple sauce of olive oil and lemon juice.

Greek. Lunch, dinner. $36-85

★★★SCHWA

1466 N. Ashland Ave., Wicker Park, 773-252-1466; www.schwarestaurant.com

Maverick chef Michael Carlson is viewed as the enfant terrible of the Chicago dining world. His eccentric Schwa became the apple of Chicago foodies' eyes, but then he abruptly closed for four months and was vague about what he did in the meantime. Thankfully, the restaurant has reopened and while its quixotic charms are still evident—tiny room, no liquor license, the cooks also serve as the waitstaff—the food is still remarkably innovative. The charismatic Carlson—who's likely to sprinkle a few uses of "dude" during your meal—offers three- and nine-course menus that feature organic ingredients and locally grown produce. The latter option includes such knockout dishes as a savory beer cheese soup with a pretzel roll, and a gently seared kona kampachi with galangal, lime and a tiny splash of maple syrup. It's a little pricey for what it is, but the cost of the meal is offset by the restaurant's BYOB policy, which allows you to carry in your own wine for a mere $2.50-per-person corkage fee. Just be sure to call ahead to snag a table; though Carlson may be unpredictable, the restaurant's popularity is not.

Contemporary American. Dinner. Closed Sunday-Monday. $36-85

★★★★SEASONS

Four Seasons Hotel Chicago, 120 E. Delaware Place, Gold Coast, 312-649-2349; www.fourseasons.com

Let other restaurants try to impress you with a stark, minimalist atmosphere. Seasons, located within the Four Seasons Hotel, goes the other way and spoils you with old-school luxury. How so? For starters, there's the marble fountain, armchair seats and deep mahogany wood trim. Then there are French-leaning prix fixe menus of four, five or six courses as well as a vegetarian option. The fare constantly changes to reflect availability of ingredients, but past favorites include Tasmanian sea trout filled with slow-cooked Kobe short ribs, and rack of Colorado lamb wrapped in eggplant and scented with toasted cumin. After a day of Mag Mile shopping, no other place in the Gold Coast feels quite as decadently classic.

Contemporary American, French. Breakfast, lunch, dinner (Tuesday-Saturday), Sunday brunch. Reservations recommended. $86 and up

★★★SEPIA
123 N. Jefferson St., West Loop, 312-441-1920; www.sepiachicago.com
A relative newcomer to the Chicago dining scene, Sepia wasted no time creating a deafening buzz in its already-happening West Loop neighborhood. Situated inside an 1890s print shop, Sepia's décor craftily mixes the old and new, much like contemporary American dishes rooted in tradition, including the pork portherhouse with bourbon, peaches and grits and the chicken with panzanella salad. Liquor aficionados flock here for the creative cocktails, which feature handmade syrups and bitters..

American. Dinner, lunch. Reservations recommended. $36-85

★★★SHANGHAI TERRACE
The Peninsula Chicago, 108 E. Superior St., River North, 312-573-6695; www.chicago.peninsula.com
The main draw at the intimate Shanghai Terrace isn't the generous menu, with its emphasis on meticulous dim sum creations, or the elegantly appointed dining room with black lacquer chairs and daring red trim. The best reason to come here is the outdoor deck, with its stunning view of the soaring buildings that surround The Peninsula hotel. The alfresco area provides the perfect place to enjoy chef Thi Ting's delicious fare, which features a dim sum sampler that includes spicy beef gyoza and foie gras and lobster dumplings. For a more complete meal, you can't go wrong with the traditional Peking duck, which includes five courses.

Asian. Lunch, dinner. Closed Sunday. Bar. $36-85

★★SHAW'S CRAB HOUSE
21 E. Hubbard St., Chicago, 312-527-2722; www.shawscrabhouse.com
Seafood. Lunch, dinner. Reservations recommended. Bar. $36-85

★★SIGNATURE ROOM AT THE 95TH
875 N. Michigan Ave., Chicago, 312-787-9596; www.signatureroom.com
American. Lunch, dinner, Sunday brunch. Reservations recommended. Children's menu. Bar. $16-35

★★★★SIXTEEN
401 N. Wabash Ave., River North, 312-924-7600; www.trumpchicagohotel.com
As you might expect, everything at Sixteen (on the 16th floor of Donald Trump's hotel) is larger-than-life. The hostesses dress like they're about to walk down a Paris runway. The views of the city through the floor-to-ceiling

windows are dazzling (and the ceiling in one of the three dining rooms is 30 feet high). Then there's the food. Chef Frank Brunacci meticulously crafts entrées like Duck Percik with two duck breasts in a date-and-kumquat chutney with black cumin, and prime tenderloin with snail ravioli and horseradish risotto. The desserts, which include Pierce Neige (a chestnut meringue accompanied by port-wine ice cream and port reduction), take so much effort that it's recommended you order them at the start of your meal. All of this is almost enough to take your eyes off the gargantuan chandelier, which comprises more than 19,000 Swarovski crystals, or the views, which, from the 16th floor in the city's best location, are larger than life.

Contemporary American. Breakfast (Sunday-Friday), lunch (Monday-Saturday), dinner, Sunday brunch. Reservations recommended. Bar. $86 and up

★★★SOLA

3868 N. Lincoln Ave., Chicago, 773-327-3868; www.sola-restaurant.com

Drawing inspiration from the sun (sol), her own independence (solo) and her roots (she's so L.A., as her friends joke), chef/owner and former surfer Carol Wallack dove headfirst into Chicago's dining scene when she opened Sola in January 2006. Wallack's focus is on freshness, so she sources all her produce from local farmers and all her seafood from Hawaii. Perhaps you'll find the culmination of these ingredients brought to your table in the form of a salad of Asian greens, housemade bacon, pineapple, rosemary and black vinegar; or halibut atop a bed of soy beluga lentils and wilted watercress, dressed with a lobster butter sauce. If these inventive takes on island-style dishes aren't enough to make you feel like wearing a grass skirt in Chicago, nothing will be.

Contemporary American, Hawaiian. Lunch (Thursday-Friday), dinner, Saturday-Sunday brunch. $36-85

★★★SPIAGGIA

980 N. Michigan Ave., Gold Coast, 312-280-2750; www.levyrestaurants.com

Any talk of Chicago's high-end Italian restaurants begins (and arguably ends) with the gorgeous Spiaggia. How many restaurants have their own cheese cave? Exactly. The elegant setting matches the caliber of the food: The multi-tiered restaurant, appropriately perched at the outset of the city's famed Magnificent Mile, offers a view of Lake Michigan and the city's most famous street. James Beard award-winning chef and partner Tony Mantuano offers an à la carte menu that includes hand rolled potato gnocchi with ricotta sauce and black truffles. There's also a tasting menu inspired by the island of Sicily, which includes items such as pasta sheets with wood-roasted sardines, fennel pollen and black currants, and desserts such as the fig cake with Sambuca gelato.

Italian. Dinner. Jacket required. $86 and up

★★★SPRING

2039 W. North Ave., Chicago, 773-395-7100; www.springrestaurant.net

Spring is Chicago restaurant star Shawn McClain's first local outpost, and some still say it's his best. The spartan dining room—the building was once a Russian bathhouse, and some of the original white tiles are still on the walls—provides a relaxing environ for McClain's celebrated seafood-orient-

ed, Asian-inflected fare. The most renowned appetizer is the seared Maine scallop and potato ravioli in a heavenly mushroom black-truffle reduction. That's just a prelude to the sophisticated entrées, which include grilled Hawaiian prawns and pork belly dumplings, and the Arctic char with toasted sesame risotto and peekytoe crab. The honeydew sorbet in a plum soup makes the perfect light capper for a remarkable meal.
Contemporary American. Dinner. Closed Monday. $36-85

★★SUSHI SAMBA RIO
504 N. Wells St., Chicago, 312-595-2300; www.sushisamba.com
Japanese. Lunch, dinner. Reservations recommended. Outdoor seating. Bar. $16-35

★★SUSHI WABI
842 W. Randolph St., West Loop, 312-563-1224; www.sushiwabi.com
From the industrial-chic exposed ductwork to the DJ spinning tunes above the dimly lit dining room, Sushi Wabi feels as much like a club as it does one of Chicago's most popular sushi restaurants. For every hipster reveling in the loft atmosphere and cool tunes, there's a sushi aficionado delving into the restaurant's fresh fish and unique creations. The maki rolls include the tried-and-true, from an expertly crafted dragon roll brushed with eel sauce to decadent specialties like the Tarantula, which bursts with soft-shell crab, avocado, chili sauce and masago mayo. Leave room for the green-tea cheesecake, which may be the world's most delicious way to enjoy antioxidants.
Japanese. Lunch (Monday-Friday), dinner. Bar. $16-35

★★★TABLE FIFTY-TWO
52 W. Elm St., Gold Coast, 312-573-4000; www.tablefifty-two.com
Art Smith will likely forever be known as Oprah's chef, although that's probably not such a bad thing. After all, it's given him the chance to open TABLE fifty-two, which provides a perfect outlet for his Southern-inflected cuisine. Each table begins the meal with piping hot, fluffy buttermilk biscuits pulled fresh from the oven. The menu boasts Smith's upgraded take on Southern classics, including fried green tomatoes layered with goat cheese, bacon and greens and cornmeal-crusted catfish with cheese grits and bacon-braised collard greens. Housed in a 19th century carriage house and featuring an open-hearth oven, Smith's restaurant is as cozy and comforting as his cuisine.
American, Southern. Lunch, dinner. Reservations recommended. $36-85

★★★TOPOLOBAMPO
445 N. Clark St., River North, 312-661-1434; www.rickbayless.com
YYou can't turn on a TV today without seeing chef Rick Bayless work his culinary magic with Mexican food—the ubiquitous chef from Chicago even won *Top Chef Masters*. But you don't have to just stare in awe if you make the trip to Topolobampo, the sleek, multicolored restaurant that serves Bayless' inventive cuisine with a monthly changing menu. Bayless isn't always in the kitchen (chef Brian Enyart is the man in the toque here), but Bayless' influence is all over the menu that uses sustainably raised veggies, meat and fish to craft stunningly imaginative Oaxacan cuisine. Favorites include Puerco

Pibil, achiote-marinated Maple Creek Farm pork served as a grill-roasted loin and a slow-cooked shoulder in banana leaves, and langosto al mojo de ajo, pan-roasted Maine lobster served with olive oil-poached garlic, giant butter beans and roasted fresh favas. It's the furthest thing from a taquería, but it's a lot more memorable.

Mexican, Southwestern. Lunch (Tuesday-Friday), dinner. Closed Sunday-Monday. Reservations recommended. $36-85

★★TRATTORIA NO. 10

10 N. Dearborn St., Chicago, 312-984-1718; www.trattoriaten.com

Given its Loop location and subterranean, Old World feel, it's surprising to learn that Trattoria No. 10 chef Douglas D'Avico is fairly progressive with his menu: He features organic and locally grown ingredients in items like handcrafted ravioli filled with asparagus tips and aged provolone topped with sun-dried tomato sauce, and butternut and acorn squash in a sweet walnut-butter sauce. Although it's big with the lunch crowd, Trattoria No. 10's low ceilings, alfresco-style murals and textured walls help the restaurant overcome its substreet-level locale and create romantic, cozy environs for dinner in a decidedly non-cozy neighborhood.

Italian. Lunch, dinner. Closed Sunday. Reservations recommended. Bar. $16-35

★★★★TRU

676 N. St. Clair St., Streeterville, 312-202-0001; www.trurestaurant.com

If you want a stellar dining experience in a large, beautifully understated room with perfectly attuned service, make a reservation at Tru, the partnership of chef Rick Tramonto and executive pastry chef Gale Gand. The gorgeous surroundings include an original Andy Warhol, and the food is equally inspiring. Tru offers different ways to take advantage of Tramonto's work, including a three-course prix fixe and a six- or nine-course "collections" tasting menu. The offerings include a delicate roasted day boat halibut with heirloom tomato and fennel, and prime beef ribeye with grilled foie gras, chanterelle mushrooms and parsley. Practically anything at Tru will delight, but we especially recommend the caviar staircase appetizer, which serves several different types of roe on an elegant glass spiral stairway. Even the bathrooms here, with their sinks made up solely of large slanted glass panels, are a sight.

Contemporary French. Dinner. Closed Sunday. Reservations recommended. Jacket required. $86 and up

★★★VIVERE

71 W. Monroe St., Chicago, 312-332-7005; www.italianvillage-chicago.com

The high end of a trio of restaurants that comprises the Loop's long-standing Italian Village, Vivere plays it cool with showy décor and luxurious meals. The food stands its ground with new takes on the familiar, such as squid ink tortellini stuffed with bass. The Italian wine list rates among the country's best, making this a solid choice for a special occasion. Live jazz is performed on Wednesday evenings.

Italian. Lunch, dinner. Closed Sunday. Reservations recommended. Children's menu. Bar. $36-85

★★★WEST TOWN TAVERN
1329 W. Chicago Ave., West Town, 312-666-6175; www.westtowntavern.com

You can get fried chicken just about anywhere, but for Susan Goss' great-grandmother's tried-and-true recipe, you have to come to the West Town Tavern. Co-owner Goss breaks out the recipe every week for the popular Fried Chicken (and Biscuit) Mondays, while serious carnivores make weekly pilgrimages here for the juicy, 10-ounce Wagyu beef creations (served on grilled focaccia with herbed mayo and grilled onions) on Burger Tuesdays. The restaurant's blond wood floors, exposed brick and warm lighting also provide a welcoming environment for the tavern's delicious contemporary American cuisine with a comfort-food touch, such as the pot roast that's braised in zinfandel, and the gently seared diver scallops served with a delicate mushroom-leek risotto.

Contemporary American. Dinner. Closed Sunday. Bar. $36-85

★★★YOSHI'S CAFE
3257 N. Halsted St., Chicago, 773-248-6160; www.yoshiscafe.com

Namesake chef Yoshi Katsumura comes from a fine-dining background, which accounts for the quality and sophistication of his French-Japanese fusion cuisine. His long-standing Lakeview café offers a relaxed atmosphere and good service. The menu changes monthly, and meanders from shrimp cappuccino soup to sirloin steak. The relaxed, minimal décor features floor-to-ceiling windows, natural wood, tile floors and a covered patio, which is a popular spot in the warm weather.

Fusion/International. Lunch, dinner. Closed Monday. Outdoor seating. Bar. $16-35

★★★ZEALOUS
419 W. Superior St., Chicago, 312-475-9112; www.zealousrestaurant.com

Charlie Trotter's protégé Michael Taus runs Zealous with a Trotter-like attention to detail and innovation. Menus change constantly, but you can expect them to be daring, with dishes such as veal paprikas with potato gnocchi and trumpet mushrooms. Put yourself in the chef's hands with a five- or seven-course tasting menu. This is event dining amplified by the thoughtful Asian-influenced décor.

American. Dinner. Closed Sunday-Monday. Reservations recommended. Bar. $36-85

SPAS

★★★★THE PENINSULA SPA BY ESPA, CHICAGO
108 E. Superior St., Chicago, 312-573-6860, 866-288-8889; www.peninsula.com

East meets Midwest at this 15,000-square-foot spa, where down-to-earth hospitality complements a full range of Asian-inspired treatments. To begin your visit, step through a giant oak door and enter the newly renovated Relaxation Lounge. The area's plush wooden beds, separated by individual curtains, set the mood for serious pampering. All treatments are exclusively designed by ESPA, an English product line focusing on high-quality, all-natural ingredients. Both mind and body get attention with the Chakra Balancing Massage ($275), which uses smooth volcanic stones to ground and balance your energy. (Sounds wacky, feels great.) Post-treatment, swim in the spa's half-Olympic size pool; its floor-to-ceiling windows provide beautiful views and a chance to find your own moment of Zen.

★★★★THE SPA AT FOUR SEASONS CHICAGO

120 E. Delaware Place, Chicago, 312-280-8800, 800-819-5053; www.fourseasons.com

This spa's plush interior makes you feel right at home—that is, if fountains and marble floors are what you're used to. White suede wall panels and soundproofed treatment rooms add to the spa's elegant feel. Put on one of the spas thick, silky robes and prepare for the royal treatment—literally. You can enjoy a facial massage with ruby-infused oil during the 80-minute Essence of Rubies Treatment ($225). In gemstone therapy, rubies promote passion and well-being; in this treatment, they just make our muscles feel like jelly. Or try the Champagne Paraffin Pedicure ($90), which begins with an antioxidant-rich grape seed oil exfoliation, and ends with a glass of bubbly. (The heated massage chairs make this decadent pedicure even more indulgent.) The gracious staff makes you feel even more relaxed. Extend your stay as much as possible by lounging in one of the day beds after your treatment.

★★★THE SPA AT THE CARLTON CLUB, RITZ-CARLTON CHICAGO

160 E. Pearson St., Chicago, 312-266-1000; www.fourseasons.com/chicagorc

With names like Azalea, Magnolia and Lilac, treatment rooms at this elegant spa are all about organic luxury. Start your visit with a trip to the sophisticated locker room, which features a cedar sauna and private vanity areas. From there, try the Aroma-Tonic Body Envelopment ($145), which begins with a full-body exfoliation and finishes with a clay and papaya cream mask to soothe dull, dry skin (perfect if you're here during the harsh winter). When the weather is nice, be sure to slather on the SPF before heading to the sun deck, where terrific views of the neighboring John Hancock Center make you feel like you're on top of the world. And considering the level of service you'll find here, it's more or less true.

★★★★THE SPA AT TRUMP

Trump International Hotel & Tower Chicago, 401 N. Wabash Ave., Chicago, 312-588-8020; www.trumpchicagohotel.com

The Donald wants to know your intentions—your spa intentions, that is. Whether you're looking to calm, balance, purify, heal or revitalize, you'll find what you need in this 23,000-square-foot den of relaxation. In concert with the property as a whole, the spa's décor is modern and sophisticated. Smooth blond wood, dim lighting and simple orchids create a comfortable, surprisingly unpretentious atmosphere. Still, it should come as no surprise that all the amenities here are the best: extra-spacious treatment rooms, deluge mood-enhancing showers (the shower lights up while water comes at you from everywhere) and an enormous health club boasting one of the most striking views in Chicago. As for the treatments, many of them focus on—what else—jewels. The Black Pearl Rejuvenation Facial ($185) combines crushed black pearls and mineral-packed oyster shell extracts to firm and tone your skin, while the Emerald Oasis Body Treatment ($325) uses mineral salt, mint and emerald-infused oils to exfoliate. If it's true that diamonds are a girl's best friend, maybe you should opt for the Purifying Diamonds Massage ($300) instead. Although you don't walk away with a rock on your finger, the precious diamond and botanical essences (who knew diamonds had essences?) will have you feeling engaged in Trump-style tranquility.

CHICAGO O'HARE AIRPORT

See also Arlington Heights, Chicago, Rosemont, Schaumburg

One of the world's busiest airports, O'Hare and neighboring Rosemont is surrounded by hotels, restaurants and entertainment facilities—a city unto itself, crossing municipal boundaries. The 18,500-seat Allstate Arena hosts professional sports and big-name musical acts, while the Rosemont Theater offers live entertainment in a more intimate environment.

WHAT TO SEE
ALLSTATE ARENA

6920 Mannheim Road, Rosemont, 847-635-6601; www.allstatearena.com

This auditorium seats 18,500 and hosts concerts, sports and other events.

CERNAN EARTH AND SPACE CENTER

2000 N. Fifth Ave., River Grove, 708-583-3100; www.criton.edu

A unique domed theater offering multimedia programs on astronomy, geography and other topics; there are also free exhibits on space exploration. Friday-Saturday evenings, matinee Sunday.

CHICAGO WOLVES

Allstate Arena, 6920 Mannheim Road, Rosemont, 800-843-9658

The Wolves are an American Hockey League farm team for the Atlanta Thrashers. The team plays its home games in the Allstate Arena, a great venue for watching hockey at prices inexpensive enough that the entire family can attend.

WHERE TO STAY
★★CHICAGO MARRIOTT SUITES O'HARE

6155 N. River Road, Rosemont, 847-696-4400, 800-228-9290; www.marriott.com

256 rooms. Restaurant, bar. Business center. Fitness center. Pool. $151-250

★★★HYATT ROSEMONT

6350 N. River Road, Rosemont, 800-633-7313, 800-233-1234; www.hyatt.com

A short drive away from O'Hare airport, this contemporary, small hotel caters to business travelers. Rooms have Wireless Internet access and spacious work areas. A complimentary airport shuttle is available 24 hours a day. 206 rooms. Restaurant. Business center. Fitness center. $151-250

★★★WESTIN O'HARE

6100 N. River Road, Rosemont, 847-698-6000; www.westin.com

This hotel is located near O'Hare International Airport and provides free shuttle service. There are several golf courses nearby. 525 rooms. Restaurant, bar. Business center. Fitness center. Pool. Pets accepted. $151-250

WHERE TO EAT
★★CARLUCCI
6111 N. River Road, Rosemont, 847-518-0990; www.carluccirestaurant.com
Italian. Lunch, dinner. Reservations recommended. Bar. $16-35

★★★MORTON'S, THE STEAKHOUSE
9525 W. Bryn Mawr Ave., Rosemont, 847-678-5155; www.mortons.com
This steakhouse chain originated in Chicago in 1978 and appeals to serious meat lovers. With a selection of steaks as well as fresh fish, lobster and chicken entrées, Morton's rarely disappoints.
Steak. Dinner. Reservations recommended. Bar. $36-85

★★★NICK'S FISHMARKET
10275 W. Higgins Road, Rosemont, 847-298-8200; www.nicksfishmarketchicago.com
This location of the Hawaiian-born seafood restaurant is one of three in the Chicago area, and features three enormous aquariums.
Seafood. Dinner. Reservations recommended. Children's menu. Bar. $36-85

DECATUR
See also Arcola, Springfield
In 1830, 21-year-old Abraham Lincoln drove through what would later become Decatur with his family to settle on the Sangamon River, a few miles west. He worked as a farmer and rail-splitter and made his first political speech in what is now Decatur's Lincoln Square. Today, the town is home to Richland Community College and Millikin University.

WHAT TO SEE
CHILDREN'S MUSEUM
55 S. Country Club Road, Decatur, 217-423-5437; www.cmofil.com
This museum features hands-on exhibits of arts, science and technology.
Daily.

FAIRVIEW PARK
620 E. Riverside Drive, Decatur, 217-422-5911; www.decatur-parks.org
This park has a swimming pool, tennis, biking trail, picnicking, playground, baseball and horseshoe pits.

MILLIKIN PLACE
Pine and Main streets, Decatur; www.millikin.edu
This housing development was laid out and landscaped in 1909 by Walter Burley Griffin, who designed Australia's capital, Canberra. The street features a Prairie school entrance, naturalized landscaping and houses by Marion Mahony, Griffin's wife, and Frank Lloyd Wright. Both Griffin and Mahony worked at Wright's famous Oak Park Studio. Numbers 1 and 3 Millikin Place are by Mahony; 2 Millikin Place is attributed to Wright.

ROCK SPRINGS CENTER FOR ENVIRONMENTAL DISCOVERY
3939 Earing Lane Rocksprings Road, Decatur, 217-423-7708;
www.maconcountyconservation.org

There are approximately 1,320 acres with hiking and self-guided interpretive trails in the center with a picnic area, shelter and asphalt bike trail. The eco-center has hands-on educational exhibits. A visitor center holds scheduled events and programs throughout year.
Daily.

SCOVILL PARK AND ZOO
71 S. Country Club Road, Decatur, 217-421-7435; www.decatur-parks.org/zoo
The zoo has more than 500 animals along with picnicking areas and a playground.
April-October, daily 10 a.m.-7 p.m.

WHERE TO STAY
★BAYMONT INN
5100 Hickory Point Frontage Road, Decatur, 217-875-5800; www.baymontinns.com
102 rooms. Complimentary breakfast. Pets accepted. $61-150

★★HOLIDAY INN
4191 Highway 36, Decatur, 217-422-8800, 800-465-4329; www.holiday-inn.com
370 rooms. Restaurant, bar. Business center. Fitness center. Pool. Tennis. $61-150

DEKALB
See also Aurora, Geneva, Oregon, Rockford, St. Charles
DeKalb, founded in 1837, was home to model Cindy Crawford and actor Richard Jenkins.

WHAT TO SEE
NORTHERN ILLINOIS UNIVERSITY
West Lincoln Highway, DeKalb, 815-753-0446; www.niu.edu
The University was founded in 1895 and currently has 22,000 students.

SPECIAL EVENT
CORN FEST
164 E. Lincoln Highway, DeKalb, 815-748-2676
This three-day street festival is devoted to corn.
Last full weekend in August.

STAGE COACH PLAYERS
126 S. Fifth St., DeKalb, 815-758-1940; www.stagecoachers.com
This community theater puts on six performances a season.
Reservations suggested. Mid-June-mid-September.

WHERE TO EAT
★★THE HILLSIDE RESTAURANT
121 N. Second St., DeKalb, 815-756-4749; www.hillsiderestaurant.com
American. Lunch, dinner. Closed Monday. Reservations recommended.

DIXON

See also Oregon

At the southernmost point of the Black Hawk Trail, Dixon sits on the banks of the Rock River. Established as a trading post and tavern by John Dixon, it now is a center for light industry. Ronald Reagan was born in nearby Tampico and grew up in Dixon.

WHAT TO SEE
JOHN DEERE HISTORIC SITE

8393 S. Main, Grand Detour, 815-652-4551; www.deere.com
The first self-scouring steel plow was made here in 1837. The site has a reconstructed blacksmith shop, restored house and gardens and natural prairie.
Early April-late November, daily.

LINCOLN STATUE PARK

100 Lincoln Statue Drive, Dixon, 815-288-3404; www.dixonil.com
This park includes the site of Fort Dixon, around which the town was built, and a statue of Lincoln as a young captain in the Black Hawk War of 1832. A plaque summarizes Lincoln's military career; at the statue's base is a bas-relief of John Dixon. Also in the park is Ronald Reagan's boyhood home, a three-bedroom house with 1920s furnishings.
April-November, daily; December-March, Saturday-Sunday.

SPECIAL EVENT
PETUNIA FESTIVAL

Dixon, 815-284-3361; www.petuniafestival.org
This festival features a carnival, parade, arts and crafts, bicycle race, tennis tournament, festival garden and fireworks.
Fourth of July week.

WHERE TO STAY
★★BEST WESTERN REAGAN HOTEL

443 Highway. 2, Dixon, 815-284-1890, 800-780-7234; www.bestwestern.com
91 rooms. Restaurant, bar. Complimentary breakfast. Fitness center. Pool. Pets accepted. $61-150

DOWNERS GROVE

See also Naperville, Oak Brook

A western Chicago suburb, this town has several houses thought to have been stops on the Underground Railroad.

WHAT TO SEE
HISTORICAL MUSEUM

831 Maple Ave., Downers Grove, 630-963-1309; www.dgparks.org
This Victorian house built in 1892 contains eight rooms of period furnishings, antiques and artifacts.
Sunday-Friday 1-3 p.m.

MORTON ARBORETUM
4100 Highway 53, Lisle, 630-968-0074; www.mortonarb.org
The Morton Arboretum, located 25 miles southwest of Chicago in the city
in Lisle, was founded in 1923 by Joy Morton of the Morton salt family. This
facility is renowned for its lush collection of trees and plants from around
the world.
Daily.

WHERE TO STAY
★★DOUBLETREE GUEST SUITES AND CONFERENCE CENTER
2111 Butterfield Road, Downers Grove, 630-971-2000, 800-222-8733;
www.doubletreedownersgrove.com
247 rooms. Restaurant, bar. Business center. Fitness center. Pool. $61-150

EFFINGHAM
See also Mattoon
This town is the seat of Effingham County. Outdoor recreation is popular
here, with Lake Sara offering fishing, boating and golfing.

WHERE TO STAY
★★BEST WESTERN RAINTREE INN
1809 W. Fayette Ave., Effingham, 217-342-4121, 800-780-7234; www.bestwestern.com
65 rooms. Restaurant, bar. Complimentary breakfast. Business center. Pool.
Pets accepted. $61-150

★COMFORT INN
1310 W. Fayette Road, Effingham, 217-342-3151, 800-228-5150;
www.comfortsuites.com
65 rooms. Complimentary breakfast. Fitness center. Pool. Pets accepted.
$61-150

★HOLIDAY INN EXPRESS
1103 Avenue of Mid-America, Effingham, 217-540-1111, 888-465-4329;
www.holiday-inn.com
118 rooms. Complimentary breakfast. Fitness center. Pool. Pets accepted.
$61-150

WHERE TO EAT
★NIEMERG'S STEAK HOUSE
1410 W. Fayette Ave., Effingham, 217-342-3921; www.niemergssteakhouse.com
American. Breakfast, lunch, dinner. Children's menu. Bar. $16-35

EVANSTON
See also Chicago, Skokie, Wilmette
Evanston sits immediately north of Chicago, occupying an enviable expanse
of land along Lake Michigan. The home to Northwestern University, Evanston boasts a multitude of art galleries, theaters, shops and restaurants. The
community is serviced by the Purple Line of Chicago's "L" system.

WHAT TO SEE
CHARLES GATES DAWES HOUSE

225 Greenwood St., Evanston, 847-475-3410; www.evanstonhistorycenter.org

The 28-room house of General Charles G. Dawes, Nobel Peace Prize winner (1926) and vice president under Calvin Coolidge.

Tours: Tuesday-Saturday.

GROSSE POINT LIGHTHOUSE

Sheridan Road and Central Street, Evanston, 847-328-6961;
www.grossepointlighthouse.net

Constructed after a Lake Michigan wreck near Evanston claimed 300 lives, guided tours of the keeper's quarters, a museum and tower are offered here. No children under age 8 permitted.

June-September, Saturday-Sunday.

LADD ARBORETUM

2024 McCormick Blvd., Evanston, 847-448-8256; www.laddarboretum.org

This arboretum has jogging and biking trails, canoeing, fishing, bird-watching and camping. There is an International Friendship Garden.

Monday-Friday.

MITCHELL MUSEUM OF THE AMERICAN INDIAN

3001 Central Park, Evanston, 847-475-1030; www.mitchellmuseum.org

This collection of more than 3,000 items of Native American art and artifacts includes baskets, pottery, jewelry, Navajo rugs, beadworkand stoneware.

Tuesday-Saturday 10 a.m.-5 p.m., Sunday noon-4 p.m.

NORTHWESTERN UNIVERSITY

633 Clark St., Evanston, 847-491-3741; www.northwestern.edu

Founded in 1851, this private university consistently ranks as one of the top in the nation. The Dearborn Observatory, built in 1888, has free public viewings. Other places of interest include the Shakespeare Garden, Norris University Center, Alice Millar Religious Center, Theatre and Interpretation Center, Mary and Leigh Block Museum of Art, Pick-Staiger Concert Hall, Ryan Field (Big Ten football) and Welsh-Ryan Arena (basketball). Guided walking tours (847-491-7271 for reservations) of the lakefront campus leave 1801 Hinman Avenue.

Tours: Academic year, one departure Monday-Saturday; July-August, two departures Monday-Friday.

WHERE TO STAY
★★★HOTEL ORRINGTON

1710 Orrington Ave., Evanston, 847-866-8700, 800-434-6835; www.hotelorrington.com

Located across from Northwestern University, this elegant hotel combines historic character with modern touches. The hotel features amenities such as an onsite fitness center and access to the Evanston Athletic Club and Henry Crown Sports Pavilion/Norris Aquatics Center.

269 rooms. Restaurant, bar. Business center. Fitness center. Pets accepted. $61-150

WHERE TO EAT
★★JILLY'S CAFE
2614 Green Bay Road, Evanston, 847-869-7636; www.jillyscafe.com
American, French. Lunch, dinner, Sunday brunch. Closed Monday. $16-35

★LAS PALMAS
817 University Place, Evanston, 847-328-2555
Mexican. Lunch, dinner. Bar. $16-35

★LUCKY PLATTER
514 Main St., Evanston, 847-869-4064; luckyplatterrestaurant.com
International. Breakfast, lunch, dinner. $16-35

★MERLE'S #1 BARBECUE
1727 Benson St., Evanston, 847-475-7766
American. Dinner. Reservations recommended. Children's menu. Bar. $16-35

★★★OCEANIQUE
505 Main St., Evanston, 847-864-3435; www.oceanique.com
As the name suggests, the focus of this restaurant is seafood. Dishes include a bouillabaisse of squid, salmon and shrimp in a saffron-scented broth. French, American. Dinner. Closed Sunday. Reservations recommended. $36-85

★★PETE MILLER'S STEAKHOUSE
1557 Sherman Ave., Evanston, 847-328-0399
Steak. Dinner. Reservations recommended. Bar. $16-35

★PRAIRIE MOON
1502 Sherman Ave., Evanston, 847-864-8328; www.prairiemoonrestaurant.com
International. Lunch, dinner, late-night, Sunday brunch. Outdoor seating. Children's menu. Bar. $16-35

★★VA PENSIERO
1566 Oak Ave., Evanston, 847-475-7779; www.va-p.com
Italian. Dinner. Outdoor seating. Bar. $16-35

FREEPORT
See also Rockford
According to legend, Freeport is named for the generosity of its pioneer settler, William Baker, who was chided by his wife for running a "free port" for everyone coming along the trail. It was the scene of the second Lincoln-Douglas debate—the site is marked by a memorial boulder and a life-size statue of Lincoln and Douglas in debate.

WHAT TO SEE
FREEPORT ARTS CENTER
121 N. Harlem Ave., Freeport, 815-235-9755
The center has a collection that includes Asian and Native American art,

European paintings and sculptures, Egyptian, Greek and Roman antiquities along with contemporary exhibits.
Tuesday-Sunday.

SILVER CREEK AND STEPHENSON RAILROAD

2954 S. Walnut St., Freeport, 815-232-2306
Trips are offered here on a 1912, 36-ton steam locomotive with three antique cabooses and a flat car.
June-August.

STEPHENSON COUNTY HISTORICAL MUSEUM

1440 S. Carroll Ave., Freeport, 815-232-8419; www.stephcohs.org
In the 1857 Oscar Taylor house, this museum features 19th-century furnishings and exhibits.
Wednesday-Sunday.

WHERE TO STAY
★COUNTRY INN & SUITES

1710 S. Dirk Drive, Freeport, 815-233-3300, 800-456-4000; www.countryinns.com
66 rooms. Complimentary breakfast. Fitness center. Pool. $61-150

★RAMADA INN

1300 E. South St., Freeport, 815-297-9700, 800-272-6232; www.ramada.com
90 rooms. Restaurant, bar. Business center. Fitness center. Pool. Pets accepted. $61-150

GALENA

See also Bellevue
A quiet town of historical and architectural interest set on terraces cut by the old Fever River, Galena was once a major crossroads for French exploration of the New World. The grand mansions standing today were built on lead and steamboat fortunes and ninety percent of the town's buildings are listed on the National Register of Historic Places.

WHAT TO SEE
BELVEDERE MANSION

1008 Park Ave., Galena, 815-777-0747
This Italianate/Steamboat Gothic mansion built in 1857 has been restored and furnished with antiques, including pieces used on set of *Gone with the Wind*. Combination ticket with Dowling House.
Daily June-October.

DOWLING HOUSE

220 N. Diagonal St., Galena, 815-777-1250
A restored stone house, the oldest in Galena, this house is authentically furnished as a trading post with primitive living quarters.
Guided tours. Combination ticket with Belvedere Mansion. Daily May-December; January-April, limited hours.

GRACE EPISCOPAL CHURCH

309 Hill St., Galena, 817-777-2590; www.gracegalena.org
A Gothic Revival church built in 1848, this building was later remodeled by
William LeBaron Jenney, father of the skyscraper.
Sunday; also by appointment.

ULYSSES S. GRANT HOME STATE HISTORIC SITE

500 Bouthillier St., Galena, 815-777-3310; www.granthome.com
This Italianate house was given to General Grant on his return from the Civil
War in 1865. It features original furnishings and Grant family items.
Wednesday-Sunday 9 a.m.-5 p.m.

WHERE TO STAY
★BEST WESTERN QUIET HOUSE & SUITES

9923 Highway 20 East, Galena, 815-777-2577, 800-937-8376; www.quiethouse.com
42 rooms. Pets accepted. Fitness center. Pool. Reservations recommended.
$61-150

★COUNTRY INN & SUITES

11134 Oldenburg Lane, Galena, 815-777-2400, 888-201-1746; www.countryinns.com
75 rooms. Complimentary breakfast. Fitness center. Pool. $61-150

★★DESOTO HOUSE HOTEL

230 S. Main St., Galena, 815-777-0090, 800-343-6562; www.desotohouse.com
55 rooms. Restaurant, bar. $61-150

★★★EAGLE RIDGE RESORT AND SPA

444 Eagle Ridge Drive, Galena, 815-777-2444, 800-892-2269; www.eagleridge.com
Located in the Galena Territories, a 6,800-acre recreational planned community adjacent to the river town of Galena, this resort has golf courses, horseback riding, hiking, bike and boat rentals. Villas and three- to eight-bedroom
homes are available.
80 rooms. Restaurant, bar. Business center. Fitness center. Pool. Spa. Pets
accepted. Golf. Tennis. $151-250

★RAMADA GALENA

11383 Highway 20 West, Galena, 815-777-2043; www.ramadagalena.com
96 rooms. Complimentary breakfast. Fitness center. Pool. $61-150

WHERE TO EAT
★BACKSTREET STEAK & CHOPHOUSE

216 S. Commerce St., Galena, 815-777-4800; www.backstreetgalena.com
Steak. Dinner. Reservations recommended. $36-85

★LOG CABIN

201 N. Main St., Galena, 815-777-0393; www.logcabingalena.com
Steak, seafood. Lunch, dinner. Children's menu. Bar. $16-35

★★WOODLANDS RESTAURANT
444 Territory Drive, Galena, 815-777-5050, 800-998-6338; www.eagleridge.com
American. Breakfast, lunch, dinner. Reservations recommended. $16-35

GALESBURG
See also Macomb
Eastern pioneers came to this area on the prairie to establish a school for the training of ministers, Knox College. The town was named for their leader, G. W. Gale. -Galesburg was an important station on the Underground Railroad. It is also the birth and burial place of poet Carl Sandburg.

WHAT TO SEE
CARL SANDBURG STATE HISTORIC SITE
331 E. Third St., Galesburg, 309-342-2361; www.sandburg.org
Located here is the restored birthplace cottage of the famous poet. Remembrance Rock, named for Sandburg's historical novel, is a granite boulder under which his ashes were placed.
Wednesday-Sunday.

LAKE STOREY RECREATIONAL AREA
1033 S. Lake Storey Road, Galesburg, 309-345-3683; www.ci.galesburg.il.us
This water park offers boat rentals, an 18-hole golf course, tennis, picnicking, a playground, gardens, concessions and camping.
Daily.

WHERE TO STAY
★★BEST WESTERN PRAIRIE INN
300 S. Soangetaha Road, Galesburg, 309-343-7151, 866-343-7151;
www.bestwestern.com
109 rooms. Restaurant, bar. Fitness center. Pool. Pets accepted. $61-150

★★RAMADA INN
29 Public Square, Galesburg, 309-343-9161, 800-272-6232; www.ramada.com
96 rooms. Restaurant, bar. Pool. Pets accepted. $61-150

WHERE TO EAT
★LANDMARK CAFE & CREPERIE
62 S. Seminary St., Galesburg, 309-343-5376; www.seminarystreet.com
American, French. Breakfast, lunch, dinner. Reservations recommended. Outdoor seating. $16-35

★PACKINGHOUSE
441 Mulberry, Galesburg, 309-342-6868; www.seminarystreet.com
Steak, seafood. Lunch, dinner. Children's menu. $16-35

GENEVA
See also Aurora, DeKalb, St. Charles, Wheaton
This quaint town has more than 100 specialty stores and a restored historic district, which has more than 200 buildings listed on the National Register

of Historic Places. Cyclists and hikers enjoy the trails that wind through the parks adjacent to the Fox River.

WHAT TO SEE
GARFIELD FARM AND INN MUSEUM
Route 38, Geneva, 630-584-8485; www.garfieldfarm.org
This 281-acre living history farm includes an 1846 brick tavern, an 1842 hay barn and an 1849 horse barn; gardens and prairie.

WHEELER PARK
822 N. First St., Geneva, 630-232-4542
This 57-acre park features flower and nature gardens, hiking, tennis, ball fields, access to a riverside bicycle trail, picnicking and miniature golf. The Geneva Historical Society Museum is located in the park.

SPECIAL EVENT
FESTIVAL OF THE VINE
Third Street and Highway 38, Geneva, 630-232-6060; www.genevachamber.com
An autumn harvest celebration, this festival features food and wine tastings, music, craft shows and antique carriage rides.
Second weekend in September.

SWEDISH DAYS
Third Street and Highway 38, Geneva, 630-232-6060; www.genevachamber.com
The Midsommar Swedish Days Festival is one of Illinois' oldest festivals. It includes a week of live music, a carnival, food, crafts and assorted entertainment for the entire family. There are parades daily, pie-eating contests, do-it-yourself crafts and a jam-packed carnival with rides and games for all ages. Be sure to drop by the local merchants, an extensive selection of antiques and unique knick-nacks are on sale.

WHERE TO STAY
★★★HERRINGTON INN
15 S. River Lane, Geneva, 630-208-7433, 800-216-2466; www.herringtoninn.com
Located in an old creamery building on the Fox River, the Herrington dates back to 1835. Each guest room in this lovingly restored limestone building has a fireplace, terrace, private bar and oversized whirlpool bath with heated marble floor.
61 rooms. Restaurant, bar. Complimentary breakfast. Business center. Fitness center. Spa. $251-350

WHERE TO EAT
★★ATWATER'S
15 S. River Lane, Geneva, 630-208-8920; www.herringtoninn.com
American. Breakfast, lunch, dinner, Sunday brunch. Reservations recommended. Outdoor seating. Bar. $16-35

★★MILL RACE INN
4 E. State St., Geneva, 630-232-2030; www.themillraceinn.com
American. Lunch, dinner, Sunday brunch. Outdoor seating. Children's menu. Bar. $16-35

GLENVIEW
See also Northbrook, Skokie, Wheeling, Wilmette
Glenview is located 20 miles north of downtown Chicago and boasts numerous shops and restaurants, desirable residential neighborhoods and exceptional public schools.

WHAT TO SEE
GROVE NATIONAL HISTORIC LANDMARK
1421 N. Milwaukee Ave., Glenview, 847-299-6096; www.thegroveglenview.org
This 124-acre nature preserve includes miles of hiking trails and three structures. On the grounds is the restored 1856 Kennicott House; the Interpretative Center, a nature center museum; and a house designed by George G. Elmslie, who studied under and worked with Louis Sullivan.
Daily. Kennicott House Tours: February-September, Sunday.

SPECIAL EVENTS
CIVIL WAR LIVING HISTORY DAYS
Grove National Historic Landmark, Glenview, 1421 Glenview Road, 847-299-6096;
www.glenview.il.us
Features realistic battle reenactment with hospital tent and camps of the period and participants in authentic clothing and uniforms. Exhibits, lectures, and house tours are highlighted.
Last weekend in July.

SUMMER FESTIVAL
Glenview Road, Glenview, 847-724-0900; www.glenviewchamber.com
The festival has entertainment, vendors and food.
Last Saturday in June.

WHERE TO EAT
★PERIYALI GREEK TAVERNA
9860 Milwaukee Ave., Glenview, 847-296-2232
Greek. Lunch, dinner. Outdoor seating. Bar. $16-35

HIGHLAND PARK
See also Chicago, Highwood, Northbrook
This lakefront suburban community is located 23 miles north of Chicago. Browse the city's pricey upscale boutiques, enjoy free summer music concerts in Port Clinton Square or dine in one of the local restaurants. Warm-weather concerts under the stars take place at Ravinia Festival, which runs from June-mid-September.

WHAT TO SEE
FRANCIS STUPEY LOG CABIN
326 Central Ave., Highland Park
This 1847 cabin is the oldest structure in town.
May-October, Saturday-Sunday; also by appointment.

RAVINIA FESTIVAL
200 Ravinia Park Road, Highland Park, 847-266-5100; www.ravinia.org
Located on the North Shore, this is the summer home of the Chicago Symphony Orchestra. Special programs include Jazz in June, the Young Artists series and Kids Concerts. While there is a 3,200-seat, open-air pavilion and two indoor venues for chamber music and smaller concerts, the majority of festivalgoers prefer the lawn, ideal for picnicking. The park offers five restaurants, a picnic catering facility, chair rentals and wine kiosks.
June-mid-September.

WHERE TO EAT
★★CAFE CENTRAL
455 Central Ave., Highland Park, 847-266-7878; www.cafecentral.net
French. Lunch, dinner. Closed Monday. Outdoor seating. Children's menu. Bar. $16-35

★★★CARLOS
429 Temple Ave., Highland Park, 847-432-0770; www.carlos-restaurant.com
Owned by husband-and-wife team Carlos and Debbie Nieto, this is an elegant and intimate restaurant. Carlos is known for its stellar haute cuisine served in classic French style: Entrées arrive topped with silver domes. The wine list has more than 3,500 international selections.
French. Dinner. Closed Tuesday. Reservations recommended. Jacket required. Bar. $36-85

HIGHWOOD
See also Highland Park, Lake Forest
Sandwiched between Highland Park and Lake Forest, this suburban community along Chicago's North Shore is known both for its many restaurants and its close association to Fort Sheridan, a former army base. Local attractions include Everts Park, the Robert McClory Bicycle Path and the 18-hole Lake County Forest Preserve golf course at the Fort Sheridan Club.

WHERE TO EAT
★★DEL RIO
228 Green Bay Road, Highwood, 847-432-4608
Italian. Dinner. Closed Sunday. Reservations recommended. $16-35

★★★FROGGY'S
306 Green Bay Road, Highwood, 847-433-7080; www.froggyscatering.com
This cheery bistro offers country French cuisine at reasonable prices, with specialties like onion soup, coq au vin and rabbit casserole. The wine list features a number of red and white Burgundies, Bordeaux and champagnes, while deca-

dent cakes and carry-out items can be purchased from the adjacent bakery. French. Lunch, dinner. Closed Sunday. Bar. $16-35

★★★GABRIEL'S
310 Green Bay Road, Highwood, 847-433-0031; www.egabriels.com
Chef/owner Gabriel Viti, formerly of Carlos' in Highland Park, turns out complex French-Italian dishes. Entrées range from grilled veal porterhouse to roasted Maine lobster with baby bok choy and ginger butter sauce. Seasonal specials and a tasting menu are also available.
French, Italian. Dinner. Closed Sunday-Monday. Reservations recommended. Outdoor seating. Bar. $36-85

HOMEWOOD
See also Chicago
Located 24 miles south of Chicago's Loop, Homewood boasts two city blocks of fascinating art. New York muralist Richard Haas refurbished older business buildings with trompe l'oeil artwork on the backs of the structures.

WHERE TO EAT
★AURELIO'S PIZZA
18162 Harwood Ave., Homewood, 708-798-8050; www.aureliospizza.com
Italian. Lunch, dinner. Outdoor seating. Children's menu. Bar. $16-35

JOLIET
See also Aurora, Lockport, Morris
The Des Plaines River, the Chicago Sanitary and Ship Canal and railroad freight lines triggered Joliet's growth as a center of industry. The canal's Brandon Road Locks, to the south of Joliet, are among the largest in the world, and the canal continues to carry millions of tons of barge traffic annually through the city. Although Joliet was named in honor of Louis Jolliet, the French-Canadian explorer who visited the area in 1673, it was incorporated in 1837 as Juliet, companion to the nearby town of Romeo (now renamed Romeoville).

WHAT TO SEE
BICENTENNIAL PARK THEATER/BAND SHELL COMPLEX
201 W. Jefferson St., Joliet, 815-724-3760; www.bicentennialpark.org
Joliet Drama Guild and other productions perform here. See outdoor concerts in the band shell during the summer on Thursday evenings.

CHALLENGE PARK XTREME
2903 Schweitzer Road, Joliet, 815-726-2800; www.challengepark.com
This 150-acre complex contains a skate park, miles of mountain biking trails and 25-paintball fields.
Wednesday-Thursday 10 a.m.-6 p.m., Friday 10 a.m.-9 p.m., Saturday 9 a.m.-9 p.m., Sunday 9 a.m.-6 p.m.; winter hours vary.

CHICAGOLAND SPEEDWAY

500 Speedway Blvd., Joliet, 815-727-7223; www.chicagolandspeedway.com

This 75,000-seat track hosts NASCAR and Indy Racing League events in mid-July and mid-September. Come on the Friday before a race for qualifying/practice day, when the admission fee is cheaper and good seats are easier to come by.

JOLIET JACKHAMMERS

Silver Cross Field, 1 Major Art Schultz Drive, Joliet, 815-726-2255;
www.jackhammerbaseball.com

The Joliet Jackhammers play in the Northern League with nine other independent teams. As is the tradition in minor league baseball, the Jackhammers' season is peppered with unusual promotions like a hospital scrubs giveaway and a Christmas in July Ornament Giveaway.
Mid-May-early September.

RIALTO SQUARE THEATRE

102 N. Chicago St., Joliet, 815-726-7171; www.rialtosquare.com

This performing arts center, designed by the Rapp brothers in 1926, is considered one of the most elaborate and beautiful of old 1920s movie palaces.
Tours: Tuesday; also by appointment.

WHERE TO STAY
★COMFORT INN

2600 W. Main St., Marion, 618-993-6221, 800-228-5150; www.choicehotels.com

122 rooms. Complimentary breakfast. Fitness center. Pool. Pets accepted. $61-150

★★HOLIDAY INN

222 Gore Road, Morris, 815-941-8700, 800-465-4329; www.holiday-inn.com

120 rooms. Restaurant, bar. Fitness center. Pool. Pets accepted. $61-150

WHERE TO EAT
★MERICHKA'S RESTAURANT

604 Theodore St., Crest Hill, 815-723-9371; www.merichkas.com

American. Lunch, dinner. $15 and under

★★ROCKWELL INN

2400 W. Highway 6, Morris, 815-942-6224; www.rockwellinn.50megs.com

American. Lunch, dinner, Sunday brunch. Reservations recommended. Children's menu. Bar. $16-35

★R-PLACE FAMILY EATERY

21 Romines Drive, Morris, 815-942-3690; www.rplaceeatery.com

American. Breakfast, lunch, dinner, late-night. Reservations recommended. Children's menu. $15 and under

★★SYL'S RESTAURANT
829 Moen Ave., Rockdale, 815-725-1977; www.sylsrestaurant.com
American. Dinner. $16-35

★★TRUTH RESTAURANT
808 W. Jefferson St., Joilet, 815-744-5901; www.truthrestaurant.com
American. Dinner. Closed Sunday-Monday. Reservations recommended.
Children's menu. Bar. $16-35

LAKE FOREST
See also Highland Park, Highwood
Lake Forest, a North Shore Chicago suburb, has long been regarded as an en-
clave of affluence and prestige. Sprawling estates spread out on bluffs overlooking Lake Michigan. It's home to Lake Forest College as well as Halas
Hall, the headquarters of the Chicago Bears. Actor Vince Vaughn is its most
famous resident. Lake -Forest's -central business district, Market Square,
was listed on the National Register of -Historic Places in 1979.

WHERE TO STAY
★★★DEER PATH INN
255 E. Illinois Road, Lake Forest, 847-234-2280, 800-788-9480; www.dpihotel.com
Patterned after a 1453 manor house in England, this half-timbered mansion
has the look of a stately residence and the feel of a weekend estate. It was
built in the 1920s by architect William C. Jones, who was instrumental in the
design of the Chicago World's Fair. Each room, named after a National Trust
property in England, is individually decorated and furnished, and many have
views of the well-manicured English garden.
55 rooms. Restaurant, bar. Business center. $151-250

WHERE TO EAT
★★BANK LANE BISTRO
670 Bank Lane, Lake Forest, 847-234-8802; www.banklanebistro.com
Contemporary American, French. Lunch, dinner. Closed Sunday. Reservations recommended. Outdoor seating. Bar. $36-85

★★★THE ENGLISH ROOM
255 E. Illinois St., Lake Forest, 847-234-2280; www.dpihotel.com
Set inside the historic Deer Path Inn, a popular destination for weekend get-
aways and fine dining since 1929, the English Room is an elegant dining
room with a traditional dinner menu that includes options like lobster bisque,
roasted rack of lamb and Dover sole. The Sunday champagne brunch is especially good here.
International. Breakfast, lunch, dinner, Sunday brunch. Reservations recommended. Outdoor seating. Bar. $36-85

★★SOUTH GATE CAFE
655 Forest Ave., Lake Forest, 847-234-8800; www.southgatecafe.com
American. Lunch, dinner, brunch. Reservations recommended. Outdoor
seating. Children's menu. Bar. $16-35

LEMONT

See also Lockport

Located in northeast Illinois, Lemont was settled in 1836 and incorporated in 1873. Limestone was the reason for the town's growth—an example of Lemont limestone can be seen today at Chicago's Water Tower.

WHAT TO SEE
COG HILL GOLF & COUNTRY CLUB

12294 Archer Ave., Lemont, 866-264-4455; www.coghillgolf.com

Easily the best course in Chicago and home to the PGA Tour's BMW Championship, the Dubsdread Course features so many bunkers that average players might think they're playing on a beach. The course is beautifully maintained and is open to the public.

RUFFLED FEATHERS GOLF CLUB

1 Pete Dye Drive, Lemont, 630-257-1000; www.ruffledfeathersgc.com

Home to the Illinois Professional Golf Association, Ruffled Feathers has been open since 1991 and was designed Pete Dye. Like Lemont neighbor Cog Hill, the course has more than 100 sand bunkers but has wide fairways to compensate.

SPECIAL EVENT
BMW CHAMPIONSHIP (FORMERLY THE WESTERN OPEN GOLF TOURNAMENT)

12294 S. Archer Ave., Lemont, 866-264-4455; www.coghillgolf.com

The third of four PGA tour tournaments that lead to the FedEx championship, the BMW Championship is a three-day, four-round event that hosts the top players in the field of golf. Tickets are available in daily, practice packs and weekly bundles.

★★★★★ ILLINOIS

WHERE TO EAT
★WHITE FENCE FARM

1376 Joliet Road, Lemont, 630-739-1720; www.whitefencefarm.com/chicago

American. Dinner. Closed Monday; also January. Children's menu. $16-35

LIBERTYVILLE

See also Gurnee, Lake Forest

Marlon Brando, Helen Hayes and Adlai Stevenson are a few of the famous personalities who have lived in Libertyville. The Roman Catholic St. Mary of the Lake Theological Seminary borders the town. There are four lakes near the village limits.

WHAT TO SEE
CUNEO MUSEUM AND GARDENS

1350 N. Milwaukee Ave., Vernon Hills, 847-362-3042; www.cuneomuseum.org

This museum is a Venetian-style mansion that features a Great Hall with arcade balconies, a chapel with stained glass and a fresco ceiling and a collection of master paintings. The grounds include fountains, gardens, sculptures and a conservatory. Tuesday-Sunday.

DAVID ADLER CULTURAL CENTER

1700 N. Milwaukee Ave., Libertyville, 847-367-0707; www.adlercenter.org

This was the summer residence of the distinguished neoclassical architect David Adler. It's now an art and music center. There are folk concerts and children's events.

LAMBS FARM

14245 W. Rockland Road, Libertyville, 847-362-4636; www.lambsfarm.org

The farm has grown from a small pet store to a nonprofit residential and vocational community that benefits adults with developmental disabilities. It includes a children's farmyard, animal nursery, miniature golf and a thrift shop. Daily.

WHERE TO EAT
★COUNTRY INN RESTAURANT AT LAMBS FARM

14245 W. Rockland Road, Libertyville, 847-362-5050; www.lambsfarm.org

American. Breakfast, lunch. Closed Monday. Outdoor seating. Children's menu. $15 and under

★★TAVERN IN THE TOWN

519 N. Milwaukee Ave., Libertyville, 847-367-5755; www.tavernlibertyville.com

American, seafood. Dinner. Closed Sunday. Bar. $36-85

LOCKPORT

See also Joliet, Lemont

Lockport was founded as the headquarters of the Illinois and Michigan Canal. In its heyday, the town boasted five different locks. The Old Canal Town National Historic District preserves several buildings from this era.

WHAT TO SEE
ILLINOIS AND MICHIGAN CANAL MUSEUM

803 S. State St., Lockport, 815-838-5080; www.willcountyhistory.org

This building was originally used as the Canal Commissioner's office. Museum includes artifacts, pictures and documents relating to the construction and operation of the canal.

Guided tours by costumed docents. February-November, noon-4 p.m.

SPECIAL EVENT
OLD CANAL DAYS

222 E. Ninth St., Lockport, 815-838-4744; www.lockportcanaldays.com

This four-day festival celebrates Lockport with pioneer craft demonstrations, horse-drawn wagon tours, Illinois and Michigan Canal walking tours and Lockport prairie tours along with entertainment and food.

Third weekend in June.

WHERE TO EAT
★★PUBLIC LANDING

200 W. Eighth St., Lockport, 815-838-6500; www.publiclandingrestaurant.com

American. Lunch, dinner. Closed Monday. Children's menu. Bar. $16-35

★★★TALLGRASS
1006 S. State, Lockport, 815-838-5566; www.tallgrassrestaurant.com
Master chef Robert Burcenski offers a well-balanced, contemporary menu. Diners can choose from three or five courses, including entrées such as grilled beef tenderloin with garlic potato puree.
French. Dinner. Closed Monday-Tuesday. Reservations recommended. Bar. $36-85

MACOMB
See also Galesburg, Nauvoo
Originally known as Washington, the town was renamed to honor General Alexander Macomb, an officer in the War of 1812. Macomb is best known as the home of Western Illinois University.

WHAT TO SEE
ARGYLE LAKE STATE PARK
640 Argyle Park Road, Macomb, 309-776-3422; dnr.state.il.us
The park has 1,700 acres with a 95-acre lake. Fishing, boating, hiking, cross-country skiing, snowmobiling, picnicking and playground are available. Daily.

WESTERN ILLINOIS UNIVERSITY
1 University Circle, Macomb, 309-298-1414; www.wiu.edu
The 1,050-acre campus, founded in 1899, includes an art gallery, agricultural experiment station and a nine-hole public golf course.

WHERE TO STAY
★★DAYS INN
1400 N. Lafayette St., Macomb, 309-833-5511, 800-329-7466; www.daysinn.com
144 rooms. Restaurant, bar. Complimentary breakfast. Pool. $61-150

WHERE TO EAT
★★CELLAR
137 S. State St., Geneseo, 309-944-2177; www.thecellar.info
Steak. Dinner. Closed Monday. Children's menu. Bar. $36-85

MCHENRY
See also Gurnee
This city is located 50 miles northwest of Chicago and was named after Major William McHenry.

WHAT TO SEE
MORAINE HILLS STATE PARK
1510 S. River Road, McHenry, 815-385-1624; www.dnr.state.il.us
The park consists of three small lakes on 1,690 acres.

WHERE TO STAY
★★HOLIDAY INN CRYSTAL LAKE
Highway 31 and Three Oaks Road, Crystal Lake, 815-477-7000, 800-465-4329; www. hicrystallake.com
197 rooms. Restaurant, bar. Business center. Fitness center. Pool. Pets accepted. $61-150

WHERE TO EAT
★★★LE VICHYSSOIS
220 W. Highway 120, Lakemoor, 815-385-8221; www.levichyssois.com
Situated across from a lake in northwest suburban Lakemoor, this inn is a retreat for classic French cuisine lovers. The chef and owner, Bernard Cretier, trained under Paul Bocuse and was an executive chef at Chicago's Maxim. The menu includes a smaller bistro menu or the larger regular menu, and either can be pared easily with selections from the wine list. Le Vichyssois is also an art gallery, so most of the oil paintings lining the walls are for sale. French. Dinner. Closed Monday-Tuesday. Reservations recommended. $36-85

NAPERVILLE
See also Aurora, Downers Grove, Wheaton
Though it's one of the fastest growing suburbs in the nation, Naperville retains the atmosphere of a small town with its core of large Victorian houses and a beautiful historic district. The downtown shopping area features more than 100 shops and restaurants in historic buildings and adjoins the Riverwalk, a 3½-mile winding brick pathway along the DuPage River.

WHAT TO SEE
DUPAGE CHILDREN'S MUSEUM
301 N. Washington St., Naperville, 630-637-8000; www.dupagechildrensmuseum.org
This museum has three floors of kid-friendly, hands-on exhibits.
Tuesday-Wednesday, Friday-Saturday 9 a.m.-5 p.m., Monday until 1 p.m., Thursday until 8 p.m., Sunday noon-5 p.m., closed late August-mid-September.

NAPER SETTLEMENT
523 S. Webster St., Naperville, 630-420-6010; www.napersettlement.org
A 13-acre living history museum, this site has 25 buildings in a village setting that depict a 19th-century northern Illinois town.
Tours are led by costumed guides April-October, Tuesday-Sunday; November-March, Monday-Friday.

WHERE TO STAY
★COURTYARD CHICAGO NAPERVILLE
1155 E. Diehl Road, Naperville, 630-505-0550, 800-228-9290; www.marriott.com
147 rooms. Restaurant. Fitness center. Pool. $61-150

★HAMPTON INN

1087 E. Diehl Road, Naperville, 630-505-1400, 800-426-7866; www.hamptoninn.com
128 rooms. Complimentary breakfast. Business center. Fitness center. Pool.
$61-150

★★★HYATT LISLE

1400 Corporetum Drive, Lisle, 630-852-1234; www.lisle.hyatt.com
Venture out for a round of golf at one of three courses within an eight-mile
radius of this hotel.
312 rooms. Restaurant, bar. Business center. Fitness center. Pool. $151-250

★★★WYNDHAM LISLE/NAPERVILLE

3000 Warrenville Road, Lisle, 630-505-1000, 800-996-3426;
www.wyndhamlislehotel.com
This suburban hotel has spacious rooms and a 17,000-square-foot fitness
center.
242 rooms. Restaurant, bar. Fitness center. Pool. $61-150

WHERE TO EAT
★★MESON SABIKA

1025 Aurora Ave., Naperville, 630-983-3000; www.mesonsabika.com
Spanish, tapas. Lunch, dinner, Sunday brunch. Outdoor seating. Children's
menu. Bar. $16-35

★★RAFFI'S ON 5TH

200 E. Fifth Ave., Naperville, 630-961-8203; www.raffison5th.com
Mediterranean. Lunch, dinner. Closed Sunday. Reservations recommended.
Bar. $16-35

NAUVOO

See also Macomb

Once the largest cities in Illinois, Nauvoo has a colorful history. When the
Mormon prophet Joseph Smith was driven out of Missouri, he came with his
Latter-day Saints to a tiny village called Commerce on a headland overlook-
ing the Mississippi River and established what was virtually an autonomous
state. A city of 8,000 houses was created and in 1841, construction began on
a great temple. A schism in the church led to riots and the persecution of the
Mormons. Joseph Smith and his brother were arrested and murdered by a
mob while in the Carthage jail. Brigham Young became leader of the Nauvoo
Mormons. When the city charter was repealed and armed clashes broke out,
Young led much of the population westward in 1846 to its final settlement in
Utah. Nauvoo became a ghost town, and the almost-completed temple was
burned by an arsonist. In 1849, the Icarians, a band of French communalists,
migrated to Nauvoo from Texas and attempted to rebuild the temple, but a
storm swept the building back into ruin. The Icarians failed to prosper and
in 1856 moved on. The city was gradually resettled by a group of Germans,
who developed the wine culture begun by the French.

★
★★ ILLINOIS
★★
★

WHAT TO SEE
BAXTER'S VINEYARDS

2010 E. Parley St., Nauvoo, 217-453-2528, 800-854-1396; www.nauvoowinery.com
The vineyards were established in 1857 and host tours and wine tastings.
Daily.

JOSEPH SMITH HISTORIC CENTER

865 Water St., Nauvoo, 217-453-2246; www.cofchrist.org/js
A 50-minute tour begins in the visitor center and includes a visit to Joseph
Smith's grave.
Daily. May-October, Monday-Saturday 9 a.m.-5 p.m., Sunday 1-5 p.m.,
November-December, Tuesday-Saturday 10 a.m.-4 p.m., January-February,
Friday and Saturday only, 10 a.m.-4 p.m., March-April, Monday-Saturday
10 a.m.-4 p.m., Sunday 1-4 p.m.

JOSEPH SMITH HOMESTEAD

This 1803 structure was the Log cabin the prophet occupied after coming to
Nauvoo in 1839 and is the town's oldest structure.
Daily.

NAUVOO RESTORATION, INC, VISITOR CENTER

Young and North Main streets, Nauvoo, 217-453-2237
This center has a 20-minute movie on Nauvoo history and information on
points of interest.
Daily.

SMITH'S MANSION

Smith lived in this refined, Federal-style frame house from 1843-1844.
Monday-Saturday 9 a.m.-5 p.m., Sunday from 1 p.m.

WHERE TO STAY
★★★HOTEL NAUVOO

1290 Mulholland St., Nauvoo, 217-453-2211; www.hotelnauvoo.com
This restored historic inn was originally a private residence.
8 rooms. Restaurant, bar. $61-150

WHERE TO EAT
★GRANDPA JOHN'S

1255 Mulholland St., Nauvoo, 217-453-2125
American. Breakfast, lunch. Closed January-February. Children's menu. $15
and under

★★★HOTEL NAUVOO

1290 Mulholland St., Nauvoo, 217-453-2211; www.hotelnauvoo.com
From mid-April-mid-November, visitors can sample the prix fixe all-Ameri-
can buffet, which includes such favorites as fried chicken and apple pie.
American. Dinner, Sunday brunch. Closed mid-November-mid-March. Bar.
$16-35

NORTHBROOK

See also Glenview, Highland Park, Wheeling

Brickyards played a major role in the prosperity and growth of this North Chicago suburb. After the Great Chicago Fire of 1871, about 300,000 bricks per day were produced here between 1915 and 1920. It's now home to many corporate headquarters, including national home goods retailer Crate & Barrel.

WHAT TO SEE
CHICAGO BOTANIC GARDEN

1000 Lake Cook Road, Glencoe, 847-835-5440; www.chicagobotanic.org
Managed by the Chicago Horticultural Society, this garden includes 300 acres of formal plantings, lakes, lagoons and wooded naturalistic areas. Daily.

RIVER TRAIL NATURE CENTER

3120 Milwaukee Ave., Northbrook, 847-824-8360, 800-870-3666; www.fpdcc.com
This park is a 300-acre nature preserve within the Forest Preserve District of Cook County.
Daily.

WHERE TO STAY
★★COURTYARD BY MARRIOTT DEERFIELD

800 Lake Cook Road, Deerfield, 847-940-8222, 800-321-2211; www.marriott.com
131 rooms. Business center. Fitness center. Pool. $61-150

★★★HYATT DEERFIELD

1750 Lake Cook Road, Deerfield, 847-945-3400, 800-633-7313; www.deerfield.hyatt.com
Want a hotel that has a cigar humidor on its heated outdoor patio? Or Starbucks coffee and breakfast pastries? Where someone will make a massage appointment for you at a nearby spa? This is the place. Wireless Internet access, a 24-hour business center and oversized desks will make business travelers happy. The rooms are sleek and contemporary with marble bathrooms.
301 rooms. Restaurant, bar. Business center. Fitness center. Pool. $61-150

★★★RENAISSANCE CHICAGO NORTH SHORE HOTEL

933 Skokie Blvd., Northbrook, 847-498-6500, 888-236-2427; www.marriott.com
Ten stories of rooms and facilities with a fun chess theme make up the Renaissance Chicago North Shore Hotel. Restaurants include Ruth's Chris Steak House and the American bistro, Rooks Corner.
385 rooms. Restaurant, bar. Business center. Fitness center. Pool. $61-150

WHERE TO EAT
★★★PRAIRIE GRASS CAFÉ

601 Skokie Blvd., Northbrook, 847-205-4433; www.prairiegrasscafe.com
Award-winning chef Sarah Stegner, most recently a chef at the Dining Room at the Ritz-Carlton Chicago, has teamed up with former colleague George Bumbaris to open this American café, a cross between casual and fine din-

ing. Hardwood floors, exposed brick walls and colorful oil paintings provide a setting for the impeccable American fare. The desserts are prepared by the best pastry chef Stegner could find—her mother.

American. Breakfast, lunch, dinner, brunch. Closed Monday. Reservations recommended. Children's menu. Bar. $36-85

OAK BROOK

See also Brookfield, Downers Grove

Known as Fullersburg in the mid-1800s, Oak Brook is the home of Butler National Golf Club. Sports and recreation have long been important in this carefully planned village—it has 12 miles of biking and hiking paths and more than 450 acres of parks and recreation land. Today, Oak Brook is a hub for international polo players and the headquarters of many major corporations.

WHAT TO SEE
FULLERSBURG WOODS ENVIRONMENTAL CENTER

3609 Spring Road, Oak Brook, 630-850-8110; www.dupageforest.com

This center has wildlife in a natural setting, an environmental center and theater, a native marsh ecology exhibit and four nature trails.

Daily.

GRAUE MILL AND MUSEUM

3800 York Road Oak Brook, Oak Brook, 630-655-2090; www.grauemill.org

A restored mill built in 1852, this was the only operating water-powered gristmill in the state and a former station of the Underground Railroad.

Mid-April-mid--November, Tuesday-Sunday 10 a.m.-4:30 p.m.

OAKBROOK CENTER

100 Oakbrook Center, Oak Brook, 630-573-0700; www.oakbrookcenter.com

This giant center has six major department stores and more than 160 shops and restaurants, all linked by gardens and fountains.

Monday-Saturday, 10 a.m.-9 p.m.; Sunday 11 a.m.-6 p.m.

SPECIAL EVENT
SUNDAY POLO

700 Oak Brook Road, Oak Brook, 630-368-6428; www.chicagopolo.com

Mid-June-mid-September.

WHERE TO STAY
★HAMPTON INN

222 E. 22nd St., Lombard, 630-916-9000, 800-426-7866; www.hamptoninn.com

128 rooms. Complimentary breakfast. Business center. Fitness center. $61-150

★★★HILTON SUITES OAKBROOK TERRACE

10 Drury Lane, Oakbrook Terrace, 630-941-0100, 800-445-8667; www.hilton.com

Adjacent to the Drury Lane Theater, this hotel is near the Oak Brook Center Mall. Each two-room suite features a sleeping room with a king or two double beds and a separate living room with a work desk and pull-out couch. 211 rooms. Restaurant, bar. Business center. Fitness center. Pool. $61-150

★★★MARRIOTT OAK BROOK HILLS RESORT
3500 Midwest Road, Oak Brook, 630-850-5555, 800-228-9290; www.marriott.com
This sprawling resort has indoor and outdoor pools, a fitness center and spa, volleyball and basketball courts and seasonal cross-country skiing. The 18-hole Willow Crest Golf Club, considered one of the Midwest's finest courses, is also on the property.
384 rooms. Restaurant, bar. Business center. Fitness center. Pool. Golf. Tennis. $151-250

WHERE TO EAT
★★BRAXTON SEAFOOD GRILL
3 Oak Brook Center Mall, Oak Brook, 630-574-2155; www.braxtonseafood.com
Seafood. Lunch, dinner, brunch. Reservations recommended. Children's menu. Bar. $16-35

★★CAFE 36
22 Calendar Court, La Grange, 708-354-5722; www.cafe36.com
French. Lunch, dinner. Closed Monday. Reservations recommended. Bar. $16-35

★★★VIE
4471 Lawn Ave., Western Springs, 708-246-2082; www.vierestaurant.com
This culinary oasis in the chain-laden suburban dining scene stands out for more than its quality (which is surprisingly high). The real selling point is for dieters. Anyone whose penchant for primo cuisine periodically sabotages his or her weight-loss plans will appreciate this: Vie's chef majored in nutrition before taking on the culinary world. And this: the housemade charcuterie plate of smoked sausage, salami, country paté, baby greens, pickled beets, apple jam and rhubarb mostarda. Where else have you seen a charcuterie plate that resembles a balanced meal? And where else have you seen rhubarb mostarda with anything?
Contemporary American. Dinner. Closed Sunday. $36-85

OAK LAWN
See also Chicago
In 1856, Oak Lawn was a settlement known as Black Oaks Grove. When the Wabash Railroad began to lay tracks through the community in 1879, an agreement was made with the railroad builder to create a permanent village. The new town of Oak Lawn was established in 1882. Now, it's a western Chicago suburb.

WHERE TO STAY
★★★HILTON OAK LAWN
9333 S. Cicero Ave., Oak Lawn, 708-425-7800; www.oaklawn.hilton.com
This is a hotel designed for business. Located just four miles from Midway airport, the hotel has a courtesy shuttle that picks up travelers curbside.

Rooms have wireless Internet access and dual-line telephones. The hotel is approximately 15 miles from downtown Chicago.

184 rooms. Restaurant, bar. Business center. Fitness center. Pool. $61-150

WHERE TO EAT

★PALERMO'S

4849 W. 95th St., Oak Lawn, 708-425-6262; www.palermos95th.com

Italian. Lunch, dinner. Closed Tuesday. Children's menu. Bar. $16-35

★WHITNEY'S GRILLE

9333 S. Cicero Ave., Oak Lawn, 708-425-7800; www1.hilton.com

American. Breakfast, lunch, dinner, Sunday brunch. Reservations recommended. Children's menu. Bar. $16-35

OAK PARK

See also Chicago

Oak Park, one of Chicago's oldest suburbs, is a village of well-kept houses and magnificent trees. The town is internationally famous as the birthplace of Ernest Hemingway and for its concentration of Prairie School houses by Frank Lloyd Wright and other modern architects of the early 20th century. Wright both lived in the town and practiced architecture from his Oak Park studio between 1889 and 1909.

WHAT TO SEE

ERNEST HEMINGWAY MUSEUM

Arts Center, 200 N. Oak Park Ave., Oak Park, 708-848-2222; www.ehfop.org

A restored 1890s Victorian home, this museum includes rare photos, artifacts and letters from the author. Walking tours of Hemingway sites, including his birthplace.

Sunday-Friday 1-5 p.m., Saturday 10 a.m.-5 p.m.; closed major holidays.

FRANK LLOYD WRIGHT HOME AND STUDIO

931 Chicago Ave., Oak Park, 708-848-1976; www.wrightplus.org

Wright built this house in 1889, when he was 22 years old. He remodeled the inside on an average of every 18 months, testing his new design ideas while creating the Prairie school of architecture in the process. This is a National Trust for Historic Preservation property.

Daily tours.

OAK PARK VISITORS CENTER

158 N. Forest Ave., Oak Park, 708-848-1500; www.oprf.com/opvc

This center offers information guidebooks, an orientation program on the Frank Lloyd Wright Prairie School of Architecture National Historic District, a recorded walking tour (fee), and admission tickets for tours of Wright's home and studio; other walking tours.

Daily.

PLEASANT HOME (JOHN FARSON HOUSE)

217 S. Home Ave., Oak Park, 708-383-2654; www.oprf.com/phf

An opulent 30-room mansion designed by prominent Prairie school architect George W. Maher in 1897, this house's second floor is home to the Oak Park/ River Forest Historical Society and Museum.

Thursday-Sunday afternoons, guided tours on the hour.

UNITY TEMPLE

875 Lake St., Oak Park, 708-848-6225

Home to a congregation of the Unitarian Universalist Church, this national landmark was designed by Frank Lloyd Wright in 1906. The church was his first Monolithic concrete structure and his first public building.

Self-guided tour, Monday-Friday afternoons; weekend tours available.

WHERE TO EAT
★★CAFE LE COQ

734 Lake St., Oak Park, 708-848-2233

French. Dinner, Sunday brunch. Closed Monday. Bar. $16-35

OREGON

See also DeKalb, Dixon, Rockford

Generations of artists have found inspiration in the scenic region surrounding Oregon. In 1898, sculptor Lorado Taft and others founded a colony for artists and writers. Located on Rock River, Oregon is the home of the Lorado Taft Field Campus of Northern Illinois University.

WHAT TO SEE
CASTLE ROCK STATE PARK

1365 W. Castle Road, Oregon, 815-732-7329; www.dnr.state.il.us

This park located on 2,000 acres offers fishing, boating, hiking skiing trails and tobogganing.

THE ETERNAL INDIAN

Rising 48 feet above brush-covered bluffs, this monumental work by Lorado Taft was constructed in 1911 of poured Portland cement. The statue is usually referred to as Black Hawk.

STRONGHOLD CASTLE

1922 Highway 2 N., Oregon, 815-732-6111; www.strongholdcenter.org

This replica of an Old English castle was built in 1929 by newspaper publisher Walter Strong and is now owned by the Presbytery of Blackhawk, Presbyterian Church.

WHITE PINES FOREST STATE PARK

Pines Road, Morris, 815-946-3717; www.dnr.state.il.us

On 385 acres, the White Pines park contains the northernmost large stand of virgin white pine in Illinois. Fishing, hiking, cross-country skiing, picnicking, concession, lodge, dining facilities, camping.

OTTAWA

See also Peru, Utica/Starved Rock State Park

Founded by the commissioners of the Illinois and Michigan Canal, Ottawa took root after the Black Hawk War of 1832. The first of the Lincoln-Douglas debates was held in the town's public square, and a monument in Washington Park marks the site. Located at the confluence of the Fox and Illinois Rivers, many industries are now located in this "Town of Two Rivers."

WHAT TO SEE
BUFFALO ROCK STATE PARK
Buffalo Rock Road, Ottawa, 815-433-2220; www.dnr.state.il.us
Part of the Illinois and Michigan Canal State Trail on 243 acres. Live buffalo. Hiking, picnicking, playground.

EFFIGY TUMULI SCULPTURE
Buffalo Rock State Park, Ottawa, 815-433-2220; dnr.state.il.us
The largest earth sculptures since Mount Rushmore were formed as part of a reclamation project on the site of a former strip mine. Fashioned with the use of earthmoving equipment, the five enormous figures—a snake, turtle, catfish, frog and water strider were deliberately designed and formed to recall similar earth sculptures done by pre-Columbian Native Americans as ceremonial or burial mounds called tumuli.
Daily.

SKYDIVE CHICAGO
Ottawa Airport, 3215 E. 1969th Road, Ottawa, 815-434-6094;
www.skydivechicago.com
Largest skydiving center in the Midwest.
Daily.

WILLIAM REDDICK MANSION
100 W. Lafayette St., Ottawa, 815-434-2737; www.state.il.us
This Italianate, antebellum mansion (built 1856-1857) has 22 rooms, ornate walnut woodwork and ornamental plasterwork. Period rooms contain many original furnishings.
Daily.

WHERE TO STAY
★HOLIDAY INN EXPRESS
120 W. Stevenson Road, Ottawa, 815-433-0029; www.hiexpress.com
70 rooms. Pool. Pets accepted. $61-150

WHERE TO EAT
★CAPTAIN'S COVE BAR AND GRILL
Starved Rock Marina, Ottawa, 815-434-0881
Steak, Seafood. Lunch, dinner. Closed January-February. Outdoor seating. Bar. $16-35

★MONTE'S RIVERSIDE INN
903 E. Norris Drive, Ottawa, 815-434-5000
American. Lunch, dinner. $16-35

PEORIA
See also Bloomington
Peoria is the oldest settlement in the state. Louis Jolliet and Father Jacques Marquette discovered the area in 1673. René Robert Cavelier and Sieur de La Salle established Fort Creve Coeur on the eastern shore of Peoria Lake (a wide stretch in the Illinois River) in 1680. Between 1691 and 1692, Henri Tonti, Francois Dauphin and Sieur de La Forest established Fort St. Louis II on a site within the city. The settlement that grew around the fort has, except for a brief period during the Fox Wars, been continuously occupied. The British flag flew over Peoria from 1763-1778 and, for a short time in 1781, the Spanish held Peoria. The city is named for the Native Americans who occupied the area when the French arrived.

WHAT TO SEE
CORN STOCK THEATRE
1700 N. Park Road, Peoria, 800-220-1185; www.cornstocktheatre.com
Theater-in-the-round summer stock under a circus-type big top with dramas, comedies and musicals. Call for schedule and pricing.
June-August.

EUREKA COLLEGE
300 E. College Ave., Eureka, 309-467-6318, 888-438-7352; www.eureka.edu
One of the first coeducational colleges in the country, this school's most famous graduate is Ronald Reagan. The grounds' Peace Garden honors Reagan's famous 1982 speech regarding the end of the Cold War.

GLEN OAK PARK AND ZOO
2218 N. Prospect Road, Peoria, 309-686-3365; www.glenoakzoo.org
This park on heavily wooded bluffs includes a zoo with more than 250 species, an amphitheater and tennis courts. Also here is the George L. Luthy Memorial Botanical Garden, which is an all-season garden.

METAMORA COURTHOUSE STATE HISTORIC SITE
113 E. Partridge, Metamora, 309-367-4470; www.illinoishistory.gov
This site has one of two remaining courthouse structures on the old Eighth Judicial Circuit, in which Abraham Lincoln practiced law for 12 years. On the first floor is a museum containing a collection of pioneer artifacts; on the second floor is the restored courtroom.
Tuesday-Saturday.

PETTENGILL-MORRON MUSEUM
1212 W. Moss Ave., Peoria, 309-674-4745; www.peoriahistoricalsociety.org
An Italianate/Second Empire mansion, built by Moses Pettengill, this house was purchased by Jean Morron in 1953 to replace her ancestral house, which was being destroyed to make way for a freeway. She moved a two-century

accumulation of household furnishings and family heirlooms, as well as such architectural pieces as the old house's cast-iron fence, chandeliers, marble mantles and brass rails from the porch.

By appointment.

SPIRIT OF PEORIA
100 N.E. Water St., Peoria, 309-637-8000, 800-676-8988; www.spiritofpeoria.com
A replica of turn-of-the-century stern-wheeler offers cruises along the Illinois River.

WILDLIFE PRAIRIE STATE PARK
3826 N. Taylor Road, Peoria, 309-676-0998; www.wildlifeprairiestatepark.org
Wildlife and nature preserve with animals native to Illinois—bears, cougars, bobcats, wolves, red foxes and more—in natural habitats along wood-chipped trails. The pioneer homestead has a working farm from the late 1800s with an authentic log cabin and one-room schoolhouse.

Daily March-mid-December.

WHERE TO STAY
★COMFORT SUITES
1812 W. War Memorial Drive, Peoria, 309-688-3800; www.comfortsuites.com
66 rooms. Complimentary breakfast. Pool. Pets accepted. $61-150

★★HOTEL PERE MARQUETTE
501 Main St., Peoria, 309-637-6500, 800-447-1676; www.hotelperemarquette.com
288 rooms. Restaurant, bar. Fitness center. Pets accepted. $61-150

★★MARK TWAIN HOTEL DOWNTOWN PEORIA
225 N.E. Adams St., Peoria, 309-676-3600, 888-325-6351; www.marktwainhotel.com
109 rooms. Complimentary breakfast. Fitness center. Pets accepted. $61-150

★STONEY CREEK INN
101 Mariners Way, East Peoria, 309-694-1300, 800-659-2220;
www.stoneycreekinn.com
165 rooms. Bar. Complimentary breakfast. Business center. Fitness center. Pool. $61-150

WHERE TO EAT
★★CARNEGIE'S
501 N. Main, Peoria, 309-637-6500, 800-474-1676; www.hotelperemarquette.com
American. Dinner. Closed Sunday. Reservations recommended. Children's menu. Bar. $16-35

PERU
See also Ottawa, Utica/Starved Rock State Park
Once a busy North-Central Illinois River port, Peru is now a commercial center for the area.

WHAT TO SEE
ILLINOIS WATERWAY VISITOR CENTER
950 N. 27th Road, Peru, 815-667-4054
Located at the Starved Rock Lock and Dam, this site offers an excellent view
across the river to Starved Rock. The history of the Illinois River from the
time of the Native Americans, the French explorers, and the construction of
canals to the modern Illinois Waterway is portrayed in a series of exhibits.
Daily.

MATTHIESSEN STATE PARK
Highways 71 and 178, Utica, 815-667-4868; www.dnr.state.il.us
This 1,938-acre park is particularly interesting for its geological formations,
which can be explored via seven miles of hiking trails. The upper area and
bluff tops are generally dry and easily hiked, but trails into the interiors of the
two dells can be difficult, especially in spring and early summer. The dells
feature scenic waterfalls.
Daily.

SPECIAL EVENTS
MENDOTA SWEET CORN FESTIVAL
Highway 34 and Illinois Avenue, Mendota, 815-539-6507; www.sweetcornfestival.com
Each year, the town serves free sweet corn at this festival. There is also a
beer garden, a queen pageant and a flea market with more than 200 dealers
represented.
Second weekend in August.

WINTER WILDERNESS WEEKEND
Routes 71 and 178, Utica, 815-667-4906
This tour departs from Starved Rock visitor center and includes guided hikes
to see the spectacular ice falls of Starved Rock. Cross-country skiing rentals
and instructions.
January.

WHERE TO STAY
★COMFORT INN
5240 Trompeter Road, Peru, 815-223-8585, 800-228-5150; www.comfortinn.com
50 rooms. Complimentary breakfast. Pool. $61-150

WHERE TO EAT
★★UPTOWN GRILL
601 First St., La Salle, 815-224-4545; www.uptowngrill.com
American. Lunch, dinner. Outdoor seating. Children's menu. Bar. $16-35

QUINCY
See also Bloomfield
Quincy, the seat of Adams County, was named for President John Quincy
Adams. Located on the east bank of the Mississippi River, the town was the
site of the sixth Lincoln-Douglas debate on October 13, 1858; a bronze bas-
relief in Washington Park marks the spot. Quincy was the second-largest city

in Illinois in the mid-19th century. Today, Quincy is known for its historical district and restored Victorian residences.

WHAT TO SEE
JOHN WOOD MANSION
425 S. 12th St., Quincy, 217-222-1835; www.adamscohistory.org
This two-story, Greek Revival mansion was the home of the founder of Quincy and a former governor of Illinois. In about 1864, the house was cut in half and moved across a special bridge to its present location.
June-August, daily; April-May, September-October, Saturday-Sunday; also by appointment.

QUINCY MUSEUM
1601 Maine St., Quincy, 217-224-7669; www.thequincymuseum.com
Located in the Newcomb-Stillwell mansion, this museum is housed in a Richardson Romanesque-style building. Rotating exhibits and a children's discovery room are featured.
Tuesday-Sunday 1-5 p.m.

WHERE TO STAY
★★HOLIDAY INN
201 S. Third St., Quincy, 217-222-2666, 800-465-4329; www.holiday-inn.com
152 rooms. Restaurant, bar. Complimentary breakfast. Pool. Pets accepted. $61-150

ROCKFORD
See also DeKalb, Freeport, Oregon
The state's second-largest city grew up on both sides of the Rock River and took its name from the ford that was used by the Galena-Chicago Stagecoach Line.

WHAT TO SEE
ANDERSON JAPANESE GARDENS
318 Spring Creek Road, Rockford, 815-229-9390; www.andersongardens.org
These formal 9-acre gardens have a waterfall, ponds, bridges, a tea house, guest house and footpaths.
Daily May-October.

BURPEE MUSEUM OF NATURAL HISTORY
737 N. Main St., Rockford, 815-965-3433; www.burpee.org
This science museum features natural history exhibits including a complete T-Rex-like skeleton called Jane, who is believed to be either a young specimen of the dinosaur or a smaller relative.
Daily.

DISCOVERY CENTER MUSEUM
Riverfront Museum Park, 711 N. Main St., Rockford, 815-963-6769;
www.discoverycentermuseum.org
This hands-on learning museum has more than 120 exhibits illustrating scientific and perceptual principles. Visitors can leave their shadow hanging on

a wall, create a bubble window, see a planetarium show, learn how a house is built, star in a TV show or visit a carboniferous coal forest. Adjacent Rock River Discovery Park features a weather station, earth and water exhibits. Daily.

ROCK CUT STATE PARK
7318 Harlem Road, Rockford, 815-885-3311; www.dnr.state.il.us
This 3,092-acre park has two artificial lakes with swimming beaches, boating, horseback trails, cross-country skiing and more.
Daily.

SPECIAL EVENTS
ILLINOIS SNOW SCULPTING COMPETITION
1401 N. Second St., Rockford, 815-987-8800; www.snowsculpting.org
Teams from throughout Illinois compete to represent the state at national and international competitions.
January.

NEW AMERICAN THEATER
118 N. Main St., Rockford, 815-964-6282
A professional theater, the troupe here produces six mainstage shows each season.
Late September-late May.

WHERE TO STAY
★★BEST WESTERN CLOCK TOWER RESORT & CONFERENCE CENTER
7801 E. State St., Rockford, 815-398-6000, 800-358-7666; www.clocktowerresort.com
247 rooms. Restaurant, bar. Business center. Fitness center. Pool. Spa. Tennis. $61-150

★★COURTYARD ROCKFORD
7676 E. State St., Rockford, 815-397-6222; www.courtyard.com
147 rooms. Business center. Fitness center. Pool. $61-150

★HAMPTON INN
615 Clark Drive, Rockford, 815-229-0404; www.rockford.hamptoninn.com
121 rooms. Complimentary breakfast. Fitness center. Pool. $61-150

WHERE TO EAT
★★GIOVANNI'S
610 N. Bell School Road, Rockford, 815-398-6411; www.giodine.com
French, Italian. Lunch, dinner. Closed Sunday. Reservations recommended. Children's menu. Bar. $36-85

★★THUNDER BAY GRILLE
7652 Potawatomi Trail, Rockford, 815-397-4800; www.thunderbaygrille.com
American. Lunch, dinner. Reservations recommended. Outdoor seating. Children's menu. Bar. $16-35

SCHAUMBURG

See also Arlington Heights, Chicago O'Hare Airport

This village has one of suburban Chicago's top shopping centers and is also the headquarters of Motorola.

WHAT TO SEE
CHICAGO ATHENAEUM AT SCHAUMBURG

190 S. Roselle Road, Schaumburg, 815-777-4444; www.chi-athenaeum.org

This museum honors the history of design in all aspects of civilization, from fashion to urban development.
Wednesday-Sunday.

WOODFIELD SHOPPING CENTER

5 Woodfield Drive, Schaumburg, 847-330-1537; www.shopwoodfield.com

This mall has more than 250 specialty shops and department stores, including Nordstrom and Lord & Taylor.
Daily.

WHERE TO STAY
★★★HYATT REGENCY WOODFIELD

1800 E. Golf Road, Schaumburg, 847-605-1234; www.hyatt.com

This hotel, with Frank Lloyd Wright-inspired public spaces and spacious guest suites, is packed with amenities, including two pools, a health club, Tre Cena Italian restaurant and a sports bar with a 9-foot video wall.
470 rooms. Restaurant, bar. Business center. Fitness center. Pool. $151-250

SKOKIE

See also Evanston, Glenview, Wilmette

In this Chicago suburb's early years, farmers produced food here for the growing city of Chicago, and market trails carved by farm wagons later became paved roads.

WHAT TO SEE
NORTH SHORE CENTER FOR THE PERFORMING ARTS

9501 Skokie Blvd., 847-679-9501; www.northshorecenter.org

This center houses two individual theaters that offer many types of performances.

WESTFIELD OLD ORCHARD

34 Old Orchard Center, Skokie, 847-673-6800; www.westfield.com

Shop at a wide array of stores linked outdoors by landscaped areas. Anchor stores include Bloomingdales, Macy's, Lord & Taylor and Nordstrom.
Monday-Saturday 10 a.m.-9 p.m., Sunday 11 a.m.-6 p.m., holiday hours vary.

WHERE TO EAT
★★CAFÉ LA CAVE

2777 Mannheim Road, Des Plaines, 847-827-7818; www.cafelacaverestaurant.com

Steak. Dinner. Bar. $16-35

★★DON'S FISHMARKET
9335 Skokie Blvd., Skokie, 847-677-3424; www.donsfishmarket.com
Seafood. Lunch, dinner. Children's menu. Bar. $16-35

★LOTAWATA CREEK
311 Salem Place, Fairview Heights, 618-628-7373; www.lotawata.com
American. Lunch, dinner. Children's menu. $16-35

SPRINGFIELD
See also Decatur
Near the geographical center of the state, Springfield, the capital of Illinois, was the home of Abraham Lincoln for a quarter of a century.

WHAT TO SEE
DANA-THOMAS HOUSE STATE HISTORIC SITE
301 E. Lawrence Ave., Springfield, 217-782-6776; www.dana-thomas.org
Designed by Frank Lloyd Wright for Springfield socialite Susan Lawrence Dana, this house is the best preserved of the architect's Prairie period. The fully restored interior has more than 100 pieces of original furniture. The house was one of the largest and most elaborate of Wright's career.
Wednesday-Sunday.

EDWARDS PLACE
700 N. 4th St., Springfield, 217-523-2631; www.springfieldart.org
Built by Benjamin Edwards (brother of Ninian Edwards, an early Illinois governor married to Mary Todd Lincoln's older sister), this Italianate mansion was Springfield's social and political center in the years before the Civil War; Lincoln addressed the public from the front gallery.
By appointment only.

HENSON ROBINSON ZOO
1101 E. Lake Drive, Springfield, 217-753-6217; www.hensonrobinsonzoo.org
A 14-acre zoo with exotic and domestic animals, penguin exhibit; contact area; picnic area.
Daily.

LINCOLN HOME NATIONAL HISTORIC SITE
413 S. Eighth St., Springfield, 217-492-4241; www.nps.gov/liho
This site is the only home Abraham Lincoln ever owned. In 1844, Abraham and Mary Lincoln purchased the house and lived there until their February 1861 departure for Washington, D.C.
Daily.

LINCOLN MEMORIAL GARDEN AND NATURE CENTER
2301 E. Lake Drive, Springfield, 217-529-1111; www.lmgnc.com
This park is an 80-acre garden of trees, shrubs and flowers native to Illinois designed in a naturalistic style by landscape architect Jens Jensen.
Tuesday-Sunday.

LINCOLN TOMB STATE HISTORIC SITE

Oak Ridge Cemetery, 1500 Monument Ave., Springfield, 217-782-2717;
www.Illinois.gov

Under a 117-foot granite obelisk, a belvedere, accessible via exterior stair-cases, offers views of a 10-foot statue of Lincoln and four heroic group-ings representing Civil War armed forces. In the center of the domed burial chamber is a monumental sarcophagus. Mary Todd Lincoln and three of four Lincoln sons are interred within the wall opposite.

Daily.

WHERE TO STAY
★COMFORT INN

3442 Freedom Drive, Springfield, 217-787-2250, 800-228-5150; www.comfortinn.com
67 rooms. Complimentary breakfast. Pool. Pets accepted. $61-150

★★COURTYARD SPRINGFIELD

3462 Freedom Drive, Springfield, 217-793-5300, 800-321-2211; www.courtyard.com
78 rooms. Fitness center. Pool. Bar. $61-150

★HAMPTON INN

3185 S. Dirksen Parkway, Springfield, 217-529-1100, 800-426-7866;
www.hamptoninn.com
124 rooms. Complimentary breakfast. Fitness center. Pool. $61-150

★★★HILTON SPRINGFIELD

700 E. Adams St., Springfield, 217-789-1530; www.hilton.com
This being the only skyscraper in Springfield, rooms here have great views of the city.
367 rooms. Restaurant, bar. Business center. Fitness center. Pool. $61-150

★★★RENAISSANCE SPRINGFIELD HOTEL

701 E. Adams St., Springfield, 217-544-8800, 800-228-9898;
www.renaissancehotels.com
With a concourse leading to the convention center and 13,000 square feet of meeting space, this hotel is popular with business travelers. Try Lindsay's Gallery Restaurant for Sunday brunch.
316 rooms. Restaurant, bar. Business center. Fitness center. Pool. $61-150

WHERE TO EAT
★★CHESAPEAKE SEAFOOD HOUSE

3045 Clear Lake Ave., Springfield, 217-522-5220; www.chesapeakeseafoodhouse.com
American, Seafood. Lunch, dinner. Children's menu. Bar. $16-35

★★MALDANER'S

222 S. Sixth St., Springfield, 217-522-4313; www.maldaners.com
American. Dinner. Closed Sunday-Monday. Bar. $16-35

ST. CHARLES
See also Aurora, DeKalb, Geneva

Located on the Fox River one hour west of Chicago, St. Charles is an affluent suburb with a charming downtown filled with antique and specialty shops housed in historic buildings.

WHAT TO SEE
FOX RIVER VALLEY TRAIL
St. Charles, 630-897-0516; www.foxrivervalleyhomes

Located among hills and historic old towns, The Fox River winds a lazy path, making it ideal for recreational canoeing. Several outfitters offer canoe rentals, and there are at least four entry points. If you have a bike, the well-maintained Fox River Trail runs parallel to the river extending as far north as Crystal Lake and as far south as Aurora. Daily.

PHEASANT RUN RESORT AND SPA
4051 E. Main St., St. Charles, 800-474-3272; www.pheasantrun.com

In terms of bang for your buck, Pheasant Run offers great golf for prices lower than most courses in the area. The course also plays only a little more than 6,300 yards, so great scores are definitely within reach. Golfers can play 18 holes for $23, cart included, from 5:30 p.m. until dark.

POTTAWATOMIE PARK
North Ave., St. Charles, 630-584-1028; www.st-charlesparks.org

This park has a mile of frontage on the Fox River and is open daily. The St. Charles Belle II and Fox River Queen paddle wheel boats offer afternoon sightseeing trips river. Boats depart from the park and follow the river trail of the Pottawatomie.

Daily June-August; May and September-mid-October, Saturday-Sunday.

WHERE TO STAY
★★★HOTEL BAKER
100 W. Main St., St. Charles, 630-584-2100, 800-284-0110; www.hotelbaker.com

Built in 1928, this hotel has traditionally decorated rooms with Egyptian cotton linens and The waterfront restaurant hosts everything from wine tastings to a Sunday champagne brunch.

53 rooms. Restaurant, bar. $251-350

WHERE TO EAT
★FILLING STATION PUB & GRILL
300 W. Main St., St. Charles, 630-584-4414; www.filling-station.com

American. Lunch, dinner. Outdoor seating. Children's menu. Bar. $15 and under

UTICA/STARVED ROCK STATE PARK
See also Ottawa, Peru

Utica is most known for being the gateway to the pristine Starved Rock State Park, located on the Illinois-Michigan Canal. The area is popular for the adventure it offers on unbeaten paths, from hiking and fishing to horseback riding and camping.

WHAT TO SEE
STARVED ROCK STATE PARK

A local favorite for recreation and outdoor sports, Starved Rock State Park, located an hour and a half southwest of Chicago in Utica, has glacial canyons, sandstone bluffs, unusual rock formations and forests. The park offers 13 miles of well-marked hiking trails, fishing and boating along the Illinois River, equestrian trails, picnicking and camping. The park has a refurbished lodge with a hotel wing with 72 luxury rooms, an indoor pool with spa and sauna, and a restaurant; 22 cabins are also available. Though it's open year-round, a prime time to visit is early spring, when waterfalls form at the heads of the more than 18 canyons and create a glittering natural spectacle. Daily.

WHERE TO STAY
★★STARVED ROCK LODGE AND CONFERENCE CENTER

Highway 178, Utica, 815-667-4211, 800-868-7625; www.starvedrocklodge.com
93 rooms. Restaurant, bar. Pool. $61-150

WAUKEGAN

See also Antioch

On the site of what was once a Native American village and a French trading post, Waukegan was first called Little Fort because of a French stockade there. In April 1860, Abraham Lincoln delivered his "unfinished speech" here—he was interrupted by a fire. Waukegan was the birthplace of comedian Jack Benny and author Ray Bradbury, who used the town as a background in many of his works.

WHERE TO STAY
★★COURTYARD CHICAGO WAUKEGAN/GURNEE

3800 Northpoint Boulevard Lakehurst Road, Waukegan, 847-689-8000, 800-321-2211; www.courtyard.com
149 rooms. Restaurant. Fitness center. Pool. $61-150

★HAMPTON INN

5550 Grand Ave., Gurnee, 847-662-1100, 800-426-7866; www.hamptoninn.com
134 rooms. Complimentary breakfast. Pool. $61-150

★★ILLINOIS BEACH RESORT AND CONFERENCE CENTER

1 Lakefront Drive, Zion, 847-625-7300, 866-452-3224; www.ilresorts.com
American. Lunch, dinner, Sunday brunch. Closed Monday. Children's menu. Bar. $151-250

WHERE TO EAT
★★COUNTRY SQUIRE

19133 W. Highway 120, Waukegan, 847-223-0121; www.csquire.com
American. Lunch, dinner, Sunday brunch. Closed Monday. Children's menu. Bar. $16-35

WHEATON

See also Geneva, Naperville

Wheaton, the seat of DuPage County, is a residential community with 39 churches and the headquarters of approximately two dozen religious publishers and organizations. The town's most famous citizens are football great Red Grange, Elbert Gary, (who created the Indiana steel city that bears his name) and evangelist Billy Graham.

WHAT TO SEE
CANTIGNY

1S151 Winfield Road, Wheaton, 630-668-5161; www.cantigny.org

This is the 500-acre estate of the late Robert R. McCormick, editor and publisher of the Chicago Tribune.

COSLEY ANIMAL FARM AND MUSEUM

1356 N. Gary Ave., Wheaton, 630-665-5534; www.museumsusa.org

This farm has a petting zoo, antique farm equipment display, railroad caboose, aviary, herb garden and outdoor education center.
Daily. April-October, Monday-Thursday 9 a.m.-4 p.m.; Friday-Sunday 10 a.m.-6 p.m.; October-November, January-March, daily 9 a.m.-4 p.m.; December, daily 9 a.m.-9 p.m.

MARION E. WADE CENTER

351 E. Lincoln, Wheaton, 630-752-5908; www.wheaton.edu

Housed here is a collection of books and papers of seven British authors: Owen Barfield, G. K. Chesterton, C.S. Lewis, George MacDonald, Dorothy L. Sayers, J. R. R. Tolkien and Charles Williams.
Monday-Saturday.

WHEATON COLLEGE

501 College Ave., Wheaton, 630-752-5000; www.wheaton.edu

This Christian liberal arts school is home to the Billy Graham Center Museum, which features exhibits on the history of evangelism in America.

WHERE TO EAT
★★GREEK ISLANDS WEST

300 E. 22nd St., Lombard, 630-932-4545; www.greekislands.net

Greek. Lunch, dinner. Outdoor seating. Bar. $16-35

WHEELING

See also Arlington Heights, Glenview, Northbrook

The Wheeling area was first occupied by the Potawatomi. Settlers arrived in 1833 and began farming the fertile prairie soil.

WHERE TO STAY
★HAWTHORN SUITES

10 Westminster Way Road, Lincolnshire, 847-945-9300, 800-527-1133; www.hawthorn.com

125 rooms. Complimentary breakfast. Business center. Fitness center. Pool. Pets accepted. $61-150

★SPRINGHILL SUITES LINCOLNSHIRE
300 Marriott Drive, Lincolnshire, 847-793-7500, 888-287-9400;
www.springhillsuites.com
161 rooms. Complimentary breakfast. Business center. Fitness center. Pool.
$61-150

★★★MARRIOTT LINCOLNSHIRE RESORT
10 Marriott Drive, Lincolnshire, 847-634-0100, 800-228-9290; www.marriott.com
This hotel has an award-winning theater-in-the-round, seasonal outdoor
sports facilities, half a dozen bars and restaurants and an open lobby with
wood beams and a roaring fire. Although the hotel hosts many business
meetings and conferences, families looking for a little R&R find it a fun
getaway.
380 rooms. Restaurant, bar. Business center. Fitness center. Pool. Golf.
Tennis. $61-150

WHERE TO EAT
★★94TH AERO SQUADRON
1070 S. Milwaukee Ave., Wheeling, 847-459-3700
American. Dinner, Sunday brunch. Closed Monday. Reservations recommended. Outdoor seating. Children's menu. Bar. $16-35

★★BOB CHINN'S CRAB HOUSE
393 S. Milwaukee Ave., Wheeling, 847-520-3633; www.bobchinns.com
Seafood. Lunch, dinner. Reservations recommended. Children's menu. Bar.
$36-85

★★DON ROTH'S
61 N. Milwaukee Ave., Wheeling, 847-537-5800; www.donroths.com
Steak. Dinner. Reservations recommended. Outdoor seating. Children's
menu. Bar. $36-85

★★★TRAMONTO'S STEAK & SEAFOOD
601 N. Milwaukee Ave., Wheeling, 847-777-6575, 800-837-8461
Chicago chef Rick Tramonto and pastry chef Gale Gand are the culinary duo
behind this contemporary steakhouse. Cozy banquettes or white linen-topped
tables fill the dining room while an impressive wine wall displays more than
1,000 bottles from around the world. The menu aptly spotlights grilled steak
and seafood from skirt steak frites with caramelized onions to spice-rubbed
yellowfin tuna. Steakhouse classics, such as creamy Caesar salad, creamed
spinach and garlic whipped potatoes accompany the entrées.
Steak, seafood. Dinner. Bar. $36-85

WILMETTE
See also Evanston, Glenview, Skokie
This tony North Shore Chicago suburb possesses an idyllic location on Lake
Michigan's shoreline. The Wilmette Park District manages 19 public parks,
including the popular Gillson Park beach.

WHAT TO SEE
BAHA'I HOUSE OF WORSHIP
100 Linden Ave., Wilmette, 847-853-2300; www.bahai.us
Spiritual center of the Baha'i faith in the United States, this remarkable nine-sided structure overlooks Lake Michigan and is surrounded by nine gardens and fountains. Exhibits and slide programs in visitor center on lower level. Daily.

GILLSON PARK
Lake and Michigan avenues, Wilmette, 847-256-9656; www.wilmettepark.org
This park contains Wilmette Beach, which has 1,000 feet of sandy shoreline, lifeguards, a beach house, sailing and Sunfish and Hobie 16 catamaran rentals. Park.
Daily.

KOHL CHILDREN'S MUSEUM
165 Green Bay Road, Wilmette, 847-512-1300; www.kohlchildrensmuseum.org
This museum offers interactive music, construction, science and arts participatory exhibits designed for children up to age eight.
Daily.

WHERE TO EAT
★★BETISE
1515 N. Sheridan Road, Wilmette, 847-853-1711; www.ylunch.com
French. Lunch, dinner, brunch. $16-35

★★CONVITO ITALIANO
1515 N. Sheridan Road, Wilmette, 847-251-3654; www.convitoitaliano.com
Italian. Dinner. $16-35

INDIANA

IF SPORTS ARE YOUR THING, INDIANA'S YOUR PLACE. WITH LEGENDARY TEAMS SUCH AS THE Super Bowl–champion Indianapolis Colts, Notre Dame's Fighting Irish and the Indiana University Hoosiers, Indiana's fabled sports legacy continues to grow. But if you're out for the ultimate Indiana sporting experience, watch racecar drivers clock 200 laps and 500 miles around Indianapolis Motor Speedway during the Indianapolis 500.

Prefer shopping to speedways? Experience first-rate stores in Indianapolis' Wholesale District; exotic dining and arts on Mass Ave; and trendy boutiques, clubs and alfresco dining in Broad Ripple Village. Buy the kids a sundae at the old-fashioned soda fountain in the Fountain Square District or stroll along the capital's family-friendly Canal and White River State Park District.

Prefer to hike on a trail than all over town? With 24 state parks, 22 fish and wildlife areas, nine reservoirs, 13 state forests and 14 nature preserves, Indiana is hardly short on places to scuff the dirt. Hike the marked trails and comb the beaches of the Indiana Dunes National Lakeshore, then rough it on 27 miles of trails on the Adventure hiking Trail in the: Harrison-Crawford State Forest.

For an idyllic getaway, the charming resort towns in Southern Indiana are your best bet, whether you're taking a family vacation or sneaking off for a romantic weekend. Browse charming craft and antique shops in the historic artist colony of Nashville, and sip and swirl your way through the Upland Wine Trail's eight wineries nearby. If you're in need of some R&R, the historic resort hotels in French Lick let you rejuvenate amid mineral springs, lush gardens, golf courses, spas and gorgeous surroundings.

If you're craving a quirkier adventure, check out wares from more than 1,000 vendors at Shipshewana's outdoor flea market (May-October), sample chocolates at the South Bend Chocolate Museum and see which Big Top biggies made it into Peru, Indiana's Circus Hall of Fame.

ANDERSON

See also Indianapolis, Muncie

This was once the site of a Delaware village in the hills south of the White River. The city was named for Kikthawenund (also called Captain Anderson), a well-known chief of the Delaware Indians. The discovery of natural gas pockets underneath the city in 1886 sparked a 10-year boom. One hundred Newport-style gaslights have been added to what is now known as historic West Eighth Street. Restored Victorian homes reflect the area's fashionable past.

WHAT TO SEE
MOUNDS STATE PARK

4306 Mounds Road, Anderson, 765-642-6627; www.moundsstatepark.org

Within this 290-acre park of rolling woodlands are several well-preserved earth formations constructed many centuries ago by a prehistoric race of

Adena-Hopewell mound builders. Their earthen structures, located on bluffs overlooking the White River, were once an important center of the ancient civilization of which very little is known. The largest structure is nine feet high and nearly 1/4 mile in circumference. Smaller structures nearby include conical mounds and a fiddle-shaped earthwork.

SPECIAL EVENT
LITTLE 500
Anderson Speedway, 1311 Pendleton Ave., Anderson, 765-642-0206
Auto races. Reservations necessary. Weekend of Indianapolis 500.

ANGOLA
This tranquil town lies in the northeastern corner of Indiana's resort area. The wooded hills surrounding Angola provide more than 100 lakes for swimming, boating and fishing in the summer and ice skating in the winter.

WHAT TO SEE
POKAGON STATE PARK
450 Lane 100 Lake James, Angola, 219-833-2012; www.in.gov/dnr
This 1,203-acre park on the shores of Lake James and Snow Lake in northern Indiana lake country offers a swimming beach, bathhouse, waterskiing, fishing, boating rentals, hiking trails, saddle barn, skiing, ice skating, tobogganing, ice fishing, picnicking, concession, camping. Nature center, wildlife exhibit, naturalist service.
Daily.

WHERE TO STAY
★★POTAWATOMI INN
6 Lane 100A Lake James, Angola, 260-833-1077, 877-768-2928
138 rooms. Restaurant. Fitness center. Pool. Beach. $61-150

AURORA
A river town located west of Cincinnati, Aurora was settled in the 1800s and has six preserved, historic churches.

WHERE TO STAY
★★GRAND VICTORIA CASINO & RESORT BY HYATT
600 Grand Victoria Drive, Rising Sun, 812-438-1234, 800-472-6311; www.hyatt.com
201 rooms. Restaurant. Business center. Fitness center. Pool. $61-150

★★★BELTERRA CASINO RESORT
777 Belterra Drive, Belterra, 812-427-7777, 888-235-8377; www.belterracasino.com
There's plenty to do at this resort, from a full-service spa and salon, to an outdoor pool, championship golf and plenty of restaurants. The 38,000-square-foot casino riverboat features 40 table games, a poker room and more than 1,600 slot machines. Rooms offer views of the Ohio River, the golf course or the hilly Indiana scenery.
600 rooms. Restaurant, bar. Business center. Fitness center. Pool. Golf. Casino. $151-250

BEDFORD

See also Bloomington, French Lick

Bedford is the center of Indiana limestone quarrying, one of the state's top industries. Limestone quarried here was used in the construction of the World War II Memorial in Indianapolis, the Empire State Building in New York and the Federal Triangle in Washington, D.C.

The headquarters of the Hoosier National Forest and Wayne National Forest are also here. Williams Dam, 11 miles southwest on Highway 450, offers fishing on the White River.

WHAT TO SEE
BLUESPRING CAVERNS

1459 Bluespring Caverns Road, Bedford, 812-279-9471; www.bluespringcaverns.com

One of the world's largest cavern systems, more than 20 miles of explored passageways and 15 miles of underground streams join to form the large river upon which tour boats travel. Electric lighting reveals many unusual sights, including eyeless blindfish and blind crawfish.

June-late October, daily; April-May, Saturday-Sunday.

HOOSIER NATIONAL FOREST

811 Constitution Ave., Bedford, 812-275-5987

Approximately 189,000 acres spread through nine counties. Swimming, boating, fishing; picnicking, hiking, horseback trails, hunting, nature study; historic sites. Campsites at Hardin Ridge Monroe County, German Ridge, Celina Lake, Tipson Lake, Indian Lake Perry Count and Springs Valley Orange County recreation areas. Campsites available on a first-come, first-served basis. Fees are charged at recreation sites for camping; entrance fee at Hardin Ridge.

BLOOMINGTON

See also Bedford, Columbus, Nashville

Home to Indiana University, Bloomington is regarded as one of America's best college towns, thanks to its relaxed atmosphere, eclectic shops and restaurants, vast cultural offerings and scenic setting. Bloomington's official population falls just short of 70,000, a figure that includes few of the 39,000 students at I.U.

Bloomington's downtown, situated a couple of blocks west of the university, is anchored by the Monroe County Courthouse. The town has a vibrant arts scene, including the Indiana University Art Museum, which was designed by I. M. Pei and boasts a collection of more than 35,000 pieces, including paintings by Monet and Picasso. Each fall, Bloomington hosts the Lotus World Music and Arts Festival, a celebration of the world's diverse cultures.

Spring brings the annual Little 500 Bicycle Race, made famous by the 1979 film Breaking Away. Many avid cyclists live in Bloomington, and they can be seen pedaling on the streets and numerous riding trails in and around town. Basketball is popular throughout Indiana, and locals take pride in the fact that I.U.'s men's program has won five national championships.

WHAT TO SEE
LITTLE 500 BICYCLE RACE
Indiana University campus, 1606 N. Fee Lane, Bloomington, 812-855-9152
This festival features bicycle and tricycle races, a golf jamboree, and live entertainment.
Late April.

WHERE TO STAY
★★COURTYARD BLOOMINGTON
310 S. College Ave., Bloomington, 812-335-8000, 800-321-2211; www.courtyard.com
117 rooms. Fitness center. Pool. $61-150

★★FOURWINDS RESORT
9301 Fairfax Road, Bloomington, 812-824-2628; www.fourwindsresort.com
This resort overlooks the Lake Monroe Reservoir and offers endless outdoor activities.
126 rooms. Restaurant, bar. Pool. Beach. $61-150

★HAMPTON INN
2100 N. Walnut St., Bloomington, 812-334-2100, 800-426-7866; www.hamptoninn.com
129 rooms. Pool. Pets accepted. $61-150

★★HOLIDAY INN
1710 N. Kinser Pike, Bloomington, 812-334-3252; www.holiday-inn.com
189 rooms. Restaurant, bar. Pool. $61-150

WHERE TO EAT
★★COLORADO STEAKHOUSE
1635 N. College Ave., Bloomington, 812-339-9979; www.colorado-steakhouse.com
Steak. Lunch, dinner. Children's menu. Bar. $16-35

★LE PETIT CAFÉ
308 W. 6th St., Bloomington, 812-334-9747;
www.bloomingpedia.org/wiki/Le_Petit_Cafe
American. Lunch, dinner. Closed Monday. $16-35

COLUMBUS
See also Bloomington, Nashville
The architectural designs of many modern buildings in Columbus have attracted international attention. In the heart of the prairie, the project was launched in the late 1930s with the commissioning of Eliel Saarinen to design a church. Since then, more than 50 public and private buildings have been designed by architects such as John Carl Warnecke, Harry Weese, I. M. Pei, Kevin Roche, Eliot Noyes and J. M. Johansen.

WHERE TO STAY
★★HOLIDAY INN
2480 Jonathan Moore Pike, Columbus, 812-372-1541, 800-465-4329;
www.holiday-inn.com
This inn offers a turn-of-the-century atmosphere.
253 rooms. Restaurant, bar. Fitness center. Pool. Pets accepted. $61-150

EVANSVILLE
See also New Harmony
Separated from Kentucky by the Ohio River, Evansville has retained some of
the atmosphere of the busy river town it once was, when steamboats cruised
the Ohio and Mississippi Rivers. Evansville is the principal transportation,
trade and industrial center of southwestern Indiana.

WHAT TO SEE
ANGEL MOUNDS STATE HISTORIC SITE
8215 Pollack Ave., Evansville, 812-853-3956; www.angelmounds.org
Largest and best-preserved group of prehistoric mounds dating back to 1100-
1450 in Indiana. Approximately 100 acres. Interpretive center has film, exhibits and artifacts; reconstructed dwellings on grounds.
Mid-March-December, Tuesday-Sunday.

EVANSVILLE MUSEUM OF ARTS, HISTORY AND SCIENCE
411 S.E. Riverside Drive, Evansville, 812-425-2406; www.emuseum.org
This museum prides itself in its permanent art, history and science exhibits;
sculpture garden; the Koch Planetarium; and its re-creation of a turn-of-the-
century village. Tours are available.
Tuesday-Sunday.

WHERE TO STAY
★HAMPTON INN
8000 Eagle Crest Blvd., Evansville, 812-473-5000, 800-426-7866;
www.hamptoninn.com
140 rooms. Complimentary breakfast. Fitness center. Pool. $61-150

★★HOLIDAY INN
4101 Highway 41 N., Evansville, 812-424-6400, 800-465-4329; www.holiday-inn.com
198 rooms. Restaurant, bar. Business center. Fitness center. Pool. $61-150

★★★MARRIOTT EVANSVILLE AIRPORT
7101 Highway 41 N., Evansville, 812-867-7999, 800-228-9290; www.marriott.com
A glass-enclosed atrium makes the lobby of this airport hotel. Rooms have
spacious work stations.
199 rooms. Restaurant, bar. Fitness center. Pool. $61-150

★SIGNATURE INN
1101 N. Green River Road, Evansville, 812-476-9626, 800-822-5252;
www.signatureinn.com
125 rooms. Complimentary breakfast. Pool. $61-150

WHERE TO EAT
★THE OLD MILL RESTAURANT
5031 New Harmony Road, Evansville, 812-963-6000
American. Lunch, dinner. $15 and under

FORT WAYNE
See also Auburn, Geneva

The Fort Wayne area is one of the most historically significant in Indiana. The point where the St. Joseph and St. Mary's Rivers meet to form the Maumee was, for many years before and after the first European explorers came to Indiana, headquarters of the Miami Native Americans. A French fort was established here around 1690 by fur traders. The settlement became known as Miami Town and Frenchtown. In 1760, English troops occupied the French fort but were driven out three years later by warriors led by Chief Pontiac. During the next 30 years, Miami Town became one of the most important trading centers in the West. President Washington sent out two armies in 1790 to establish a fort for the United States at the river junction, but both armies were defeated. A third American army, under General "Mad Anthony" Wayne, succeeded and set up a post called Fort Wayne across the river from Miami Town. Today, Fort Wayne is the second largest city in Indiana.

WHAT TO SEE
ALLEN COUNTY FORT WAYNE HISTORICAL SOCIETY MUSEUM
302 E. Berry St., Fort Wayne, 260-426-2882; www.fwhistorycenter.com
There are exhibits on six themes: earliest times to the Civil War; 19th-century industrialization 1860s-1894; culture and society 1894-1920; 20th-century technology and industry 1920-present; old city jail and law enforcement 1820-1970; and ethnic heritage. There are also special temporary exhibits. Tuesday-Sunday.

FOELLINGER-FREIMANN BOTANICAL CONSERVATORY
1100 S. Calhoun St., Fort Wayne, 260-427-6440; www.botanicalconservatory.org
Showcase house with seasonally changing displays of colorful flowers; Tropical house with exotic plants; Arid house with cacti and other desert flora native to Sonoran Desert. There is also a natural cascading waterfall. Daily.

FORT WAYNE CHILDREN'S ZOO
3411 Sherman Blvd., Fort Wayne, 260-427-6800; www.kidszoo.com
This museum is especially designed for children, with exotic animals, pony rides, a train and parent-child contact area. The 22-acre African Veld allows animals to roam free while visitors travel by miniature safari cars. Spend time in the tropical rain forest; 5-acre Australian Outback area with dugout canoe ride; and observe kangaroos and Tasmanian devils. Late April-mid-October, daily.

WHERE TO STAY
★★COURTYARD FORT WAYNE
1619 W. Washington Center Road, Fort Wayne, 260-489-1500, 800-321-2211;
www.courtyard.com
142 rooms. Fitness center. Pool. $61-150

★★HOLIDAY INN
300 E. Washington Blvd., Fort Wayne, 260-422-5511, 800-465-4329;
www.holiday-inn.com
208 rooms. Restaurant, bar. Fitness center. Pool. $61-150

★★★HILTON FORT WAYNE CONVENTION CENTER
1020 S. Calhoun St., Fort Wayne, 260-420-1100, 800-445-8667; www.hilton.com
Located in downtown Fort Wayne, this hotel and convention center has rooms
decorated with contemporary furnishings. The hotel also has an onsite fitness
center and indoor pool.
250 rooms. Restaurant, bar. Fitness center. Pool. Pets accepted. $61-150

★★★MARRIOTT FORT WAYNE
305 E. Washington Center Road, Fort Wayne, 260-484-0411, 800-228-9290;
www.marriott.com
Rooms at this Fort Wayne hotel have been updated with luxury linens and
beds. Try Red River Steaks and BBQ Restaurant for a pleasurable dining
experience.
222 rooms. Restaurant, bar. Fitness center. Pool. Pets accepted. $151-250

★SIGNATURE INN
1734 W. Washington Center, Fort Wayne, 260-489-5554, 800-822-5252
102 rooms. Complimentary breakfast. Pool. $61-150

WHERE TO EAT
★DON HALL'S FACTORY
5811 Coldwater Road, Fort Wayne, 260-484-8693; www.donhalls.com
American. Lunch, dinner. Children's menu. Bar. $16-35

★★FLANAGAN'S
6525 Covington Road, Fort Wayne, 260-432-6666; www.eatatflanagans.com
Flanagan's Irish Pub has antique décor, a pleasant garden gazebo, and a car-
ousel. The countdown is on until St. Patrick's Day.
Irish, American. Lunch, dinner. Children's menu. Bar. $16-35

FRENCH LICK
See also Bedford
In the early 18th century, this was the site of a French trading post. The post,
and the existence of a nearby salt lick, influenced the pioneer founders of the
later settlement to name it French Lick.

Today, this small community is a well-known health and vacation resort
centered around the French Lick springs and surrounding woodlands. The
water contains a high concentration of minerals.

WHERE TO STAY
★★★FRENCH LICK SPRINGS RESORT & SPA

8670 W. Highway 56, French Lick, 812-936-9300, 888-936-9360; www.FrenchLick.com
This historic resort is set among gardens, mineral springs and blooming flowers, and it features comfortable suites, golf, tennis and a spa.
443 rooms. Restaurants, bar. Fitness center. Pool. Spa. Golf. Tennis. $61-150

★★★WEST BADEN SPRINGS HOTEL

8538 West Baden Ave., French Lick, 812-936-9300; www.frenchlick.com
This more than 100-year-old property recently underwent a massive restoration. When it was built in 1902, this grand structure with its massive domed roof (deemed architecturally impossible to build at the time) was considered one of the finest hotels in the country. The number of rooms has been reduced by half to create spacious retreats with plush beds topped with luxury bedding. The spa offers cutting edge treatments as well as the original Pluto mineral water baths, drawn from local springs.
246 rooms. Restaurant, bar. Fitness center. Pool. Spa. Pets accepted. Casino. Golf. Tennis. $151-250

GARY

See also Hammond
An industrial center located on Lake Michigan just outside Chicago, Gary is probably best known for its most famous residents, Michael Jackson and the Jackson family.

WHERE TO EAT
★★★MILLER BAKERY CAFE

555 S. Lake St., Gary, 219-938-2229
Located in the Miller Beach area, this charming restaurant's name comes from its setting in a renovated bakery building. The kitchen serves up mostly modern American fare, with specialties including pasta and seafood dishes. International. Lunch, dinner. Closed Monday. Reservations recommended. $16-35

GOSHEN

See also Nappanee
This historic town is located in the heart of Amish country and surrounded by farmland.

WHERE TO STAY
★★COURTYARD GOSHEN

1930 Lincolnway East, Goshen, 574-534-3133, 800-321-2211; www.courtyard.com
91 rooms. Restaurant. Fitness center. Pool. $61-150

★★★ESSENHAUS INN AND CONFERENCE CENTER

240 Highway 20, Middlebury, 574-825-9471, 800-455-9471; www.essenhaus.com
Essenhaus Inn and Conference Center is surrounded by Amish countryside in northern Indiana. Comfortable guest rooms have refrigerators, and some

feature balconies. Within walking distance is the Village Shops, carriage rides, a covered bridge and miniature golf.

40 rooms. Restaurant. $151-250

GREENCASTLE

See also Terra Haute

Greencastle is located within 15 miles of two man-made lakes—Raccoon Lake Reservoir and Cataract Lake. It is also the home of DePauw University, a small liberal arts school.

WHERE TO STAY
★★★WALDEN INN

2 W. Seminary St., Greencastle, 765-658-1000, 800-225-8655; www.waldeninn.com

Located within minutes of DePauw University and the area's covered bridges, this country inn has warmth and charm.

54 rooms. Restaurant. Fitness center. $61-150

WHERE TO EAT
★★★DIFFERENT DRUMMER

2 W. Seminary St., Greencastle, 765-653-2761; www.waldeninn.com

Located inside the Walden Inn, this restaurant serves classic fare such as chicken cordon bleu, roasted eggplant with spinach, lamb chops and veal medallions. Appetizers include warm duck breast pâté.

International. Breakfast, lunch, dinner. Bar. $16-35

HAMMOND

See also Gary, Valparaiso

Hammond is one of the Calumet area's industrial cities on the southwest shore of Lake Michigan. The Indiana-Illinois state line is two blocks from Hammond's business district and separates it from its neighbor community, Calumet City, Illinois. Hammond is also adjacent to Chicago.

WHERE TO STAY
★★BEST WESTERN NORTHWEST INDIANA INN

3830 179th St., Hammond, 219-844-2140, 800-937-8376; www.bestwestern.com

111 rooms. Restaurant, bar. Complimentary breakfast. Fitness center. Pool. $61-150

WHERE TO EAT
★★CAFE ELISE

435 Ridge Road, Munster, 219-836-2233

American. Lunch, dinner. Closed Monday. Children's menu. Bar. $16-35

INDIANAPOLIS

See also Anderson, Greenfield

The present site of Indianapolis was an area of rolling woodland when it was selected by a group of 10 commissioners as the location of the new Indiana state capital on June 7, 1820. Only scattered Native American villages and two white settler families were located in the region at the time. The city was laid out in the wheel pattern of Washington, D.C.

The annual 500-mile Formula One automobile race at the Indianapolis Motor Speedway has brought international fame to the city. Indianapolis has also been called the nation's amateur sports capital and has hosted more than 400 national and international amateur sporting events.

In the middle of Indianapolis is Circle Centre Mall, which is home not only to the largest mall in the area but also to the Indianapolis Artsgarden, which has concerts, botanical displays and other cultural events. Also downtown are the RCA Dome, home to the Indianapolis Colts, Conseco Fieldhouse, home of the Indiana Pacers, and Victory Field, where the Indianapolis Indians play. Victory Field is consistently voted one of the top ballparks in minor-league baseball.

WHAT TO SEE

CHILDREN'S MUSEUM OF INDIANAPOLIS

3000 N. Meridian St., Indianapolis, 317-334-3322; www.childrensmuseum.org
The largest of its kind, this outstanding children's museum has exhibits covering science, culture, space, history and exploration. The largest gallery, the Center for Exploration, is designed for ages 12 and up.
March-August, daily 10 a.m.-5 p.m.; September-February, Tuesday-Sunday 10 a.m.-5 p.m.

CITY MARKET

222 E. Market St., Indianapolis, 317-634-9266; www.indianapoliscitymarket.com
This renovated marketplace was constructed in 1886. Shops in the building and two adjacent areas sell smoked meats, dairy products, specialty baked goods, fruits and ethnic foods. Live music is featured on Wednesdays and Fridays in the summer.
Monday-Friday 6 a.m.-6 p.m.

COLONEL ELI LILLY CIVIL WAR MUSEUM

1 Monument Circle, Indianapolis, 317-232-7615; www.in.gov
At this museum underneath the Soldiers and Sailors Monument on downtown's Monument Circle, displays describe Hoosier involvement in the Civil War. Exhibits include photos, letters and diaries of Indiana soldiers.
Wednesday-Sunday 10 a.m.-6 p.m.

EASLEY WINERY

205 N. College Ave., Indianapolis, 317-636-4516; www.easleywine.com
Visit for a wine tasting, also peruse the outdoor garden and gift shop. Tours are available.
Monday-Saturday 9 a.m.-6 p.m., Sunday noon-4 p.m.

INDIANAPOLIS MOTOR SPEEDWAY AND HALL OF FAME MUSEUM

4790 W. 16th St., Indianapolis, 317-484-6747; www.indianapolismotorspeedway.com
Site of the famous 500-mile automobile classic held each year the Sunday before Memorial Day. Many innovations in modern cars have been tested at races here. The oval track is 2½ miles long and lined by grandstands, paddocks and bleachers. Designated a National historic Landmark, the Hall of

Fame Museum displays approximately 75 cars, including a 1957 SSI Corvette and the Marmon "Wasp," which, with Ray Harroun behind the wheel, won the first Indy 500 in 1911.
Daily.

INDIANAPOLIS MUSEUM OF ART
4000 Michigan Road, Indianapolis, 317-920-2659; www.ima-art.org
Extensive collections with many special exhibits. Tours are avilable.
Tuesday-Sunday.

MADAME WALKER THEATRE CENTER
617 Indiana Ave., Indianapolis, 317-236-2099
The Walker Theatre, erected and embellished in an African and Egyptian motif, was built in 1927 as a tribute to Madame C. J. Walker, America's first self-made female millionaire. The renovated theater now features theatrical productions, concerts and other cultural events. The center serves as an educational and cultural center for the city's African-American community.
Tours are available by appointment.

INDIANAPOLIS 500
Indianapolis Motor Speedway, 4790 W. 16th St., Indianapolis, 317-484-6780;
www.indianapolismotorspeedway.com
This 500-mile auto race is the nation's premier event for racing. Watching and partying from the track's inner circle is a popular annual event.
Sunday before Memorial Day.

INDIANAPOLIS ZOO
1200 W. Washington St., Indianapolis, 317-630-2001; www.indyzoo.com
This zoo includes the state's largest aquarium, an enclosed whale and dolphin pavilion and more than 3,000 animals from around the world. horse-drawn streetcar and miniature train rides. There are stroller and locker rentals available.
Daily.

NCAA HALL OF CHAMPIONS
700 W. Washington St., Indianapolis, 800-735-6222
This center celebrates intercollegiate athletics through photographs, video presentations and displays covering 22 men's and women's sports and all NCAA championships. The 25,000-square-foot area contains two levels of interactive displays and multimedia presentations.
Monday-Saturday 10 a.m.-5 p.m.; Sunday noon-5 p.m.; September-May, closed Monday.

PRESIDENT BENJAMIN HARRISON HOME
1230 N. Delaware St., Indianapolis, 317-631-1888; www.presidentbenjaminharrison.org
This is the former residence of the 23rd president of the United States. Guided tours depart every 30 minutes and take visitors through 16 rooms with original furniture, paintings and the family's personal effects.
Monday-Saturday 10 a.m.-3:30 p.m.; closed first three weeks in January, 500 Race Day.

WHERE TO STAY

★★★CANTERBURY HOTEL

123 S. Illinois St., Indianapolis, 317-634-3000, 800-538-8186;
www.canterburyhotel.com

Since the 1850s, this hotel has been Indianapolis' leading hotel. Mahogany furniture and traditional artwork decorate the guest rooms. The restaurant dishes up American and continental favorites for breakfast, lunch and dinner while the traditional afternoon tea is a local institution.

104 rooms. Restaurant. Fitness center. $251-350

★★COURTYARD INDIANAPOLIS DOWNTOWN

601 W. Washington St., Indianapolis, 317-573-6534, 800-321-2211;
www.courtyard.com

297 rooms. Restaurant, bar. Business center. Pool. $61-150

★★★CONRAD INDIANAPOLIS

50 W. Washington St., Indianapolis, 317-713-5000; www.conradindianapolis.com

An oasis in the heart of the bustling city, the Conrad Indianapolis oozes elegance as soon as you walk in: The lobby's breathtaking crushed-glass chandelier is a replica of the one hanging in the New York Metropolitan Opera House. The Capital Grille serves culinary delights, and Spa Chakra offers exclusive Guerlain therapies. The Conrad's rooms, decked out in cozy golds, reds and greens, feature flat-screen HD plasma televisions, wireless keyboards, three telephones each (one cordless) and 500-thread-count Italian Anichini bed linens. And if you must tear yourself away from all the amenities, a skybridge connects the hotel's meeting spaces with the Artsgarden, Circle Centre Mall and the Indiana Convention Center.

241 rooms. Restaurant. Business center. Fitness center. Pool. Spa. Pets accepted. $151-250

★COURTYARD INDIANAPOLIS AT THE CAPITOL

320 N. Senate Ave., Indianapolis, 317-684-7733, 800-321-2211; www.courtyard.com

124 rooms. Business center. Pool. $61-150

★★★CROWNE PLAZA HOTEL UNION STATION

123 W. Louisiana St., Indianapolis, 317-631-2221, 888-303-1746;
www.crowneplaza.com/ind/downtown

Located in historic Union Station, this hotel offers 26 authentic Pullman sleeper train cars for overnight stays, and each one is named for a famous personality from the early 1900s. Full of Old World charm and modern convenience, this hotel is within walking distance of downtown restaurants and sports and cultural hot spots.

273 rooms. Restaurant, bar. Fitness center. Pool. Business center. $61-150

★★DOUBLETREE GUEST SUITES

11355 N. Meridian St., Carmel, 317-844-7994, 800-222-8733; www.doubletree.com

137 rooms. Restaurant, bar. Fitness center. Pool. $61-150

★HAMPTON INN

105 S. Meridian St., Indianapolis, 317-261-1200, 800-426-7866; www.hamptoninn.com

180 rooms. Complimentary breakfast. Fitness center. $61-150

★★HILTON GARDEN INN INDIANAPOLIS DOWNTOWN

10 E. Market St., Indianapolis, 317-955-9700; hiltongardeninn.hilton.com

180 rooms. Restaurant, bar. Complimentary Fitness center. Pool. $61-150

★★★HYATT REGENCY INDIANAPOLIS

1 S. Capitol Ave., Indianapolis, 317-632-1234; www.hyatt.com

This hotel is located eight miles from the Indianapolis International Airport and connected to the Indiana Convention Center, RCA Dome and Circle Centre Mall by a skywalk.

497 rooms. Restaurant, bar. Business center. Fitness center. Pool. $151-250

★★★MARRIOTT INDIANAPOLIS DOWNTOWN

350 W. Maryland St., Indianapolis, 317-822-3500, 877-640-7666; www.marriott.com

Superior customer service is the hallmark of this downtown hotel. Guest rooms are tastefully decorated with modern furnishings. The onsite Champions Sports Bar features more than 30 TVs, making it the perfect spot to watch a big race or game.

622 rooms. Restaurant, bar. Business center. Fitness center. Pool. $61-150

★★★OMNI SEVERIN HOTEL

40 W. Jackson Place, Indianapolis, 317-634-6664; www.omnihotels.com

This historic hotel is connected to the Circle Centre Mall and located opposite Union Station. Rooms feature luxury linens and stocked refreshment centers.

424 rooms. Restaurant, bar. Business center. Fitness center. Pool. Pets accepted. $151-250

★★★SHERATON HOTEL AND SUITES

8787 Keystone Crossing, Indianapolis, 317-846-2700; www.sheraton.com

Connected to the city's most upscale mall, Keystone Crossing, this hotel is close to several restaurants and a nearby Bally's Health Club. The hotel has rooms and suites that feature refrigerators, wet bars and spacious seating areas.

506 rooms. Restaurant, bar. Business center. Pool. Pets accepted. $61-150

★★★THE WESTIN INDIANAPOLIS

50 S. Capitol Ave., Indianapolis, 317-262-8100; www.westin.com

Located near the IMAX Theater and connected to the RCA Dome and a shopping center, this hotel is convenient for business and leisure travelers. Rooms have plush, duvet-topped beds and views of the city.

573 rooms. Restaurant, bar. Business center. Fitness center. Pool. Pets accepted. $61-150

WHERE TO EAT

★ARISTOCRAT PUB

5212 N. College Ave., Indianapolis, 317-283-7388

American. Lunch, dinner, Sunday brunch. Outdoor seating. Children's menu. Bar. $16-35

★CAFE PATACHOU

4911 N. Pennsylvania St., Indianapolis, 317-925-2823; www.cafepatachou.com

American. Breakfast, lunch, brunch. Outdoor seating. Children's menu. $15 and under

★★★CHANTECLAIR

2501 S. High School Road, Indianapolis, 317-243-1040

This eatery, located on the top floor of the Holiday Inn Select, is not a typical hotel restaurant. Classic French dishes like steak Diane and Dover sole make up the menu, while candlelight and violinists set the mood. Jackets for men are suggested, but not required.

French. Dinner. Closed Sunday. Reservations recommended. Bar. $36-85

★★DADDY JACK'S

9419 N. Meridian St., Indianapolis, 317-843-1609; www.konajacksindy.com

American. Lunch, dinner. Closed Sunday. Reservations recommended. Outdoor seating. Bar. $16-35

★★GLASS CHIMNEY

12901 Old Meridian St., Carmel, 317-844-0921; www.glasschimneyanddeeters.com

French, American. Dinner. Closed Sunday. Outdoor seating. Bar. $36-85

★★HOLLYHOCK HILL

8110 N. College Ave., Indianapolis, 317-251-2294; www.hollyhockhill.com

American. Lunch (Sunday), dinner. Closed Monday. Children's menu. Bar. $16-35

★LOON LAKE LODGE

6880 E. 82nd St., Indianapolis, 317-845-9011; www.loonlakelodge.com

American. Lunch, dinner, Sunday brunch. Children's menu. Bar. $16-35

★★★THE OCEANAIRE SEAFOOD ROOM

30 S. Meridian St., Indianapolis, 317-955-2277; www.theoceanaire.com

This modern seafood house is located in downtown Indianapolis and is a popular choice for power lunches. The menu changes daily and features fresh seafood from ahi tuna to black bass. The oyster bar features mollusks from both the Atlantic and Pacific Oceans.

Seafood. Lunch, dinner. Reservations recommended. Bar. $36-85

★★PALOMINO

49 W. Maryland St., Indianapolis, 317-974-0400; www.palomino.com

Mediterranean. Lunch, dinner. Reservations recommended. Outdoor seating. Children's menu. Bar. $16-35

★★★RESTAURANT AT THE CANTERBURY
123 S. Illinois St., Indianapolis, 317-634-3000, 800-538-8186;
www.canterburyhotel.com
Located downtown in the Canterbury hotel, this eatery is decorated more like an English club than a restaurant. American Continental cuisine is the focus here, with classics like Steak Diane and surf and turf served at dinner. American, Continental. Breakfast, lunch, dinner, brunch. Reservations recommended. $36-85

★★RICK'S CAFE BOATYARD
4050 Dandy Trail, Indianapolis, 317-290-9300; www.rickscafeboatyard.com
International. Lunch, dinner, Sunday brunch. Outdoor seating. Children's menu. Bar. $16-35

★★ST. ELMO STEAK HOUSE
127 S. Illinois St., Indianapolis, 317-635-0636; www.stelmos.com
Steak. Dinner. Reservations recommended. Bar. $36-85

★YATS
5463 College Ave., Indianapolis, 317-253-8817; www.yatscajuncreole.com
Cajun-Creole menu. Lunch, dinner. Outdoor seating. $15 and under

KOKOMO
See also Logansport, Marion
This lively manufacturing center is where Elwood Haynes invented the first clutch-driven automobile with an electric ignition. Since then, Kokomo manufacturers have invented several more useful items, from the first pneumatic rubber tire to canned tomato juice. Chrysler and Delphi-Delco Electronics have plants here, which manufacture automotive entertainment systems, semiconductor devices, transmissions and aluminum die castings. Indiana University has a branch here, and Grissom Air Reserve Base is located 14 miles north of town.

WHAT TO SEE
ELWOOD HAYNES MUSEUM
1915 S. Webster St., Kokomo, 765-456-7500; www.inkokomo.com/community
This museum was the home of Elwood Haynes, creator of one of the earliest American automobiles. Includes memorabilia, 1905 and 1924 Haynes cars and the Haynes Stellite alloy used in spaceships.
Daily.

SEIBERLING MANSION
1200 W. Sycamore St., Kokomo, 765-452-4314; www.howardcountymuseum.org
This late Victorian mansion houses exhibits of historical and educational interest, county history, manufacturing artifacts.
Tuesday-Sunday afternoons; closed January.

WHERE TO STAY
★BEST WESTERN SIGNATURE INN
4021 S. Lafountain St., Kokomo, 765-455-1000, 800-822-5252; www.bestwestern.com
101 rooms. Complimentary breakfast. Fitness center. Pool. $61-150

★★CLARION HOTEL
1709 E. Lincoln Road, Kokomo, 765-459-8001
132 rooms. Restaurant, bar. Fitness center. Pool. $61-150

★HAMPTON INN
2920 S. Reed Road, Kokomo, 765-455-2900, 800-426-7866;
www.hamptoninnkokomo.com
105 rooms. Complimentary breakfast. Fitness center. Pool. Pets accepted.
$61-150

WHERE TO EAT
★★SYCAMORE GRILLE
115 W. Sycamore St., Kokomo, 765-457-2220; www.sondyssycamoregrille.com
Lunch, dinner. Closed Sunday. Children's menu. Bar. $16-35

LA PORTE
See also Michigan City, South Bend, Valparaiso
This busy manufacturing center is a popular resort area. City lakes offer fishing, ice fishing, snowmobiling and other recreational activities. Seven lakes with fishing and boating facilities border the town on the north and west. The area's chief industrial products are industrial fans, coil coating, corrugated and plastic containers, rubber products and iron and metal castings.

WHERE TO STAY
★★★ARBOR HILL
263 W. Johnson Road, La Porte, 219-362-9200; www.arborhillinn.com
Built in 1910, this historic Greek Revival inn welcomes guests with its fusion of old-world, turn-of-the-century charm and luxurious modern amenities. Nearby attractions include the Prime Outlet Mall, Notre Dame and Lake Michigan.
12 rooms. Complimentary breakfast. $61-150

★BEST VALUE
444 Pine Lake Ave., La Porte, 219-362-4585, 888-298-2054; www.bestvalueinn.com
146 rooms. Restaurant, bar. Complimentary breakfast. Fitness center. Pool. Pets accepted. $61-150

LAFAYETTE
See also Crawfordsville
Lafayette, a farming community on the east bank of the Wabash River, was named for the Marquis de Lafayette, who served as a general under George Washington in the Revolutionary War. On the west bank of the river in West Lafayette is Purdue University. Established as an agricultural college in 1869, Purdue is known for its engineering school.

WHAT TO SEE
PURDUE UNIVERSITY
504 Northwestern Ave., West Lafayette, 765-494-4636; www.purdue.edu
This Big Ten conference member has 38,208 students and more than 140 major buildings on 1,579 acres.

TIPPECANOE BATTLEFIELD MUSEUM AND PARK
200 Battleground Ave., Battle Ground, I-65 at Highway 43 exit, 765-567-2147;
www.tcha.mus.in.us
This is the site of the 1811 battle in which soldiers and local militia led by General William H. Harrison, territorial governor of Indiana, who defeated a confederation of Native Americans. The Wabash Heritage Trail begins here. Daily.

WOLF PARK
4004 E. 800 N., Battle Ground, 765-567-2265; www.wolfpark.org
Education-research facility; home to several packs of wolves, a small herd of bison, some coyotes and foxes. See wolves close at hand as they eat and socialize.
May-November, Tuesday-Sunday afternoons.

WHERE TO STAY
★★BEST WESTERN
4343 Highway 26 E., Lafayette, 765-447-0575; www.bestwestern.com
124 rooms. Restaurant, bar. Fitness center. Pool. Pets accepted. $61-150

★FAIRFIELD INN
4000 Highway 26 E., Lafayette, 765-449-0083, 888-236-2427; www.fairfieldinn.com
79 rooms. Complimentary breakfast. Pool. $61-150

★JAMESON INN
4320 Highway 26 E., Lafayette, 765-447-4142, 800-526-3766; www.signatureinn.com
121 rooms. Complimentary breakfast. Business center. Fitness center. Pool. Pets accepted. $61-150

★★UNIVERSITY INN CONFERENCE CENTER AND SUITES
3001 Northwestern Ave., West Lafayette, 765-463-5511, 800-777-9808;
www.uiccwl.com
259 rooms. Restaurant, bar. Fitness center. Pool. $61-150

LOGANSPORT
See also Kokomo
Located where the Wabash and Eel Rivers meet, Logansport is situated in the agricultural heartland. The town was named in honor of James Logan, nephew of the famous Shawnee chief, Tecumseh. Logan was fatally wounded by British-led Native Americans after serving with distinction as leader of a company of scouts fighting for the United States in the War of 1812.

WHERE TO STAY
★★HOLIDAY INN
3550 E. Market St., Logansport, 574-753-6351, 800-465-4329; www.holiday-inn.com
95 rooms. Restaurant, bar. Pool. Pets accepted. $61-150

MARION
See also Kokomo
A farm town, Marion is located on the banks of the Mississinewa River. Indiana Wesleyan University, established in 1920, is located here. Film legend James Dean is from Marion.

WHAT TO SEE
MATTHEWS COVERED BRIDGE
Third and Front streets, Matthews, 765-998-2928
This 175-foot-long bridge spans the Mississinewa River.

WHERE TO STAY
★COMFORT INN
1345 N. Baldwin Ave., Marion, 765-651-1006; www.comfortsuites.com
62 rooms. Complimentary breakfast. Fitness center. Pool. Pets accepted. $61-150

MERRILLVILLE
See also Gary, Hammond, Valparaiso
Once a thriving stopoff point for the many wagon trains headed west, Merrillville has abandoned its rural beginnings to become a leader in commercial and industrial development.

WHERE TO STAY
★FAIRFIELD INN
8275 Georgia St., Merrillville, 219-736-0500, 800-228-2800; www.fairfieldinn.com
112 rooms. Complimentary breakfast. Pool. $61-150

★★RADISSON HOTEL AT STAR PLAZA
800 E. 81st Ave., Merrillville, 219-769-6311, 800-333-3333; www.radisson.com
343 rooms. Restaurants, bar. Business center. Fitness center. Pool. $151-250

WHERE TO EAT
★GAMBA RISTORANTE
455 E. 84th Drive, Merrillville, 219-736-2203; www.gambaristorante.com
Italian. Lunch, dinner. Closed Sunday. Reservations recommended. $16-35

MICHIGAN CITY
See also La Porte
This is Indiana's summer playground on the southeast shore of Lake Michigan. Located in the famous Indiana sand dunes region, Michigan City offers miles of fine beaches. For fishermen, the lake has coho salmon from late March to November, as well as chinook salmon, lake trout and perch.

WHAT TO SEE
BARKER MANSION

631 Washington St., Michigan City, 219-873-1520; www.emichigancity.com

This 38-room mansion (circa 1900) was modeled after an English manor house. Tours are available.

June-October, daily; November-May, Monday-Friday.

THE LUBEZNIK CENTER FOR THE ARTS

101 W. Second St., Michigan City, 219-874-4900; www.lubeznikcenter.org

Paintings, sculptures and graphic art exhibits of regional, national and international origin can be viewed here.

Tuesday-Sunday.

LIGHTHOUSE PLACE OUTLET CENTER

601 Wabash St., Michigan City, 219-879-6506;

www.premiumoutlets.com/lighthouseplace

This center has more than 135 outlet stores, including J. Crew and Polo Ralph Lauren.

Daily.

WASHINGTON PARK ZOO

115 Lakeshore Drive, Michigan City, 219-873-1510; www.washingtonparkzoo.com

In addition to animal observation, there is a swimming beach, yacht basin, marina, fishing, picnic facilities, concession, tennis courts, and an observation tower.

Daily. Amphitheater: June-August, Thursday-Sunday.

OLD LIGHTHOUSE MUSEUM

Heisman Harbor Road, Michigan City, 219-872-6133; www.oldlighthousemuseum.org

This is the site of the launching of the first submarine on the Great Lakes in 1845.

March-December, Tuesday-Sunday.

WHERE TO STAY
★★BLUE CHIP HOTEL AND CASINO

2 Easy St., Michigan City, 219-879-7711, 888-879-7711; www.bluechip-casino.com

184 rooms. Restaurant, bar. Business center. Fitness center. Pool. Casino.
$61-150

MUNCIE

See also Anderson

This area was once the home of the Munsee tribe of the Delaware Indians. The town became a farming center during the first half of the 19th century, but with the construction of railroads and the discovery of natural gas, it became an industrial city.

Ball Corporation, which for years produced the classic Ball jars, has its international headquarters in Muncie. The five Ball brothers took an active part in the city's life and contributed substantially to Ball State University. Muncie became famous in the 1930s as the subject of Robert and Helen

Lynd's sociological studies of a "typical" small city: Middletown and Middletown in Transition.

WHERE TO STAY
★★BEST VALUE INN
3400 S. Madison St., Muncie, 765-288-1911, 888-315-2378; www.bestvalueinn.com
148 rooms. Restaurant, bar. Complimentary breakfast. Pool. Pets accepted. $61-150

★★CLUBHOUSE INN
420 S. High St., Muncie, 765-741-7777
130 rooms. Restaurant, bar. Pool. Pets accepted. $61-150

★SIGNATURE INN
3400 N. Chadam Lane, Muncie, 765-284-4200, 800-822-5252; www.signatureinn.com
101 rooms. Complimentary breakfast. Fitness center. Pool. Pets accepted. $61-150

NASHVILLE
See also Bloomington, Columbus
Driving south from Indianapolis on State Road 135, the scenery quickly evolves from bland to beautiful as the pavement, at first level and unbending, begins to rise, fall and gently curve. On either side of the road, fields give way to dense forests. Within an hour, travelers arrive at the charming village of Nashville in Brown County. This area is also known as the art colony of the Midwest, a moniker earned in the early 1900s when the area was one of six art colonies established in the United States. The impressionist painter T. C. Steele moved here in 1907, and his homestead, the House of the Singing Winds, is now a state historic site. Many artists followed Steele's lead and moved to Brown County, and today Nashville is filled with shops and galleries featuring the works of local artists. Like the larger city of the same name, Nashville has a vibrant country music scene. Two popular venues include the Little Nashville Opry and the Country Time Music hall.

WHERE TO STAY
★★BROWN COUNTY INN
Highway 46, Nashville, 812-988-2291, 800-772-5249; www.browncountyinn.com
99 rooms. Restaurant, bar. Pool. Tennis. $61-150

★★THE SEASONS LODGE
560 Highway 46 E., Nashville, 812-988-2284, 800-365-7327; www.seasonslodge.com
80 rooms. Restaurant, bar. Pool. $61-150

WHERE TO EAT
★THE ORDINARY
61 S. Van Buren St., Nashville, 812-988-6166
Lunch, dinner. Closed Monday, except in October. Children's menu. Bar. $16-35

NEW HARMONY

See also Evansville

During the first half of the 19th century, this was the site of two social experiments in communal living. A town was founded here by religious leader George Rapp and members of the Harmony Society, who came from Germany and settled in Harmony, Pa. In 1814, the society moved to Indiana. The deeply religious members believed in equality, mutual protection and common ownership of property. They practiced celibacy and believed in the imminent return of Christ. In a 10-year period, they transformed 30,000 acres of dense forest and swampland into farms and a town that was the envy of the surrounding region. In 1825, the group returned to Pennsylvania and sold Harmony to Robert Owen, a Welsh social reformer and communal idealist. Owen, with his four sons and geologist William Maclure, attempted to organize a new social order, eliminating financial exploitation, poverty and competition. He tried to establish a model society in New Harmony, with equal opportunities for all, full cooperative effort and advanced educational facilities to develop the highest type of human beings. Within a short time, many of the world's most distinguished scientists, educators, scholars and writers came to New Harmony, which became a scientific center for America.

Though Owen's original experiment failed, mainly because of his absence from the community and rivalry among his followers, the scientists and educators stayed on. The first U.S. Geological Survey was done here, and the Smithsonian Institution has its origins in this community.

The town is in a rural area surrounded by rich farmland. Historic New Harmony and the New Harmony State historic Sites are dedicated to the founders of this community. Many of the buildings and old homes still dominate New Harmony today.

WHAT TO SEE
ATHENEUM VISITORS CENTER

North and Arthur streets, New Harmony, 812-682-4474, 800-231-2168;
www.newharmony.org

The orientation area in this building was designed by Richard Meier. There is an educational documentary film. All tours begin here.
April-October, daily; March, November-December, hours vary; closed January-February.

HARMONIST CEMETERY

West, Arthur and North streets, New Harmony, 800-231-2168

Buried here in unmarked graves dating from 1814 to 1824 are 230 members of the Harmony Society. Site includes several prehistoric Woodland mounds and an apple orchard.

LABYRINTH

Main Street, New Harmony, 800-231-2168

This circular maze of shrubbery was created to symbolize the twists and choices along life's pathway.

ROBERT HENRY FAUNTLEROY HOUSE
West and Church streets, New Harmony, 800-231-2168
Harmonist family residence (1822-1840) was enlarged and restyled by Robert and Jane Owen Fauntleroy. The house museum contains period furniture. Hours vary.

THRALL'S OPERA HOUSE
Church Street, New Harmony, 800-231-2168
Originally the Harmonist Dormitory Number 4, this building was later converted to a concert hall by Owen descendants.
Show times vary.

ROOFLESS CHURCH
North and Main streets, New Harmony, 800-231-2168
This interdenominational church, designed by Philip Johnson in 1959, commemorates New Harmony's religious heritage.

WHERE TO STAY
★★NEW HARMONY INN
504 North St., New Harmony, 812-682-4431, 800-782-8605; www.newharmonyinn.com
90 rooms. Restaurant, bar. Fitness center. Pool. Tennis. $61-150

WHERE TO EAT
★★RED GERANIUM
504 North St., New Harmony, 812-682-4431, 800-782-8605; www.newharmonyinn.com
Lunch, dinner. Closed Monday. Bar. $16-35

PLYMOUTH
See also South Bend
Plymouth is a farming and industrial center. Southwest of the town was the site of the last Potawatomi village in this area. The chief, Menominee, refused to surrender his village to white settlers. The surviving men, women and children were removed by the government and sent to Kansas in 1838. So many members of the tribe died of malaria that fresh graves were left at every campsite during their journey.

WHERE TO STAY
★★RAMADA INN
2550 N. Michigan St., Plymouth, 574-936-4013, 800-272-6232; www.ramada.com
108 rooms. Pets accepted. Restaurant, bar. Pool. $61-150

RICHMOND
See also Muncie
Established by Quakers, this city on the Whitewater River is one of Indiana's leading industrial communities.

WHAT TO SEE
HAYES REGIONAL ARBORETUM
801 Elks Road, Richmond, 765-962-3745; www.hayesarboretum.org
This is a 355-acre site with trees, shrubs and vines native to this region. Also enjoy its 40-acre beech-maple forest. There is an auto tour that navigates 3½ miles of the site. There is a Fern garden, spring house, hiking trails, bird sanctuary, nature center with exhibits, and a gift shop.
Tuesday-Sunday.

INDIANA FOOTBALL HALL OF FAME
815 N. A St., Richmond, 765-966-2235; www.geocities.com/indfoothall
Learn about the history of football in Indiana; exhibits include photos, plaques, and memorabilia of more than 300 inductees. Indiana high schools, colleges and universities are represented.
Monday-Friday, also by appointment.

WHERE TO STAY
★KNIGHTS INN RICHMOND
3020 E. Main St., Richmond, 765-966-1505
44 rooms. Complimentary breakfast. Pool. $61-150

WHERE TO EAT
★★OLDE RICHMOND INN
138 S. Fifth St., Richmond, 765-962-2247; www.oldrichmondinn.net
American. Lunch, dinner. Outdoor seating. Children's menu. Bar. $16-35

★TASTE OF THE TOWN
1616 E. Main St., Richmond, 765-935-5464
Italian. Lunch, dinner. Closed Monday. Children's menu. Bar. $16-35

SOUTH BEND
See also La Porte, Plymouth
South Bend is probably most famous, at least in the eyes of football fans, for being the home of the Fighting Irish of the University of Notre Dame. A visit to the campus, distinguished by the massive golden dome of the Administration Building, is worth the trip. Indiana University also has a branch here.

Two Frenchmen, Peré Jacques Marquette and Louis Jolliet, were the first Europeans to explore the South Bend area. In 1679, the famous French explorer Rene-Robert Cavelier proceeded from here with 32 men to the Mississippi River. During a second trip in 1681, Cavelier negotiated a peace treaty between the Miami and Illinois Confederations under an oak tree known as the Council Oak. The first permanent settlers arrived in 1820, when Pierre Freischuetz Navarre set up a trading post for the American Fur Company.

South Bend was founded in 1823 by Alexis Coquillard who, with his partner Francis Comparet, bought a fur trading agency from John Jacob Astor. Joined by Lathrop Taylor, another trading post agent, Coquillard was instrumental in promoting the European settlement of the area and in the construction of ferries, dams and mills, which began the industrial development of the town.

INDIANA ★★★★★

WHAT TO SEE
NOTRE DAME STADIUM
Juniper and Edison streets, South Bend, 574-631-5267

Few sports arenas have as much history and tradition as Notre Dame Stadium. The stadium has hosted several national championship teams and some of the greatest players and coaches in collegiate history. It was expanded in 1997 to hold more than 80,000 fans and is well attended—if not sold out—for almost every regular-season game.

WHERE TO STAY
★★HOLIDAY INN CITY CENTER
213 W. Washington St., South Bend, 574-232-3941, 800-465-4329;
www.holiday-inn.com

176 rooms. Restaurant, bar. Business center. Fitness center. Pool. $61-150

★★INN AT SAINT MARY'S
53993 State Road 933, South Bend, 574-232-4000, 800-947-8627;
www.innatsaintmarys.com

150 rooms. Bar. Complimentary breakfast. Business center. Fitness center. Pool. $61-150

★★★MARRIOTT SOUTH BEND
123 N. St. Joseph St., South Bend, 574-234-2000, 800-328-7349; www.marriott.com

This downtown South Bend hotel has a nine-story atrium and lobby decorated in an Art Deco style. A skywalk connects the hotel to the Century Center Convention and Civic Complex, and the downtown location makes it accessible to local businesses, attractions and schools, including, the University of Notre Dame.

298 rooms. Restaurant, bar. Business center. Fitness center. Pool. Pets accepted. $61-150

★★MORRIS INN
Notre Dame Avenue, South Bend, 574-631-2000; www.morrisinn.com

92 rooms. Restaurant, bar. Complimentary breakfast. Business center. Fitness center. $61-150

★SIGNATURE INN
215 Dixie Way S., South Bend, 574-277-3211; www.signatureinn.com

123 rooms. Complimentary breakfast. Business center. Fitness center. Pool. Pets accepted. $61-150

WHERE TO EAT
★★★THE CARRIAGE HOUSE DINING ROOM
24460 Adams Road, South Bend, 574-272-9220; www.carriagehousedining.com

A historic church is the setting for this South Bend gem, where an inventive American menu is complemented by professional, friendly service. All dishes, including signatures like hickory-smoked salmon, beef Wellington with Burgundian sauce, and steak Diane with dauphinoise potatoes, are prepared using classic French techniques as well as fresh, seasonal produce.

American. Dinner. Closed Sunday-Monday; also early January. Outdoor seating. Bar. $36-85

★★DAMON'S GRILL
52885 Highway 933 N., South Bend, 574-272-5478
Barbecue. Lunch, dinner. Children's menu. Bar. $16-35

★★★LA SALLE GRILL
115 W. Colfax, South Bend, 574-288-1155; www.lasallegrill.com
This acclaimed restaurant in downtown South Bend offers such creative American dishes as grilled Amish chicken with honey and raisin barbecue sauce and black pepper mashed potatoes. The dining room has high ceilings and tables topped with white linens and imported crystal. Its wine list includes nearly 350 selections.
American. Dinner. Closed Sunday. Bar. $36-85

★★MORRIS INN UNIVERSITY
Notre Dame Ave., South Bend, 574-631-2000; www.morrisinn.nd.edu
American, French. Breakfast, lunch, dinner. Closed mid-December-early January. Reservations recommended. Children's menu. Bar. $16-35

★★★TIPPECANOE PLACE
620 W. Washington St., South Bend, 574-234-9077; www.tippe.com
This 1880s stone mansion once owned by the Studebaker family is now an elegant restaurant. The menu features classics like filet mignon or roasted salmon with mustard-basil glaze. The extensive wine list features bottles from around the world, but spotlights winemakers from California.
American. Lunch, dinner, Sunday brunch. Reservations recommended. Children's menu. Bar. $16-35

140 TERRE HAUTE
See also Bloomington
Terre Haute was founded as a river town on the lower Wabash River and has become an important industrial, educational and cultural center.

The plateau on which the city is built was named Terre Haute or "high land" by the French, who governed this area until 1763. The dividing line that separated the French provinces of Canada and Louisiana runs through this section. American settlers arrived with the establishment of Fort Harrison in 1811. Many wagon trains with westbound settlers passed through here.

Novelist Theodore Dreiser, author of Sister Carrie and An American Tragedy, and his brother, Paul Dresser, composer of Indiana's state song, "On the Banks of the Wabash," lived here. Eugene V. Debs founded the American Railway Union, the first industrial union in America, in Terre Haute. The city is the home of Rose-Hulman Institute of Technology, established in 1874.

WHERE TO STAY
★FAIRFIELD INN
475 E. Margaret Ave., Terre Haute, 812-235-2444; www.fairfieldinn.com
62 rooms. Complimentary breakfast. Pool. $61-150

★★HOLIDAY INN
3300 Dixie Bee Highway, Terre Haute, 812-232-6081, 800-465-4329;
www.holiday-inn.com
230 rooms. Restaurant, bar. Fitness center. Pool. Pets accepted. $61-150

VALPARAISO
See also Hammond, La Porte
This northern Indiana town, located two hours from Chicago, has a quaint and historic town center.

WHERE TO STAY
★BEST WESTERN EXPRESSWAY INN
760 Morthland Drive, Valparaiso, 219-464-8555, 800-321-2211; www.bestwestern.com
48 rooms. Complimentary breakfast. Fitness center. Pets accepted. $61-150

★★COURTYARD VALPARAISO
2301 E. Morthland Drive, Valparaiso, 219-465-1700; www.courtyard.com
111 rooms. Restaurant. Fitness center. Pool. $61-150

★★INDIAN OAK RESORT & SPA
558 Indian Boundary Road, Chesterton, 219-926-2200, 800-552-4232;
www.indianoak.com
61 rooms. Restaurant. Complimentary breakfast. Business center. Fitness center. Pool. $61-150

WHERE TO EAT
★BILLY JACK'S CAFE & GRILL
2904 N. Calumet Ave., Valparaiso, 219-477-3797; www.billyjacks.com
Italian, Southwestern. Lunch, dinner. Children's menu. Bar. $16-35

★BISTRO 157
157 Lincolnway, Valparaiso, 219-462-0992; www.bistro157.net
International. Lunch, dinner. Closed Monday. Outdoor seating. $16-35

★★DISH RESTAURANT
3907 Calumet Ave., Valparaiso, 219-465-9221; www.dishrestaurant.net
American. Lunch, dinner. Closed Sunday. Bar. $16-35

★DON QUÌJOTE
119 E. Lincolnway, Valparaiso, 219-462-7976; www.donquijoterestaurant-in.com
Spanish. Lunch, dinner. Closed Sunday. Reservations recommended. Outdoor seating. Children's menu. $16-35

★★STRONGBOW INN
2405 E. Route 30, Valparaiso, 219-462-5121; www.strongbowinn.com
American. Lunch, dinner. Children's menu. Bar. $16-35

OHIO

NOT EVERY VACATION LEAVES YOU FEELING AS SPRIGHTLY AS A YOUTH. BUT WITH ITS renowned art museums and orchestras, quaint Lake Erie resorts and famous amusement parks, Ohio can bring out the kid in you, no matter what your age.

Between fishing on Lake Erie and the area's miles of hiking trails, Northeast Ohio is an ideal stop for nature lovers. For the ultimate outdoor adventure, visit Cuyahoga Valley National Park, covering 33,000 acres along the banks of the Cuyahoga River. Whether you like sweating it out on steep backcountry slopes, cycling or taking a stroll on the groomed Ohio and Erie Canal Towpath Trail, the park offers something for all outdoor enthusiasts.

Because you're already in the neighborhood, and in a sporting mood, make a stop at the Pro Football Hall of Fame in nearby Canton and learn about the game's heroes.

Or continue on to Cleveland, where a rich arts scene, stellar sports teams and diverse neighborhoods make it one of the Midwest's most unique cities. Enjoy a night at the theater at Playhouse Square or experience University Circle, where you can see famed paintings at the Cleveland Museum of Art, explore 10 acres of landscaped gardens at the Cleveland-Botanical Garden and hear the Cleveland Orchestra's symphonic sounds at Severance Hall.

Prefer rock to Ravel? No problem. Head to the Rock and Roll Hall of Fame and Museum. Perched on Cleveland's lakefront, it houses some of the world's most legendary rock 'n' roll memorabilia, including Janis Joplin's car and Jimi Hendrix' guitars.

If you'd rather feel the beat of feet stomping in a deafening stadium, don scarlet and gray and hasten to Ohio State University in Columbus. The state's capital and largest city is home not only to the Columbus Museum of Art and a popular ethnic dining scene but also the Ohio State Buckeyes—and their storied football and basketball history.

For a fun family getaway, a trip to southern Ohio is a must. Take a whitewater rafting trip down the Ohio River, learn about Ohio's integral role in the anti-slavery movement at Cincinnati's National Underground Railroad Freedom Center and get a thrill on one of 80 roller coasters, water rides and other attractions at nearby Paramount's Kings Island.

Want even more amusement? Make your way to Cedar Point in Sandusky. The second oldest amusement park in North America boasts the most rides and some of the highest and fastest coasters in the world.

AKRON

See also Cleveland, Kent

Once called the "rubber capital of the world," Akron is the headquarters for four major rubber companies, including Goodyear and Firestone.

Akron owes its start to the Ohio and Erie Canal, which was opened in 1827. The town was already thriving when Dr. Benjamin Franklin Goodrich launched the first rubber plant here in 1870. When automobiles were invented, Akron became a boomtown. Though industry isn't quite what it once was, the signs of the city's past affluence can still be seen.

WHAT TO SEE
HALE FARM AND VILLAGE

2686 Oak Hill Road, Bath, 330-666-3711, 800-589-9703; www.wrhs.org

Hale Farm and Village includes an authentic Western Reserve house circa 1825, and other authentic buildings in the village setting depict northeastern Ohio's rural life in the mid-1800s.

June-August, Wednesday-Saturday 11 a.m.-5 p.m., Sunday noon-5 p.m.;
September and October, Saturday 11 a.m.-5 p.m., Sunday noon-5 p.m.

QUAKER SQUARE

135 S. Broadway, Akron, 330-253-5970; www.quakersquare.com

Shopping, restaurants and an entertainment center can be found in the original mills and silos of the Quaker Oats Company. Historical displays include famous Quaker Oats advertising memorabilia.

Monday-Thursday 10 a.m.-8 p.m., Saturday 10 a.m.-9 p.m., Sunday 10 a.m.-6 p.m.

STAN HYWET HALL AND GARDENS

714 N. Portage Path, Akron, 330-836-5533; www.stanhywet.org

This Tudor Revival manor house built by F. A. Seiberling, co-founder of Goodyear Tire & Rubber, contains 65 rooms with antiques and art, with some pieces dating from the 14th century. More than 70 acres of grounds and gardens.

Tuesday-Sunday 10 a.m.-6 p.m.

WHERE TO STAY
★BEST WESTERN EXECUTIVE INN

2677 Gilchrist Road, Akron, 330-794-1050, 800-528-1234; www.bestwestern.com

112 rooms. Complimentary breakfast. Fitness center. Pool. $61-150

★★★HILTON AKRON-FAIRLAWN

3180 W. Market St., Akron, 330-867-5000, 800-445-8667;
www.akronfairlawn.hilton.com

This locally owned hotel is located in the Akron suburb of Fairlawn. Rooms are large and feature marble bathrooms.

203 rooms. Restaurant, bar. Business center. Fitness center. Pool. $61-150

★★HOLIDAY INN

4073 Medina Road, Akron, 330-666-4131, 800-465-4329; www.holiday-inn.com

165 rooms. Restaurant. Fitness center. Pool. $61-150

★★★ QUAKER SQUARE INN

135 S. Broadway St., Akron, 330-253-5970; www.quakersquareakron.com

Constructed from 19th-century silos and mills that once produced or stored oats for Quaker Oats Company, this historic hotel (which has round guest rooms) is a landmark for Akron. There's also a large entertainment complex with restaurants and shops connected to the hotel.

91 rooms. Restaurant, bar. Complimentary breakfast. Business center. Fitness center. Pool. $61-150

★★RADISSON INN AKRON-FAIRLAWN
200 Montrose West Ave., Akron, 330-666-9300, 800-333-3333; www.radisson.com
128 rooms. Restaurant, bar. Fitness center. Pool. $61-150

WHERE TO EAT
★★★LANNING'S
826 N. Cleveland-Massillon Road, Akron, 330-666-1159; www.lannings-restaurant.com
On the banks of Yellow Creek, this fine dining room offers fresh fish and
hand-cut steaks and has been in business since 1967. Everything is made in-
house, including salad dressings, sauces, soups, breads and desserts.
American. Dinner. Closed Sunday. Reservations recommended. Bar. $36-85

★★★TANGIER
532 W. Market St., Akron, 330-376-7171, 800-826-4437; www.thetangier.com
This local gem is considered one of Ohio's top spots for live music, from jazz
to light rock. Listen to the entertainment while sampling the eclectic Middle
Eastern cuisine.
American, Middle Eastern. Lunch, dinner. Closed Sunday. Reservations
recommended. Outdoor seating. Children's menu. Bar. $36-85

ASHTABULA
See also Cleveland
This modern harbor at the mouth of the Ashtabula River is an important shipping
center for coal and iron ore. Popular pastimes here are swimming and fishing.

WHERE TO STAY
★COMFORT INN
1860 Austinburg Road, Austinburg, 440-275-2711, 877-424-6423;
www.comfortinn.com
119 rooms. Restaurant, bar. Complimentary breakfast. Fitness center. Pool.
Pets accepted. $61-150

WHERE TO EAT
★★EL GRANDE
2145 W. Prospect St., Ashtabula, 440-998-2228
American, Italian. Lunch, dinner. Closed Sunday-Monday. $16-35

ATHENS
See also Columbus
The founding in 1804 of Ohio University, the oldest college in what was
the Northwest Territory, created the town of Athens. Life in this small town
revolves around the almost 30,000 students who attend the school.

WHERE TO STAY
★AMERIHOST INN
20 Home St., Athens, 740-594-3000, 800-434-5800; www.amerihostinn.com
102 rooms. Complimentary breakfast. Business center. Fitness center. Pool.
$61-150

★★OHIO UNIVERSITY INN AND CONFERENCE CENTER
331 Richland Ave., Athens, 740-593-6661; www.ouinn.com
139 rooms. Restaurant, bar. Pool. Pets accepted. $61-150

AURORA
See also Akron, Cleveland, Kent
This small city situated between Cleveland and Akron attracts visitors for its Geauga Lake theme park (which has everything from roller coasters to waterslides) and the premium outlets located here.

WHERE TO STAY
★★★THE BERTRAM INN AND CONFERENCE CENTER
600 N. Aurora Road, Aurora, 330-995-0200, 877-995-0200; www.thebertraminn.com
This sprawling resort attracts large conferences. Rooms are decorated with traditional furnishings. The onsite Leopard Restaurant is acclaimed for its creative cooking—the menu includes everything from Kurobuta pork chop with branded apples to Guanciale wrapped pheasant with spiced pumpkin cream.
162 rooms. Restaurant, bar. Business center. Fitness center. Pool. $151-250

BEACHWOOD
See also Cleveland
This eastern Cleveland suburb has some of the areas best shopping, thanks to the Beachwood Place Mall and many stores surrounding it.

WHERE TO STAY
★★COURTYARD CLEVELAND BEACHWOOD
3695 Orange Place, Beachwood, 216-765-1900, 800-321-2211; www.beachwoodcourtyard.com
113 rooms. Restaurant, bar. Business center. Fitness center. Pool. $61-150

★★EMBASSY SUITES
3775 Park East Drive, Beachwood, 216-765-8066, 800-362-2779; www.embassysuites.com
216 rooms. Restaurant, bar. Complimentary breakfast. Business center. Fitness center. Pool. $151-250

WHERE TO EAT
★★★RISTORANTE GIOVANNI
25550 Chagrin Blvd., Beachwood, 216-831-8625; www.giovanniscleveland.com
Dine in a romantic setting at this restaurant, which serves fine classic Italian dishes and pastas. Enjoy a good cigar with dessert.
Italian. Lunch, dinner. Closed Sunday. Reservations recommended. Jacket required. Bar. $36-85

CAMBRIDGE
See also Newark
Cambridge, an important center for the glassmaking industry, was named by settlers who came from England's Isle of Guernsey. At one time a center

of mining and oil, it is located at the crossroads of three major federal highways.

WHERE TO STAY
★BEST WESTERN CAMBRIDGE
1945 Southgate Parkway, Cambridge, 740-439-3581, 800-528-1234;
www.bestwestern.com
95 rooms. Bar. Complimentary breakfast. Pool. Pets accepted. $61-150

★★RAMADA CAMBRIDGE
2248 Southgate Parkway, Cambridge, 740-432-7313, 800-272-6232; www.ramada.com
108 rooms. Restaurant, bar. Complimentary breakfast. Business center. Fitness center. Pool. Pets accepted. $61-150

WHERE TO EAT
★BEARS DEN
13320 E. Pike, Cambridge, 740-432-5285
American. Dinner. Closed Sunday. $15 and under

★THEO'S
632 Wheeling Ave., Cambridge, 740-432-3878; www.theosrestaurant.us
Eclectic. Lunch, dinner. Closed Sunday. Bar. $16-35

CANTON
See also Akron, New Philadelphia, Wooster
In 1867, president-to-be William McKinley opened a law office in Canton and later conducted his "front porch campaign" for the presidency here. After his assassination, his body was brought back to Canton for burial. Because of his love for the red carnation, it was made the state flower.

This large steel-processing city, important a century ago for farm machinery, is in the middle of rich farmland on the edge of "steel valley" where the three branches of Nimishillen Creek come together. It's also home to the Pro Football Hall of Fame.

WHAT TO SEE
PRO FOOTBALL HALL OF FAME
2121 George Halas Drive Northwest, Canton, 330-456-8207; www.profootballhof.com
This museum, a five-building complex, is dedicated to the game of football and its players. It houses memorabilia, a research library, a movie theater and a museum store.
June-August, daily 9 a.m.-8 p.m.; September-May, daily 9 a.m.-5 p.m.

WHERE TO STAY
★★COURTYARD CANTON
4375 Metro Circle N.W., Canton, 330-494-6494, 877-867-7666; www.marriott.com
150 rooms. Restaurant, bar. Business center. Fitness center. Pool. $61-150

★HAMPTON INN

5335 Broadmoor Circle N.w., Canton, 330-492-0151, 800-426-7866;
www.hamptoninn.com

107 rooms. Complimentary breakfast. Business center. Fitness center. $61-150

★★HOLIDAY INN

4520 Everhard Road N.w., Canton, 330-494-2770, 800-465-4329; www.holiday-inn.com

194 rooms. Restaurant, bar. Fitness center. Pool. $61-150

WHERE TO EAT
★JOHN'S

2749 Cleveland Ave., Canton, 330-454-1259; www.johnsgrille.com

American. Breakfast, lunch, dinner. Closed Sunday. Bar. $15 and under

★★★LOLLI'S

4801 N.W. Dressler Road, Canton, 330-492-6846, 877-465-6554;
www.lollisrestaurant.net

This restaurant and banquet center in the Belden Village Mall hosts many of the area's special events and has space for up to 375 people. Try reserving a table at the weekly murder mystery dinner theater.

Italian, Seafood. Dinner. Closed Sunday-Thursday. Bar. $16-35

CHILLICOTHE

See also Columbus

Chillicothe, first capital of the Northwest Territory, became the first capital of Ohio in 1803. Among the early settlers from Virginia who helped Ohio achieve statehood were Edward Tiffin, first state governor, and Thomas Worthington, governor and U.S. senator. Greek revival mansions built for these statesmen can be seen on Chillicothe's Paint Street.

WHERE TO STAY
★COMFORT INN

20 N. Plaza Blvd., Chillicothe, 740-775-3500, 877-424-6423; www.comfortinn.com

99 rooms. Bar. Complimentary breakfast. Fitness center. Pool. Pets accepted. $61-150

★HAMPTON INN

100 N. Plaza Blvd., Chillicothe, 740-773-1616, 800-426-7866; www.hamptoninn.com

71 rooms. Complimentary breakfast. Business center. Fitness center. Pool. $61-150

WHERE TO EAT
★DAMON'S

10 N. Plaza Blvd., Chillicothe, 740-775-8383; www.damons.com

American. Lunch, dinner. Children's menu. Bar. $16-35

CINCINNATI

See also Hamilton, Lebanon, Mason

Cincinnati was a busy frontier riverboat town and one of the largest cities in the nation when poet Henry Wadsworth Longfellow called it the "queen city of the West." Although other cities farther west have since outstripped it in size, Cincinnati is still the Queen City to its inhabitants and to the many visitors who rediscover it. With a wealth of fine restaurants, a redeveloped downtown with a Skywalk, its own Montmartre in Mount Adams and the beautiful Ohio River, Cincinnati has a cosmopolitan flavor uniquely its own.

Early settlers chose the site because it was an important river crossroads used by Native Americans. In 1790, Arthur St. Clair, governor of the Northwest Territory, changed the name of Losantiville to Cincinnati in honor of the revolutionary officers' Society of Cincinnati. Despite smallpox, insects, floods and crop failures, approximately 15,000 settlers came in the next five years. They had the protection of General Anthony Wayne, who broke the resistance of the Ohio Native Americans. In the early 1800s, a large influx of immigrants, mostly German, settled in the area.

During the Civil War, the city was generally loyal to the Union, although its location on the Mason-Dixon line and the interruption of trade with the South caused mixed emotions. After the Civil War, prosperity brought art, music, a new library and a professional baseball team. A period of municipal corruption in the late 19th century was ended by a victory for reform elements and the establishment of a city manager form of government, which has earned Cincinnati the title of America's best-governed city.

Today, the city is the home of two universities and several other institutions of higher education and has its own symphony orchestra, opera and ballet. Major hotels, stores, office complexes, restaurants, entertainment centers and the Cincinnati Convention Center are now connected by a skywalk system, making the city easy to walk, even in winter.

WHAT TO SEE
CINCINNATI BALLET
Aronoff Center, 1555 Central Parkway, Cincinnati, 513-621-5219;
www.cincinnatiballet.com
This company performs a five-series program at the Aronoff Center of both contemporary and classical works.
October-May, December (show vary).

CINCINNATI OPERA
Cincinnati Music Hall, 1241 Elm St., Cincinnati, 513-241-2742;
www.cincinnatiopera.com
The nation's second oldest opera company offers a summer season; capsulized English translations are projected above the stage for all operas.
Mid-June-mid-July.

CINCINNATI SYMPHONY ORCHESTRA
Cincinnati Music Hall, 1241 Elm St., Cincinnati, 513-381-3300;
www.cincinnatisymphony.org
The fifth-oldest orchestra presents symphony and pops programs.
September-May.

CINCINNATI ZOO AND BOTANICAL GARDEN

3400 Vine St., Cincinnati, 513-281-4700, 800-944-4776; www.cincyzoo.org

More than 700 species can be seen in a variety of naturalistic habitats, including the world-famous gorillas and white Bengal tigers. The Cat House features 16 species of cats; the Jungle Trails exhibit is an indoor-outdoor rain forest. Rare okapi, walrus, Komodo dragons and giant eland also are on display. Enjoy the participatory children's zoo, animal shows, elephant and camel rides. There are also picnic areas, and an onsite restaurant.
Daily, hours vary.

EDEN PARK

950 Eden Park Drive, Cincinnati, www.cincinnati-oh.gov

More than 185 acres initially called "the Garden of Eden." Ice skating on Mirror Lake. The Murray Seasongood Pavilion features spring and summer band concerts and other events. There are four overlooks with scenic views of the Ohio River, the city and Kentucky hillsides.

HARRIET BEECHER STOWE HOUSE

224 W. Liberty St., Cincinnati, 513-632-5120; www.harrietbeecherstowecenter.org

The author of Uncle Tom's Cabin lived here from 1832 to 1836 and it has since been completely restored with some original furnishings.
Tuesday-Thursday, by appointment only.

MUSEUM OF NATURAL HISTORY & SCIENCE

1301 Western Ave., Cincinnati, 513-287-7000; www.cincymuseum.org

This museum depicts the natural history of the Ohio Valley with a wilderness trail with Ohio flora and fauna, and a full-scale walk-through replica of a cavern with a 32-foot waterfall. Kids love the Children's Discovery Center.
Monday-Saturday 10 a.m.-5 p.m., Sunday 11 a.m.-6 p.m.

WILLIAM HOWARD TAFT NATIONAL HISTORIC SITE

2038 Auburn Ave., Cincinnati, 513-684-3262; www.nps.gov/wiho

This is the birthplace and boyhood home of the 27th president and chief justice of the United States. Four rooms with period furnishings; other rooms contain exhibits on Taft's life and careers.
Daily 8 a.m.-4 p.m.

WHERE TO STAY

★BAYMONT INN AND SUITES

10900 Crowne Point Drive, Cincinnati, 513-771-6888, 877-229-6668;
www.baymontinns.com

130 rooms. Complimentary breakfast. Pool. Pets accepted. $61-150

★★★★CINCINNATIAN HOTEL

601 Vine St., Cincinnati, 513-381-3000, 800-942-9000; www.cincinnatianhotel.com

Open since 1882, the Cincinnatian hotel was one of the first hotels in the world to have elevators and incandescent lighting; it is now listed on the National Register of Historic Places. The accommodations are lovingly maintained and incorporate modern technology, like Internet access and multiline telephones. Furnishings lean toward the contemporary, while some rooms feature balconies and fireplaces. The eight-story atrium of the Cricket Lounge serves afternoon tea and evening cocktails. The fine dining and impeccable service at the Palace Restaurant make it one of the top tables in town.

146 rooms. Restaurant, bar. Fitness center. Pets accepted. $151-250

★★COURTYARD CINCINNATI BLUE ASH

4625 Lake Forest Drive, Cincinnati, 513-733-4334, 800-321-2211; www.courtyard.com

Designed for business travelers but also family friendly; this stylish, affordable hotel is conveniently located near major highways and about 15 minutes from downtown. The casual lobby features plenty of overstuffed seating and a large flat-screen TV. The well-appointed guest rooms are spacious and wired for work needs.

149 rooms. Business center. Fitness center. Pool. $61-150

★★EMBASSY SUITES

4554 Lake Forest Drive, Blue Ash, 513-733-8900, 800-362-2779;
www.embassysuites.com

235 rooms. Restaurant, bar. Complimentary breakfast. Fitness center. Pool. $151-250

★★★HILTON CINCINNATI NETHERLAND PLAZA

35 W. Fifth St., Cincinnati, 513-421-9100, 800-445-8667; www.hilton.com

The Hilton Cincinnati Netherland Plaza is a showpiece of Art Deco design in the heart of the city. Listed on the National Register of Historic Places, this elegant hotel marries historic character with modern amenities. The hotel's Palm Court Restaurant is one of the city's most fashionable dining rooms.

561 rooms. Restaurant, bar. Business center. Fitness center. Pool. $151-250

★★HOLIDAY INN CINCINNATI EASTGATE

4501 Eastgate Blvd., Cincinnati, 513-752-4400, 800-465-4329; www.holiday-inn.com

247 rooms. Restaurant, bar. Business center. Fitness center. Pool. Pets accepted. $61-150

★★★HYATT REGENCY CINCINNATI

151 W. Fifth St., Cincinnati, 513-579-1234, 800-233-1234; www.cincinnati.hyatt.com

This well-appointed, moderately priced hotel is located across from the convention center and connected to the business district and a shopping mall by an enclosed skywalk. The bright and airy atrium lobby has a huge skylight and fountain. One restaurant serves breakfast and lunch buffets, while a sports bar offers pool tables and traditional bar food.

486 rooms. Restaurant, bar. Business center. Fitness center. Pool. $151-250

★★★MARRIOTT CINCINNATI AIRPORT

2395 Progress Drive, Hebron, Kentucky, 859-586-0166; www.marriott.com

This airport has a fitness center, indoor pool and rooms updated with plush beds and linens. Complimentary shuttle service to the airport is available 24 hours a day.

295 rooms. Restaurant. Business center. Fitness center. Pool. $151-250

★★★MARRIOTT CINCINNATI NORTH

6189 Muhlhauser Road, West Chester, 513-874-7335, 800-228-9290;
www.marriott.com

Located near Interstate 75 between Cincinnati and Dayton, this hotel is ideal for business travelers. Guest rooms and suites have traditional furniture, luxury bedding and 24-hour room service.

295 rooms. Restaurant, bar. Business center. Fitness center. Pool. $151-250

★★★MILLENNIUM HOTEL CINCINNATI

150 W. Fifth St., Cincinnati, 513-352-2100, 866-866-8086; www.millenniumhotels.com

Business travelers choose this downtown hotel for amenities like an onsite car rental desk and the enclosed skywalk leading to the convention center. Rooms are decorated with natural wood and glass furnishings and have ergonomic desk chairs. A poolside bar and grill livens up warmer months.

872 rooms. Restaurant, bar. Business center. Fitness center. Pool. Pets accepted. $61-150

★★VERNON MANOR HOTEL

400 Oak St., Cincinnati, 513-281-3300, 800-543-3999; www.vernon-manor.com

177 rooms. Restaurant, bar. Business center. Fitness center. Pets accepted. $61-150

★★★THE WESTIN CINCINNATI

21 E. Fifth Street, Cincinnati, 513-621-7700, 800-937-8461; www.westin.com

Overlooking the city's Fountain Square and within steps of restaurants, museums and other cultural attractions, this stylish 456-room hotel is connected to a shopping center and the convention center by an enclosed skywalk. Guest rooms feature subdued contemporary furnishings. The onsite restaurant serves American fare and the lounge offers pub food in a sports bar setting.

456 rooms. Restaurant, bar. Business center. Fitness center. Pool. Pets accepted. $151-250

WHERE TO EAT

★AGLAMESIS BROS

3046 Madison Road, Cincinnati, 513-531-5196; www.aglamesis.com

Deli. Lunch, dinner. Children's menu. $15 and under

★★★CELESTIAL

1071 Celestial St., Cincinnati, 513-241-4455; www.thecelestial.com

This restaurant's name could just as easily refer to its stunning view of the Ohio River and city as to its street address. Dining takes place in a clubby atmosphere of carved wood. Stop at the Incline Lounge to sip a cocktail and watch the sunset.

Steak. Dinner. Reservations recommended. Outdoor seating. Bar. $16-35

★CHRISTY'S AND LENHARDT'S

151 W. McMillan Ave., Cincinnati, 513-281-3600; www.christysandlenhardts.com

German, Hungarian. Lunch, dinner, late-night. Closed Sunday-Monday. Reservations recommended. Outdoor seating. Bar. $16-35

★★FERRARI'S LITTLE ITALY
7677 Goff Terrace, Madeira, 513-272-2220; www.ferrarilittleitaly.com
Italian. Lunch, dinner. Reservations recommended. Outdoor seating. Children's menu. Bar. $36-85

★★GERMANO'S
9415 Montgomery Road, Cincinnati, 513-794-1155; www.germanosrestaurant.com
Italian. Lunch, dinner. Closed Sunday-Monday. Reservations recommended. $36-85

★★GRAND FINALE
3 E. Sharon Road, Glendale, 513-771-5925; www.grandfinale.info
American. Lunch, dinner, Sunday brunch. Closed Monday. Reservations recommended. Outdoor seating. Children's menu. Bar. $36-85

★HOUSE OF TAM
889 W. Galbraith Road, Cincinnati, 513-729-5566
Chinese. Lunch, dinner. Closed Sunday. $16-35

★★IRON HORSE RESTAURANT
40 Village Square, Glendale, 513-772-3333; www.ironhorseinn.com
American. Lunch, dinner. Outdoor seating. Children's menu. Bar. $16-35

★★JEANRO
413 Vine St., Cincinnati, 513-621-1465; www.bistrojeanro.com
French. Lunch, dinner. Reservations recommended. Bar. $36-85

★LE BOXX CAFE
819 Vine St., Cincinnati, 513-721-5638; www.leboxxcafe.com
American. Lunch. Closed Saturday-Sunday. Bar. $15 and under

★MECKLENBURG GARDENS
302 E. University, Cincinnati, 513-221-5353; www.mecklenburgs.net
German. Lunch, dinner. Closed Sunday. Reservations recommended. Outdoor seating. Children's menu. Bar. $16-35

★★MONTGOMERY INN
9440 Montgomery Road, Montgomery, 513-791-3482; www.montgomeryinn.com
American. Lunch, dinner. Children's menu. Bar. $16-35

★★MONTGOMERY INN AT THE BOATHOUSE
925 Riverside Drive, Cincinnati, 513-721-7427; www.montgomeryinn.com
American. Lunch, dinner. Outdoor seating. Children's menu. Bar. $16-35

★★NATIONAL EXEMPLAR
6880 Wooster Pike, Mariemont, 513-271-2103; www.nationalexemplar.com
American. Breakfast, lunch, dinner. Reservations recommended. Children's menu. Bar. $16-35

★★NICOLA'S
1420 Sycamore St., Cincinnati, 513-721-6200; www.nicolasrestaurant.com
Italian. Dinner. Closed Sunday. Reservations recommended. Outdoor seating. Bar. $36-85

★★★ORCHIDS AT PALM COURT
35 W. Fifth St., Cincinnati, 513-421-9100; www.hilton.com
The Orchids at Palm Court, located in the Hilton Cincinnati Netherland Plaza, has an elegant dining room with friendly, accommodating service. Menu standouts include the phyllo venison wrapped in bacon. On Fridays and Saturdays, a jazz trio and pianist perform.
American. Dinner, Sunday brunch. Reservations recommended. Children's menu. Bar. $16-35

★★★THE PALACE
601 Vine St., Cincinnati, 513-381-3000, 800-942-9000; www.palacecincinnati.com
This elegant restaurant inside the Cincinnatian hotel is now under the direction of Alsatian chef Romuald Jung. The menu features traditional, French-influenced dishes such as rack of lamb with fava beans and fingerling potatoes, or prime ribeye with potato purée.
American. Breakfast, lunch, dinner. Closed Sunday. Reservations recommended. Children's menu. Bar. $36-85

★★★THE PHOENIX RESTAURANT
812 Race St., Cincinnati, 513-721-8901; www.thephx.com
Built in 1893, this traditional restaurant serves dinner in the wood-paneled President's Room, while the rest of the historic building, which is adorned with two elegant chandeliers, is used for weddings or special events. The menu features steaks and other classics like the grilled pork chop with walnut stuffing and sage beurre blanc.
Continental. Dinner. Closed Sunday-Tuesday. Reservations recommended. Bar. $36-85

★★★PRECINCT
311 Delta Ave., Cincinnati, 513-321-5454, 877-321-5454; www.jeffruby.com
This restaurant, housed in a former police precinct that was used from the 1900s to the 1940s, offers steakhouse classics—from aged Angus beef to the perfect rib eye broiled to perfection and seasoned with a secret spice mix. At night, the exterior of this historic building is bathed in neon light. Dishes such as steak Diane, fettuccine and Bananas Foster are prepared tableside.
Steak. Dinner. Reservations recommended. Bar. $86 and up

★★★PRIMAVISTA
810 Matson Place, Cincinnati, 513-251-6467; www.pvista.com
The view of Cincinnati from its floor-to-ceiling windows is one reason to dine at Primavista, but it's not the only one. A menu of creative but classic Italian fare including fresh seafood, meat and veal specialties as well as pizzas and pasta dishes are featured. Dishes include pine nut crusted salmon over fettuccine with pesto cream sauce and roasted tomatoes, filet mignon

broiled and served with calamari and linguine tossed in fresh cream, pancetta, egg and green peas.
Italian. Dinner. Reservations recommended. Bar. $36-85

CLEVELAND

See also Akron, Aurora, Beachwood, Kent, Lorian, Mentor, Oberlin

Ohio's second-largest city extends 50 miles east and north along the shore of Lake Erie and 25 miles south inland. It is a combination of industrial flats, spacious suburbs, wide principal streets and an informal spirit, due partially to its diverse population. Many nationalities have contributed to the city's growth—Poles, Italians, Croats, Slovaks, Serbs, Lithuanians, Germans, Irish, Romanians, Russians and Greeks. In the past, the various national groupsd-divided regionally, but this is less true today.

Cleveland's history is peppered with industrial giants—John D. Rockefeller, the Mathers of iron and shipping, Mark Hanna of steel and political fame, the Van Sweringens and others. The village, founded by Moses Cleaveland, profited from the combination of Great Lakes transportation and fertile farm land. At the time, northern Ohio was still almost entirely unoccupied, and growth was slow. Not until 1827, when the Ohio Canal was opened to join Lake Erie with the Ohio River, did the town start to expand. Incoming supplies of coal and iron ore jump-started a manufacturing industry. The boom era after World War I brought bedroom communities like Shaker Heights, one of the more affluent suburbs; the Terminal Tower Group of buildings downtown and the Group Plan, with civic buildings surrounding a central mall.

The layout of the city is systematic. All the main avenues lead to the Public Square Tower City Center where the Terminal Tower is located. The east-west dividing line is Ontario Street, which runs north and south through the square. Euclid Avenue is the main business street running through Cleveland and many of its suburbs. Many of the early buildings have been razed and replaced by planned urban architecture, including "Millionaire's Row" and the magnificent mansions on Euclid Avenue.

Sports is a favorite pastime here, whether it's Cleveland Browns football (so beloved the city sued to stop the team from leaving for Baltimore in the 1990s; the team still went, but the city kept the name and launched an expansion franchise in 1999), Indians baseball or Cavaliers basketball. In 1995, the Rock and Roll Hall of Fame opened on the city's lakefront in an I. M. Pei-designed building. This and new stadiums for all three sports teams continue to draw visitors to the city's downtown.

WHAT TO SEE
CLEVELAND BOTANICAL GARDEN

11030 E. Blvd., Cleveland, 216-721-1600; www.cbgarden.org

Meander through these aromatic herb, rose, perennial, wildflower, Japanese and reading gardens.
April-October, Monday-Saturday 10 a.m.-5 p.m., Sunday noon-5 p.m.;
November-March, Tuesday-Saturday 10 a.m.-5 p.m., Sunday noon-5 p.m.

CLEVELAND METROPARKS

4101 Fulton Parkway, Cleveland, 216-635-3200; www.clemetparks.com

Established in 1917, this park system circles the city with more than 20,000 acres of land in 14 reservations, their connecting parkways and the Cleveland Metroparks Zoo. Bike paths lace throughout the park, and driving through the heavily wooded areas is a favorite fall pastime. Also available are swimming, boating and fishing, picnic areas and play fields; hiking and bridle trails, stables; golf courses; tobogganing, sledding, skating and cross-country skiing areas; eight outdoor education facilities offer nature exhibits and programs.

CLEVELAND METROPARKS ZOO

3900 Wildlife Way, Cleveland, 216-661-6500; www.clemetzoo.com

The seventh-oldest zoo in the country; this zoo has more than 3,300 animals. Includes mammals, land and water birds; animals displayed in naturalized settings. More than 600 animals and 7,000 plants are featured in the 2-acre Rainforest exhibit.

Daily 10 a.m.-5 p.m.

CLEVELAND MUSEUM OF ART

11150 E. Blvd., Cleveland, 216-421-7340; www.clemusart.com

Extensive collections of approximately 30,000 works of art represent a wide range of history and culture. Included are arts of the Islamic Near East, the pre-Columbian Americas and European and Asian art; also African, Indian, American, ancient Roman and Egyptian art. Also check out frequent concerts, lectures, special exhibitions, films, and the onsite cafe.

Tuesday, Thursday, Saturday-Sunday 10 a.m.-5 p.m.; Wednesday, Friday 10 a.m.-9 p.m.

★
★
★ OHIO
★
★

CLEVELAND MUSEUM OF NATURAL HISTORY

1 Wade Oval, Cleveland, 216-231-4600, 800-317-9155; www.cmnh.org

Discover the dinosaurs, mammals, birds, geological specimens, and historic gems. There are also exhibits on prehistoric Ohio, North American native cultures, and ecology. Explore the Wood Garden, with live animals.

Monday-Saturday 10 a.m.-5 p.m., Wednesday until 10 p.m., Sunday noon-5 p.m.

155

CLEVELAND ORCHESTRA

Severance Hall, 11001 Euclid Ave., Cleveland, 216-231-1111;
www.clevelandorchestra.com

One of the world's finest orchestras. International soloists and guest conductors are featured each season. During summer months, the orchestra performs at Blossom Music Center, approximately 28 miles south via Interstate 71.

Mid-September-mid-May, Tuesday and Thursday-Sunday.

FREDERICK C. CRAWFORD AUTO-AVIATION MUSEUM

Magnolia Drive and East 108th, Cleveland, 216-721-5722; www.wrhs.org

This museum has an extensive collection of antique cars, planes, and 20th-century motorcycles and bicycles.

Monday-Saturday 10 a.m.-5 p.m., Sunday noon-5 p.m.

GREAT LAKES SCIENCE CENTER

601 Erieside Ave., Cleveland, 216-694-2000; www.greatscience.com

More than 400 hands-on exhibits explain scientific principles and topics specifically relating to the Great Lakes region. It also features an Omnimax domed theater.

Daily 10 a.m.-5 p.m.

PLAYHOUSE SQUARE CENTER

1501 Euclid Ave., Cleveland, 216-241-6000, 800-766-6048; www.playhousesquare.org

Five restored theaters form the nation's second-largest performing arts and entertainment center. Performances include theater, Broadway productions, popular and classical music, ballet, opera, children's theater and concerts. Show times vary.

ROCK AND ROLL HALL OF FAME AND MUSEUM

1 Key Plaza, Cleveland, 216-781-7625, 888-764-7625; www.rockhall.com

A striking composition of geometric shapes, this I. M. Pei-designed building is the permanent home of the Rock and Roll Hall of Fame. More than 50,000 square feet of exhibition areas explore rock's ongoing evolution and its impact on culture. Also check out the interactive database of rock and roll songs; videos; working studio with DJs conducting live broadcasts; and exhibits on rhythm and blues, soul, country, folk and blues music.

Daily 10 a.m.-5:30 p.m.

WHERE TO STAY

★★★BARICELLI INN

2203 Cornell Road, Cleveland, 216-791-6500; www.baricelli.com

This charming 1896 brownstone with individually decorated rooms is known for its superb restaurant, where the chef serves American cuisine with a European flare.

7 rooms. Complimentary breakfast. Restaurant. $151-250

★★★CLEVELAND AIRPORT MARRIOTT

4277 W. 150th St., Cleveland, 216-252-5333, 800-228-9290; www.marriott.com

This hotel is located near Cleveland Hopkins Airport and 10 miles from downtown. It is near tennis courts, golf courses and attractions.

371 rooms. Restaurant, bar. Fitness center. Pool. $151-250

★★★DOUBLETREE HOTEL CLEVELAND SOUTH

6200 Quarry Lane, Independence, 216-447-1300; www.doubletree1.hilton.com

A contemporary stay in a country setting, this hotel located just south of Cleveland includes an amphitheater, an indoor-outdoor pool, a fitness facility and Shula's Steak 2 Restaurant. Local attractions such as Progressive Field (formerly Jacob's Field) are just a short drive away.

193 rooms. Restaurant, bar. Fitness center. Pool. Business center. $61-150

★★★EMBASSY SUITES

1701 E. 12th St., Cleveland, 216-523-8000, 800-362-2779; www.embassysuites.com

Located in downtown Cleveland, this all-suite hotel is two blocks away from the Galleria and Playhouse Square and just seven blocks away from the Rock and Roll Hall of Fame.

268 rooms. Restaurant, bar. Complimentary breakfast. Business center. Fitness center. Pool. $151-250

★★★GLIDDEN HOUSE INN

1901 Ford Drive, Cleveland, 216-231-8900, 800-759-8358; www.gliddenhouse.com

With its location on the campus of Case Western Reserve University, this charming inn is close to the medical centers—including the Cleveland Clinic—and attractions of the school. The contemporary guest rooms have plasma TVs and luxury bedding.

60 rooms. Restaurant, bar. Business center. Fitness center. $61-150

★★HILTON GARDEN INN

1100 Carnegie Ave., Cleveland, 216-658-6400, 877-782-9444;
www.hiltongardeninn.com

240 rooms. Restaurant, bar. Business center. Fitness center. Pool. $61-150

★HOWARD JOHNSON CLEVELAND AIRPORT

16644 Snow Road, Brook Park, 216-676-5200, 800-446-4656;
www.howardjohnson.com

135 rooms. Complimentary breakfast. Fitness center. Pool. Pets accepted. $61-150

★★★HYATT REGENCY CLEVELAND AT THE ARCADE

420 Superior Ave., Cleveland, 216-575-1234, 800-233-1234; www.cleveland.hyatt.com

Attached to the 1890 Cleveland Arcade, one of America's first indoor shopping malls, this hotel has updated rooms featuring Portico bath products and luxury linens. The onsite-spa offers a complete menu of services.

293 rooms. Restaurant, bar. Business center. Fitness center. $61-150

★★★INTERCONTINENTAL HOTEL & CONFERENCE CENTER

9801 Carnegie Ave., Cleveland, 216-707-4100, 888-424-6835;
www.intercontinental.com

This hotel has rooms with flatscreen TVs, minibars, easy chairs and Audley bath amenities. There's a state-of-the-art fitness facility and well-equipped business center, and the friendly staff will arrange everything from laundry and dry cleaning to babysitting. The Rock and Roll Hall of Fame, Cleveland Art Museum and Cleveland Clinic are all nearby.

299 rooms. Restaurant, bar. Business center. Fitness center. Spa. $251-350

★★RADISSON HOTEL CLEVELAND AIRPORT

25070 Country Club Blvd., North Olmsted, 440-734-5060, 800-333-3333;
www.radisson.com

Though this hotel is actually located about a 10-minute drive from the airport, it still caters to business travelers with its high-speed Internet access, spacious work areas and upgraded plush beds. The Great Northern Mall and its many shops and restaurants are nearby.

140 rooms. Restaurant, bar. Fitness center. Pool. Pets accepted. $61-150

★★★★THE RITZ-CARLTON, CLEVELAND

1515 W. Third St., Cleveland, 216-623-1300, 866-372-7868; www.ritzcarlton.com

Adjacent to Cleveland's Tower City Center and close to the Cleveland Indians' Progressive Field (formerly Jacobs Field), this elegant hotel offers downtown visitors a place to stay in style. The guest rooms, with city and water views, are luxuriously appointed, from the marble-clad bathrooms to the plush terry robes. Even pets are pampered here, with cookies upon check-in, a personalized water bowl and pet room-service menu; walking service is available for a fee. All-day dining at Muse features a seafood-heavy menu dotted with updated comfort-food like truffled macaroni and cheese. By day, the Lobby Lounge serves afternoon tea, while in the evening live entertainment attracts hotel guests and locals alike.

206 rooms. Restaurant, bar. Business center. Fitness center. Pool. Spa. Pets accepted. $251-350

★★SHERATON INDEPENDENCE HOTEL

5300 Rockside Road, Independence, 216-524-0700, 800-325-3535;
www.sheratoninn.com

179 rooms. Restaurant, bar. Business center. Fitness center. Pool. Tennis. Pets accepted. $61-150

★★★WYNDHAM CLEVELAND AT PLAYHOUSE SQUARE

1260 Euclid Ave., Cleveland, 216-615-7500, 800-996-3426;
www.wyndhamcleveland.com

The city's historic theaters are located just around the corner from this downtown hotel. Rooms are spacious with plenty of work space and feature Herman Miller Aeron desk chairs.

205 rooms. Restaurant, bar. Fitness center. Pool. $61-150

WHERE TO EAT

★★★BARICELLI INN

2203 Cornell Road, Cleveland, 216-791-6500; www.baricelli.com

Located in University Circle's Little Italy neighborhood, this inn and Italian restaurant are perched on a bluff in a large, turn-of-the-century brownstone mansion. The Little Italy location delivers romantic, old-world charm, and the seasonal menu features thoughtful preparations of local ingredients.

Continental. Dinner. Closed Sunday. Outdoor seating. $16-35

★CABIN CLUB

30651 Detroit Road, Westlake, 440-899-7111; www.hrcleveland.com

Seafood, Steak. Lunch, dinner. Reservations recommended. Children's menu. Bar. $36-85

★CAFE SAUSALITO

1301 E. Ninth St., Cleveland, 216-696-2233; www.cafesausalito.com

Seafood. American. Lunch, dinner. Closed Saturday-Sunday. $16-35

★★DON'S LIGHTHOUSE GRILLE

8905 Lake Ave., Cleveland, 216-961-6700; www.donslighthouse.com

American, seafood. Lunch, dinner. Bar. $16-35

★GREAT LAKES BREWING CO.
2516 Market Ave., Cleveland, 216-771-4404; www.greatlakesbrewing.com
American. Lunch, dinner. Closed Sunday. Outdoor seating. Children's menu.
Bar. $16-35

★GUARINO'S
12309 Mayfield Road, Cleveland, 216-231-3100; www.guarinoscleveland.blogspot.com
Italian, American. Lunch, dinner. Reservations recommended. Outdoor seating. Children's menu. Bar. $16-35

★JOHN Q'S STEAKHOUSE
55 Public Square, Cleveland, 216-861-0900; www.johnqssteakhouse.com
Steak. Lunch, dinner. Outdoor seating. Children's menu. Bar. $36-85

★★★JOHNNY'S BAR
3164 Fulton Road, Cleveland, 216-281-0055; www.johnnyscleveland.com
Johnny's Bar has consistently been named the No.1 restaurant in Cleveland.
It is listed in the Zagat Survey Guide as one of the top restaurants in America.
Additionally, the restaurant is a recipient of the Wine Spectator's Award of
Excellence and is recognized by DiRoNA as a distinguished fine dining
establishment. Patrons can expect large portions, a variety of dishes and a
selection of over 850 fine wines.
Italian. Lunch, dinner. Closed Sunday. Reservations recommended. Bar.
$36-85

★LEMON GRASS
2179 Lee Road, Cleveland Heights, 216-321-0210; www.lemongrassrestaurant.net
Thai. Lunch, dinner. Outdoor seating. Bar. $16-35

★★★MORTON'S, THE STEAKHOUSE
1600 W. Second St., Cleveland, 216-621-6200; www.mortons.com
This branch of the national steakhouse chain offers more than 10 different
cuts of perfectly prepared steaks and plenty of classics from Caesar salad to
creamed spinach to go with them. Traditional desserts such as thick, creamy
cheesecake and warm apple pie complete the experience.
Steak. Dinner. Bar. $36-85

★PLAYERS ON MADISON
14523 Madison Ave., Lakewood, 216-226-5200; www.playersonmadison.com
Italian. Dinner, Sunday brunch. Bar. $16-35

★★★SANS SOUCI
24 Public Square, Cleveland, 216-696-5600; www.sanssoucicleveland.com
Fine cuisine is served in this comfortable dining room, which has exposed
beams and a stone hearth. This Renaissance hotel space is sectioned into
intimate rooms where classic cooking is served.
Mediterranean. Dinner. Bar. $36-85

COLUMBUS

See also Lancaster, Newark, Springfield

Columbus was created to be the capital of Ohio. The streets here are attractive, broad and tree-lined and are the perfect setting for the nation's largest public university, Ohio State University.

With its more than 50,000 students, Ohio State influences much of what happens in Columbus, as does the state government. The people of Columbus are civic-minded, sports-minded and cultured. The city has more than 1,130 churches and congregations and 12 colleges and universities.

WHAT TO SEE
COLUMBUS MUSEUM OF ART

480 E. Broad St., Columbus, 614-221-6801; www.columbusmuseum.org
Collections focus on 19th- and 20th-century European and American paintings, sculptures, works on paper and decorative arts; contemporary sculpture; 16th- and 17th-century Dutch and Flemish Masters. Galleries are arranged chronologically.
Tuesday-Sunday.

OHIO STATE CAPITOL

High and Broad streets, Columbus, 614-728-2695; www.statehouse.state.oh.us
This capitol building has a group of bronze statues by Levi T. Scofield at its northwest corner that depict Ohio soldiers and statesmen under Roman matron Cornelia. Her words, "These are my jewels," refer to Grant, Sherman, Sheridan, Stanton, Garfield, Hayes and Chase, who stand below her. There's an observation window on 40th floor of State Office Tower Building, across from the rotunda.
Daily.

OPERA COLUMBUS

Palace Theatre, 117 Naghten, Columbus, 614-469-0939; www.operacolumbus.org
There is English translation projected onto screen above the stage.
October-May.

WHERE TO STAY
★BEST WESTERN FRANKLIN PARK SUITES-POLARIS

2045 Polaris Parkway, Columbus, 614-396-5100, 800-528-1234; www.bestwestern.com
64 rooms. Bar. Complimentary breakfast. Business center. Fitness center. Pool. $61-150

★BEST WESTERN SUITES

1133 Evans Way Court, Columbus, 614-870-2378, 888-870-2378;
www.bestwestern.com
66 rooms. Complimentary breakfast. Fitness center. Pool. $61-150

★★CLARION HOTEL DUBLIN

600 Metro Place N., Dublin, 614-764-2200; www.crowneplaza.com
217 rooms. Restaurant, bar. Fitness center. Pool. Pets accepted. $61-150

★★★THE BLACKWELL

2110 Tuttle Park Place, Columbus, 614-247-4000, 866-247-4003;
www.theblackwell.com

Talk about higher learning: This hotel isn't near a college, it's on the campus of Ohio State University. The Blackwell features simply decorated, comfortable rooms with pillow-top mattresses and plush comforters on the beds, and good-sized bathrooms. The hotel also houses a conference center.

151 rooms. Restaurant, bar. Business center. $151-250

★★★COLUMBUS MARRIOTT NORTH

6500 Doubletree Ave., Columbus, 614-885-1885, 800-228-9290; www.marriott.com

This hotel is situated close to such attractions as the Polaris Amphitheater, Columbus Zoo and Center of Science and Industry.

300 rooms. Restaurant, bar. Business center. Fitness center. Pool. $61-150

★★COURTYARD COLUMBUS DOWNTOWN

35 W. Spring St., Columbus, 614-228-3200, 800-321-2211; www.marriott.com

149 rooms. Restaurant, bar. Fitness center. Pool. $61-150

★★★CROWNE PLAZA

33 E. Nationwide Blvd., Columbus, 614-461-4100, 800-227-6963;
www.crowneplaza.com

Connected to the Columbus Convention Center, this hotel is perfectly located near the city's top attractions. With a convenient shuttle service, guests are just minutes away from downtown.

377 rooms. Restaurant, bar. Business center. Fitness center. Pool. $61-150

★★EMBASSY SUITES

2700 Corporate Exchange Drive, Columbus, 614-890-8600, 800-362-2779;
www.embassysuites.com

This hotel, with a beautiful atrium setting, is perfect for guests who want extra space and comfort. With its two-room suites, guests can also enjoy a complimentary breakfast, an evening reception to unwind and much more.

221 rooms. Restaurant, bar. Complimentary breakfast. Business center. Fitness center. Pool. $61-150

★FAIRFIELD INN & SUITES

3031 Olentangy River Road, Columbus, 614-267-1111, 800-228-2800;
www.fairfieldinn.com

163 rooms. Restaurant, bar. Complimentary breakfast. $61-150

★★★HYATT ON CAPITOL SQUARE

75 E. State St., Columbus, 614-228-1234, 800-233-1234; www.hyatt.com

This hotel is in the downtown area across from Capitol Park and connected to the Columbus City Center shopping and historic Ohio Theater. The health club overlooks the State Capitol.

400 rooms. Restaurant, bar. Business center. Fitness center. $151-250

★★★HYATT REGENCY COLUMBUS

350 N. High St., Columbus, 614-463-1234, 800-233-1234; www.hyatt.com
Connected to the Columbus Convention Center, this hotel is conveniently located for both business and leisure travel. The luxurious guest suites are spacious. The hotel also houses a deli, café and 63,000 square feet of meeting space.
631 rooms. Restaurant, bar. Business center. Fitness center. Pool. $151-250

★★★THE LOFTS

55 E. Nationwide Blvd., Columbus, 614-461-2663, 800-735-6387; www.55lofts.com
Located in downtown Columbus, the 100-year-old warehouse that houses this hotel has been energized with contemporary design. Clean, simple lines and furnishings create an uncluttered look in the guest rooms, while Frette linens and Aveda bath products make everything more comfortable.
44 rooms. Restaurant, bar. Complimentary breakfast. Fitness center. Pool.
$151-250

★★★MARRIOTT COLUMBUS NORTHWEST

5605 Paul G. Blazer Memorial Parkway, Dublin, 614-791-1000, 800-228-9290;
www.marriott.com
This hotel is located in one of Columbus' fastest-growing entertainment and business districts. Nearby attractions include the Columbus Zoo, Murfield Village and Golf Club and Anheuser Busch Brewery.
303 rooms. Restaurant, bar. Business center. Fitness center. Pool. $61-150

WHERE TO EAT
★★ALEX'S BISTRO

4681 Reed Road, Columbus, 614-457-8887
French. Lunch, dinner. Closed Sunday. Reservations recommended. Bar.
$16-35

★★BEXLEY'S MONK

2232 E. Main St., Bexley, 614-239-6665; www.bexleysmonk.com
Continental. Lunch, dinner. Bar. $36-85

★CAP CITY DINER-GRANDVIEW

1299 Olentangy River Road, Columbus, 614-291-3663; www.cameronmitchell.com
American. Lunch, dinner, Sunday brunch. Outdoor seating. Children's menu.
Bar. $16-35

★★★HANDKE'S CUISINE

520 S. Front St., Columbus, 614-621-2500; www.chefhandke.com
Located in the brewery district, this restaurant is set in a former 19th-century brewery, with three dining rooms and vaulted ceilings. The menu includes dishes like grilled tenderloin with morels, potatoes and French green beans.
International. Dinner. Closed Sunday. Reservations recommended. $36-85

★★HUNAN HOUSE

2350 E. Dublin-Granville Road, Columbus, 614-895-3330
Chinese. Lunch, dinner. Bar. $16-35

★★HUNAN LION
2038 Bethel Road, Columbus, 614-459-3933
Chinese, Thai. Lunch, dinner. Bar. $16-35

★KATZINGER'S DELICATESSEN
475 S. Third St., Columbus, 614-228-3354; www.katzingers.com
Deli. Breakfast, lunch, dinner. Outdoor seating. Children's menu. $15 and
under

★★★L'ANTIBES
772 N. High St., Columbus, 614-291-1666; www.lantibes.com
Sophisticated French fare served in an unpretentious atmosphere defines dining at this small restaurant. The sweetbreads are the talk of the town.
French. Dinner. Closed Sunday-Monday; also last week in January and one
week in July. Reservations recommended. $36-85

★★LINDEY'S
169 E. Beck St., Columbus, 614-228-4343; www.lindeys.com
American. Lunch, dinner, brunch. Reservations recommended. Outdoor
seating. Children's menu. Bar. $16-35

★★★MORTON'S, THE STEAKHOUSE
280 N. High St., Columbus, 614-464-4442; www.mortons.com
For the freshest lobster and steaks, this branch of the national chain is a sure
bet. Professional service and a club-like setting make for a seamless dining
experience at Morton's.
Steak. Dinner. Reservations recommended. Bar. $36-85

★OLD MOHAWK
819 Mohawk St., Columbus, 614-444-7204; www.theoldmohawk.com
American. Lunch, dinner. Bar. $16-35

★★★REFECTORY
1092 Bethel Road, Columbus, 614-451-9774; www.therefectoryrestaurant.com
Housed in a historic church, this fine French restaurant is known as one of
the area's most romantic. For a great deal, try chef Richard Blondin's three-
course bistro menu served Monday through Thursday in the lounge or on the
outdoor patio.
French. Dinner. Closed Sunday. Reservations recommended. Outdoor seating. Bar. $36-85

★★RIGSBY'S CUISINE VOLATILE
698 N. High St., Columbus, 614-461-7888
Italian. Lunch, dinner. Closed Sunday. Reservations recommended. Bar.
$16-35

★★RJ SNAPPERS
700 N. High St., Columbus, 614-280-1070; www.rjsnappers.com
Seafood. Dinner. Reservations recommended. Children's menu. Bar. $16-35

★★SCHMIDT'S SAUSAGE HAUS
240 E. Kossuth St., Columbus, 614-444-6808; www.schmidthaus.com
German. Lunch, dinner. Children's menu. Bar. $16-35

★★TONY'S ITALIAN RISTORANTE
16 W. Beck St., Columbus, 614-224-8669; www.tonysitalian.net
Italian. Lunch, dinner. Closed Sunday. Reservations recommended. Outdoor seating. Bar. $16-35

DAYTON

See also Lebanon, Mason, Miamisburg, Springfield

Dayton is located on a fork of the Miami River, which curves through the city from the northeast, uniting with the Stillwater River half a mile above the Main Street Bridge. The Mad River flows from the east and Wolf Creek from the west to join the others four blocks away. Dayton has 28 bridges crossing these rivers.

The first flood, in 1805, started a progression of higher levees. In 1913, a disastrous flood took 361 lives and property worth $100 million and inspired a flood-control plan effective to date.

Though the city itself can seem like something of a ghost town these days, with most of the action happening in the suburbs, plenty of famous residents have put the city on the map, including Orville and Wilbur Wright, inventors of the airplane.

WHAT TO SEE
FORT ANCIENT STATE MEMORIAL
6123 State Route 350, Oregonia, 513-932-4421; www.ohiohistory.org
Fort Ancient is one of the largest and most impressive prehistoric earthworks of its kind in the United States. The Fort Ancient earthworks were built by the Hopewell people between 100 BC and AD 500. This site occupies an elevated plateau overlooking the Little Miami River Valley. Its massive earthen walls, more than 23 feet high in places, enclose an area of 100 acres. Within this area are earth mounds once used as calendar markers and other archaeological features. Relics from the site and the nearby prehistoric Native American village are displayed in Fort Ancient Museum, hiking trails, picnic facilities.
March-November, daily.

WHERE TO STAY
★★★CROWNE PLAZA
33 E. Fifth St., Dayton, 937-224-0800, 800-227-6963; www.crowneplaza.com
Located in the business district, this hotel is adjacent to the convention center and near many local attractions. The rooftop restaurant, with views of the city, serves dinner nightly.
291 rooms. Restaurant, bar. Fitness center. Pool. $61-150

★★DOUBLETREE GUEST SUITES
300 Prestige Place, Dayton, 937-436-2400, 800-222-8733; www.doubletree.com
137 rooms. Restaurant, bar. Fitness center. Pool. Pets accepted. $61-150

★FAIRFIELD INN

6960 Miller Lane, Dayton, 937-898-1120, 800-228-2800; www.fairfieldinn.com
131 rooms. Complimentary breakfast. Pool. $61-150

★★★MARRIOTT DAYTON

1414 S. Patterson Blvd., Dayton, 937-223-1000, 800-450-8625; www.marriott.com
Rooms at this hotel, located just outside downtown, have been updated with plush new beds and luxury bedding. Fitness and business centers are just a few of the amenities.
399 rooms. Restaurant, bar. Business center. Fitness center. Pool. Pets accepted. $61-150

WHERE TO EAT
★AMBER ROSE

1400 Valley St., Dayton, 937-228-2511; www.theamberrose.com
American, European. Lunch, dinner. Closed Sunday. Bar. $16-35

★★B. R. SCOTESE'S

1375 N. Fairfield Road, Beavercreek, 937-431-1350
Italian. Dinner. Closed Sunday. Children's menu. Bar. $16-35

★BARNSIDER

5202 N. Main St., Dayton, 937-277-1332; www.barnsider-restaurant.com
Steak. Dinner. Children's menu. Bar. $16-35

★★BRAVO! ITALIAN KITCHEN

2770, Miamisburg Centerville Road, Centerville, 937-439-1294; www.bestitalianusa.com
Italian. Lunch, dinner. Children's menu. Bar. $16-35

★CHINA COTTAGE

6290 Far Hills Ave., Dayton, 937-434-2622; www.chinacottagerestaurant.com
Chinese. Lunch, dinner. Bar. $16-35

★★EL MESON

903 E. Dixie Drive, West Carrolltown, 937-859-8229; www.elmeson.net
Latin American, Spanish. Lunch (Monday-Friday), dinner. Closed Sunday; also first three weeks in January. Reservations recommended. Outdoor seating. Bar. $16-35

★★J. ALEXANDER'S

7970 Washington Village Drive, Dayton, 937-435-4441; www.jalexanders.com
American. Lunch, dinner. Children's menu. Bar. $16-35

★★JAY'S

225 E. Sixth St., Dayton, 937-222-2892; www.jays.com
Seafood. Dinner. Children's menu. Bar. $16-35

★★★L'AUBERGE
4120 Far Hills Ave., Dayton, 937-299-5536; www.laubergedayton.com
For more than 20 years, serious lovers of classic French fare have dined at L'Auberge. Owner Josef Reif has succeeded in creating an elegant restaurant filled with flowers. The food spotlights seasonal ingredients of the region, prepared with a light, classic French hand.
French, Seafood. Lunch (Monday-Friday), dinner. Closed Sunday. Outdoor seating. Jacket required. Bar. $36-85

★★LINCOLN PARK GRILLE
580 Lincoln Park Blvd., Dayton, 937-293-6293
American. Lunch, dinner. Closed Sunday. Outdoor seating. Bar. $16-35

★★OAKWOOD CLUB
2414 Far Hills Ave., Oakwood, 937-293-6973; www.oakwoodclub.com
Seafood, Steak. Dinner. Closed Sunday. Bar. $16-35

★★PINE CLUB
1926 Brown St., Dayton, 937-228-5371; www.thepineclub.com
Steak. Dinner. Closed Sunday. Children's menu. Bar. $16-35

DELAWARE
See also Columbus, Marion, Mount Vernon
Delaware, on the Olentangy River, is a college town, trading center for farmers and site of diversified industry. The area was chosen by Native Americans as a campsite because of its mineral springs. The Mansion house—a famous sulphur-spring resort built in 1833—is now Elliot hall, the first building of Ohio Wesleyan University. There is a legend that President Rutherford B. Hayes (a native of Delaware) proposed to his wife, Lucy Webb, one of the school's first coeds, at the sulphur spring.

WHERE TO EAT
★BRANDING IRON
1400 Stratford Road, Delaware, 740-363-1846
American, Steak. Dinner, Sunday brunch. Closed Monday; also first two weeks in August. Children's menu. Bar. $16-35

★BUN'S OF DELAWARE
14 W. Winter St., Delaware, 740-363-3731
American. Lunch, dinner. Children's menu. Bar. $16-35

EAST LIVERPOOL
See also Steubenville
Located where Ohio, Pennsylvania and West Virginia meet on the Ohio River, East Liverpool was called Fawcett's Town after its first settler arrived until 1860. Its clay deposits determined its destiny as a pottery center; everything from dinnerware to brick is produced here.

GRANVILLE

See also Columbus, Newark

Founded in 1805 by settlers who moved here from Granville, Massachusetts and Granville, Connecticut, this city retains a classic small-town American charm.

WHERE TO EAT
★★★BUXTON INN DINING ROOM

313 E. Broadway, Granville, 740-587-0001; www.buxtoninn.com

This restaurant serves classic dishes like porterhouse steaks or salmon with lemon caper sauce. The tavern serves a more casual menu of bar favorites like burgers or French onion soup.

American, French. Lunch, dinner, Sunday brunch. Closed Monday. Bar. $16-35

KENT

See also Akron, Aurora, Cleveland

Home to Kent State University, this small town outside Akron is a typical college town with plenty of restaurants and boutiques catering to the many students who attend the school.

WHERE TO STAY
★★UNIVERSITY INN

540 S. Water St., Kent, 330-678-0123; www.kentuniversityinn.com

107 rooms. Restaurant. Pool. $61-150

WHERE TO EAT
★★PUFFERBELLY LTD.

152 Franklin Ave., Kent, 330-673-1771; www.pufferbellyltd.com

American. Lunch, dinner, Sunday brunch. Reservations recommended. Children's menu. Bar. $16-35

LANCASTER

See also Columbus, Newark

Centrally located in the middle of the state, this city of 35,000 has a well-preserved historic downtown. General William Tecumsah Sherman, the famed union Civil War leader, was born in Lancaster.

WHERE TO STAY
★★★GLENLAUREL

14940 Mount Olive Road, Rockbridge, 740-385-4070, 800-809-7378;
www.glenlaurel.com

This Scottish country inn is located on a 140-acre estate and has a series of waterfalls, a private gorge and 50-foot rock cliffs on its grounds.

16 rooms. Restaurant. Complimentary breakfast. No children under 13. $251-350

WHERE TO EAT
★★★SHAW'S
123 N. Broad St., Lancaster, 740-654-1842, 800-654-2477; www.shawsinn.com
This charming restaurant is located in historic Lancaster. The menu features regional specials from Southwestern to country French. Fresh fish is flown in from Boston, and tangy ribs and steaks are cooked to perfection.
Continental. Lunch, dinner. Outdoor seating. Bar. $16-35

LEBANON
See also Cincinnati, Dayton, Mason
Some of the early settlers around Lebanon were Shakers who contributed much to the town's culture and economy. Though their community, Union Village, was sold more than 50 years ago and is now a retirement home, local interest in the Shakers and their beliefs still thrives.

WHERE TO STAY
★★★GOLDEN LAMB
27 S. Broadway, Lebanon, 513-932-5065; www.froglegking.com, www.goldenlamb.com
This national historic inn, built in 1803, has an outstanding collection of authentic shaker antiques, many of which are used daily in the dining room.
18 rooms. Restaurant, bar. Complimentary breakfast. $61-150

WHERE TO EAT
★★GOLDEN LAMB RESTAURANT
27 S. Broadway, Lebanon, 513-932-5065; www.goldenlamb.com
American. Lunch, dinner. Children's menu. Bar. $16-35

★★HOUSTON INN
4026 Highway, 42 S., Lebanon, 513-398-7377; www.froglegking.com
American. Lunch, dinner. Closed Monday; late December-early January. Children's menu. Bar. $16-35

MANSFIELD
See also Mount Vernon, Wooster
A pioneer log blockhouse, built as protection against Native Americans during the War of 1812, still stands in South Park in the city's western section. Named for Jared Mansfield, U.S. Surveyor General, this is a diversified industrial center 75 miles southwest of Cleveland. John Chapman, better known as Johnny Appleseed, lived and traveled in Richland County for many years. Pulitzer Prize–winning novelist Louis Bromfield was born here and later returned to conduct agricultural research at his 914-acre Malabar Farm.

WHERE TO STAY
★COMFORT INN
500 N. Trimble Road, Mansfield, 419-529-1000, 800-424-6423; www.comfortinn.com
114 rooms. Bar. Complimentary breakfast. Pool. Pets accepted. $61-150

★★HOLIDAY INN

116 Park Ave. West, Mansfield, 419-525-6000, 800-465-4329; www.holiday-inn.com
139 rooms. Restaurant, bar. Fitness center. Pool. $61-150

MARIETTA

See also Newark
General Rufus Putnam's New England flotilla, arriving at the junction of the Muskingum and Ohio Rivers for western land-buying purposes, founded Marietta, the oldest settlement in Ohio. Its name is a tribute to Queen Marie Antoinette who offered French assistance to the American Revolution. Most of the landmarks are along the east side of the Muskingum River. Front Street is approximately the eastern boundary of the first stockade, which was called Picketed Point. Later, the fortification called Campus Martius was erected and housed General Putnam, Governor Arthur St. Clair and other public officials.

One of the most important Ohio River ports in steamboat days, Marietta is now a beautiful tree-filled town and the home of Marietta College.

WHERE TO STAY
★COMFORT INN

700 Pike St., Marietta, 740-374-8190, 800-424-6423; www.comfortinn.com
120 rooms. Restaurant, bar. Complimentary breakfast. Fitness center. Pool. Pets accepted. $61-150

★★HOLIDAY INN

701 Pike St., Marietta, 740-374-9660, 800-465-4329; www.holiday-inn.com
109 rooms. Restaurant, bar. Pool. $61-150

★★LAFAYETTE HOTEL

101 Front St., Marietta, 740-373-5522, 800-331-9336; www.lafayettehotel.com
77 rooms. Restaurant, bar. Pets accepted. $61-150

WHERE TO EAT
★★★THE GUN ROOM

101 Front St., Marietta, 740-373-5522; www.lafayettehotel.com
The traditional American menu at this Lafayette hotel restaurant is as much a draw as the room's ornate, 19th-century riverboat décor and antique gun collection. The adjacent Riverview Lounge offers great Ohio River views. American, Seafood. Breakfast, lunch, dinner, Sunday brunch. Children's menu. Bar. $36-85

MARION

See also Columbus
Both agricultural and industrial, Marion's growth was influenced by the Huber Manufacturing Company, which introduced the steam shovel in 1874. Marion is also the center of a major popcorn-producing area. Its best-known citizen was Warren G. Harding, owner and publisher of the Star. Later, he became a state senator, lieutenant governor and 29th president of the United States.

WHAT TO SEE
PRESIDENT WARREN G. HARDING HOME AND MUSEUM

380 Mount Vernon Ave., Marion, 740-387-9630, 800-600-6894

Built during Harding's courtship with Florence Mabel Kling, this was the site of their marriage in 1891. Harding administered much of his 1920 "front porch campaign" for presidency from the front of the house. The museum, at the rear of the house, was once used as the campaign's press headquarters. June-August, Wednesday-Sunday; April-May and September-October, Saturday-Sunday.

WHERE TO STAY
★COMFORT INN

256 Jamesway, Marion, 740-389-5552, 800-424-6423; www.comfortinn.com

56 rooms. Complimentary breakfast. Pool. Pets accepted. $61-150

MASON

See also Cincinnati, Dayton, Hamilton, Lebanon

This Cinncinatti suburb is the home of the vast amusement park Kings Island, which is known for its cutting-edge roller coasters.

WHAT TO SEE
PARAMOUNT'S KINGS ISLAND

6300 Kings Island Drive, Mason, 513-754-5700, 800-288-0808; www.pki.com

Premier seasonal family theme park. Facility includes 350 acres with more than 100 rides and attractions, such as the outer limits thrill ride and flight of fear, an indoor roller coaster.
Late May-early September, daily; mid-April-late May, Friday-Sunday; early September-October, select weekends.

WHERE TO STAY
★★★KINGS ISLAND RESORT & CONFERENCE CENTER

5691 Kings Island Drive, Mason, 513-398-0115, 800-727-3050;
www.kingsislandresort.com

Located across the street from Paramount's Kings Island theme park, resort offers 13,000 square feet of meeting space and various recreational facilities. Visit the Main Street Grill for the weekend prime rib buffet.
284 rooms. Restaurant, bar. Fitness center. Pool. Tennis. $61-150

★★★MARRIOTT CINCINNATI NORTHEAST

9664 Mason-Montgomery Road, Mason, 513-459-9800, 800-228-9290;
www.marriott.com

This hotel is ideal for both business travelers and visitors to nearby Kings Island. Other local attractions include the Beach Waterpark and the Golf Center at Kings Island.
302 rooms. Restaurant, bar. Business center. Fitness center. Pool. $61-150

MENTOR

See also Cleveland

Site of the first Lake County settlement, Mentor was once an agricultural center. James A. Garfield lived here before his election as U.S. president. The town is now a popular commuter community for those who work in Cleveland.

WHAT TO SEE
LAWNFIELD JAMES A. GARFIELD NATIONAL HISTORIC SITE
8095 Mentor Ave., Mentor, 440-255-8722; www.nps.gov-jaga
This was the 20th president's last house before the White House. It includes two floors of original furnishings and a memorial library containing his books and desk. On the grounds are his campaign office, carriage house and picnic area. Daily.

WHERE TO STAY
★★RADISSON HOTEL & SUITES CLEVELAND-EASTLAKE
35000 Curtis Blvd., Eastlake, 440-953-8000, 800-333-3333; www.radisson.com
126 rooms. Restaurant, bar. Business center. Fitness center. Pool. $61-150

WHERE TO EAT
★★MOLINARI'S
8900 Mentor Ave., Mentor, 440-974-2750; www.molinaris.com
Italian. Lunch, dinner. Closed Sunday-Monday. Bar. $16-35

MIAMISBURG
See also Dayton
Located near Dayton, this city is home to large corporations such as LexisNexis. The Miamisburg Mound, a large conical structure attributed to the Adena culture can be found here.

WHERE TO STAY
★★COURTYARD DAYTON SOUTH/MALL
100 Prestige Plaza, Miamisburg, 937-433-3131, 800-321-2211; www.courtyard.com
146 rooms. Restaurant, bar. Business center. Fitness center. Pool. $61-150

★★HOLIDAY INN
31 Prestige Plaza Drive, Miamisburg, 937-434-8030, 800-465-4329; www.holiday-inn.com
195 rooms. Restaurant, bar. Fitness center. Pool. Pets accepted. $61-150

WHERE TO EAT
★BULLWINKLE'S TOP HAT BISTRO
19 N. Main St., Miamisburg, 937-859-7677; www.usbistroco.com
American. Lunch, dinner. Children's menu. Bar. $16-35

MILAN
See also Oberlin, Sandusky
Settlers from Connecticut founded Milan, building houses with the hallmarks of New England architecture. A canal connecting the town with Lake Erie was built in 1839, making Milan one of the largest shipping centers in the Midwest at that time. The town is the birthplace of inventor Thomas Edison.

WHAT TO SEE
THOMAS A. EDISON BIRTHPLACE MUSEUM

9 Edison Drive, Milan, 419-499-2135; www.tomedison.org

This is the two-story redbrick house where the inventor Thomas Edison spent his first seven years. Contains some original furnishings, inventions and memorabilia. Guided tours.

April-October, Tuesday-Sunday; February-March and November-December, Wednesday-Sunday; hours vary by month.

WHERE TO STAY
★COMFORT INN

11020 Milan Road, Milan, 419-499-4681, 800-424-6423; www.comfortinn.com

101 rooms. Complimentary breakfast. Pool $61-150

MOUNT VERNON

See also Newark

Descendants of the first settlers from Virginia, Maryland, New Jersey and Pennsylvania still live in this town. The seat of Knox County, Mount Vernon is in the largest sheep-raising county east of the Mississippi.

Johnny Appleseed owned two lots in the original village plot at the south end of Main Street. Daniel Decatur Emmett, author and composer of "Dixie," was born here. Many buildings in town feature Colonial-style architecture.

WHERE TO STAY
★★HISTORIC CURTIS INN ON THE SQUARE

12 Public Square, Mount Vernon, 740-397-4334; www.historiccurtisinn.com

72 rooms. Restaurant, bar. Pets accepted. $61-150

★★★WHITE OAK INN

29683 Walhonding Road, Danville, 740-599-6107, 877-908-5923;
www.whiteoakinn.com

Enjoy the peace and quiet at this inn, which is located in a turn-of-the-century farmhouse with original white oak woodwork. Breakfast and dinner are served daily.

10 rooms. Complimentary breakfast. No chidren under 13. $151-250

NEW PHILADELPHIA

See also Canton

New Philadelphia, the seat of Tuscarawas County, and its neighbor Dover still reflect the early influences of the German-Swiss who came here from Pennsylvania. Some of the earliest town lots in New Philadelphia were set aside for German schools.

WHERE TO STAY
★★★ATWOOD LAKE RESORT AND CONFERENCE CENTER

2650 Lodge Road, New Philadelphia, 330-735-2211, 800-362-6406;
www.atwoodlakeresort.com

This hilltop resort overlooking a lake provides a unique retreat. Each room has either a view of the lake or countryside. Boat rentals are available through the hotel, and harbor cruises are available through the nearby marina. Private airstrip, heliport. A Muskingum Watershed Conservancy District facility. 104 rooms. Restaurant, bar. Fitness center. Pool. Golf. Tennis. $61-150

★★HOLIDAY INN

131 Bluebell Drive S.w., New Philadelphia, 330-339-7731, 800-465-4329; www.holiday-inn.com
106 rooms. Restaurant, bar. Fitness center. Pool. Spa. Pets accepted. $61-150

NEWARK

See also Columbus, Lancaster, Mount Vernon
This industrial city on the Licking River attracts many visitors because of its large group of prehistoric mounds. Construction of the Ohio and Erie Canal began here on July 4, 1825, with Governor DeWitt Clinton of New York as the official groundbreaker and speaker. The Ohio Canal was then built north to Lake Erie and south to the Ohio River.

WHAT TO SEE
MOUNDBUILDERS STATE MEMORIAL

65 Messimer Drive, Newark, 740-344-1920, 800-600-7174
The Great Circle has walls from 8 to 14 feet high with burial mounds in the center. The museum contains Hopewell artifacts.
Museum: June-August, Wednesday-Sunday; September-October, Friday-Sunday. Park: April-October.

NEWARK EARTHWORKS

South 21st Street and Highway 79, Newark, 740-344-1920, 800-600-7174
This group of earthworks was originally one of the most extensive of its kind in the country, covering an area of more than four square miles. The Hopewell society used their geometric enclosures for social, religious and ceremonial purposes. Remaining portions of the Newark group are Octagon Earthworks and Wright Earthworks, with many artifacts of pottery, beadwork, copper, bone and shell exhibited at the nearby Moundbuilders Museum.

OCTAGON EARTHWORKS

North 30th Street, Newark, 740-344-1920, 800-600-7174
The octagon-shaped enclosure encircles 50 acres that include small mounds and is joined by parallel walls to a circular embankment.

WRIGHT EARTHWORKS

James and Waldo streets, Newark, 740-344-1920, 800-600-7174
One-acre earthworks have a 100-foot wall remnant, an important part of the original Newark group.

WHERE TO STAY
★★BUXTON INN

313 E. Broadway, Granville, 740-587-0001; www.buxtoninn.com
26 rooms. Restaurant. Complimentary breakfast. $61-150

★★CHERRY VALLEY LODGE
2299 Cherry Valley Road, Newark, 740-788-1200, 800-788-8008;
www.cherryvalleylodge.com
200 rooms. Restaurant, bar. Fitness center. Pool. Pets accepted. $151-250

WHERE TO EAT
★★BUXTON INN
313 E. Broadway, Granville, 740-587-0001; www.buxtoninn.com
American. Breakfast, lunch, dinner, brunch. $15 and under

★★CHERRY VALLEY LODGE SUNFLOWERS RESTAURANT
2299 Cherry Valley Road, Newark, 740-788-1200; www.cherryvalleylodge.com
American. Breakfast, lunch, dinner, brunch. Children's menu. Bar. $36-85

★DAMON'S
1486 Granville Road, Newark, 740-349-7427; www.damons.com
American. Lunch, dinner. Children's menu. Bar. $16-35

★NATOMA
10 N. Park, Newark, 740-345-7260; www.thenatoma.com
American, Steak. Lunch, dinner. Closed Sunday. Bar. $16-35

NILES

See also Akron
This southwestern Ohio town, located on the Mahoning River, was named in the 1840s for the editor of a Baltimore newspaper. The town has a stadium that hosts the Mahoning Valley Scrappers, the AA farm team for the Cleveland Indians.

WHERE TO EAT
★★★ALBERINI'S
1201 Youngstown-Warren Road, Niles, 330-652-5895; www.alberinis.com
Husband-wife team Richard and Gilda Alberini preside over this popular Italian restaurant. The restaurant has a cigar room and a pleasant, glass patio. Italian. Lunch, dinner. Closed Sunday. Reservations recommended. Bar. $16-35

OBERLIN

See also Cleveland
Oberlin College and the town were founded together. Oberlin was the first college to offer equal degrees to men and women and the first in the United States to adopt a policy against discrimination because of race. The central portion of the campus forms a six-acre public square, called Tappan Square, in the center of the town.

Charles Martin Hall, a young Oberlin graduate, discovered the electrolytic process of making aluminum in Oberlin. The Federal Aviation Agency maintains an Air Traffic Control Center here.

WHERE TO STAY
★★OBERLIN INN

7 N. Main St., Oberlin, 440-775-1111, 800-376-4173; www.oberlininn.com
67 rooms. Restaurant. Pets accepted. $61-150

OXFORD

See also Cincinnati, Hamilton, Mason

This small town exists primarily because of Miami University, which was founded here in 1809. The university was established following a land grant in 1792 from George Washington for a western college and was named after the Miami Indians who lived in the area. The campus is considered one of the most picturesque in the country, with almost all buildings built in the same brick neo-Georgian style. Miami has been called everything from a "public ivy" for its academic excellence to the "cradle of coaches" for its outstanding football program. Famous alumni include 23rd President Benjamin Harrison and Pittsburgh Steelers quarterback Ben Roethlisberger.

WHERE TO STAY
★BEST WESTERN SYCAMORE INN

6 E. Sycamore St., Oxford, 513-523-0000, 800-523-4678; www.bestwestern.com
61 rooms. Complimentary breakfast. Fitness center. Pool. $61-150

★HAMPTON INN

5056 College Corner Pike, Oxford, 513-524-0114, 800-426-7866;
www.hamptoninn.com
66 rooms. Complimentary breakfast. Business center. Fitness center. Pool. $61-150

★★HUESTON WOODS RESORT

5201 Lodge Road, College Corner, 513-664-3500, 800-282-7275;
www.huestonwoodsresort.com
92 rooms. Restaurant, bar. Fitness center. Pool. Golf. Tennis. $61-150

PAINESVILLE

See also Ashtabula, Cleveland

This northeastern Ohio town is located close to Cleveland and a short drive from Lake Erie beaches.

WHERE TO STAY
★★★RENAISSANCE QUAIL HOLLOW RESORT

11080 Concord Hambden Road, Painesville, 440-497-1100, 800-468-3571; www.
quailhollowresort.com

Located outside Cleveland, this resort has 36 holes of golf, a spa and many other onsite recreational facilities. The elegant dining room serves classically prepared dishes.
176 rooms. Restaurant, bar. Business center. Fitness center. Pool. Golf. Tennis. $61-150

WHERE TO EAT
★★RIDER'S INN
792 Mentor Ave., Painesville, 440-942-2742; www.ridersinn.com
Features fare from original 19th-century recipes.
American. Lunch, dinner, Sunday brunch. Outdoor seating. Children's menu.
Bar. $16-35

PORT CLINTON
See also Put-in-Bay, Sandusky, Toledo
This lakeshore town is the departure point for ferries to the Lake Erie islands.

WHERE TO STAY
★FAIRFIELD INN
3760 E. State Road, Port Clinton, 419-732-2434, 800-228-2800; www.fairfieldinn.com
64 rooms. Complimentary breakfast. Business center. Fitness center. Pool.
$61-150

WHERE TO EAT
★★GARDEN AT THE LIGHTHOUSE
226 E. Perry St., Port Clinton, 419-732-2151; www.gardenrestaurant.com
American. Dinner. Closed Sunday, September-May. Outdoor seating. Children's menu. Bar. $16-35

PORTSMOUTH
See also Chillicothe
Portsmouth is the leading firebrick and shoelace center of southern Ohio. At the confluence of the Ohio and Scioto rivers 100 miles east of Cincinnati, it is -connected to South Portsmouth, Kentucky, by bridge. The Boneyfiddle historic District in downtown Portsmouth includes many antique and specialty shops. Portsmouth was the childhood home of cowboy movie star Roy Rogers and baseball's Branch Rickey.

WHERE TO STAY
★★DAYS INN
3762 Highway 23, Portsmouth, 740-354-2851, 800-329-7466; www.daysinn.com
100 rooms. Restaurant, bar. Pool. Pets accepted. $61-150

★★RAMADA
711 Second St., Portsmouth, 740-354-7711, 800-272-6232; www.ramada.com
96 rooms. Restaurant. Complimentary breakfast. Fitness center. Pool. Pets accepted. $61-150

PUT-IN-BAY
See also Port Clinton, Sandusky
On South Bass Island in Lake Erie, this village is an all-year resort that can be reached by ferry from Port Clinton. The area claims the best smallmouth black bass fishing in America in spring and walleye and perch fishing at other

times of the year. In summer, the area teams with boaters who come here to party at the many bars and restaurants near the town's marina.

WHAT TO SEE
PERRY'S CAVE

979 Catawba Ave., Put-in-Bay, 419-285-2283; www.perryscave.com

Commodore Perry is rumored to have stored supplies here before the Battle of Lake Erie in 1813; later, prisoners were kept here for a short time. The cave is 52 feet below the surface and measures 208 feet by 165 feet; the temperature is 50 F. It has an underground stream that rises and falls with the level of Lake Erie. Picnic areas and a twenty-minute guided tour are available.

June-August, daily; March-May, September-November, Friday-Sunday; December-February, by appointment.

PERRY'S VICTORY AND INTERNATIONAL PEACE MEMORIAL

2 Bay View Ave., Put-in-Bay, 419-285-2184; www.nps.gov/pev

This Greek Doric granite column is 352 feet tall and commemorates Commodore Oliver Hazard Perry's 1813 victory over the British naval squadron at the Battle of Lake Erie, near Put-in-Bay. The United States gained control of the lake, preventing a British invasion. The 3,986-mile U.S.-Canadian boundary, which passes near here through the lake, is the longest unfortified border in the world. Children under 16 are only permitted with an adult.

May-mid-October, daily.

SANDUSKY

See also Port Clinton, Put-in-Bay, Sandusky

On a flat slope facing 18-mile-long Sandusky Bay, this town stretches for more than six miles along the waterfront. Originally explored by the French, the town was named by the Wyandot "Sandouske," meaning "at the cold water." When the amusement park Cedar Point opened here in 1870, Sandusky became a center for summertime tourism.

WHAT TO SEE
CEDAR POINT

1 Cedar Point Drive, Sandusky, 419-627-2350; www.cedarpoint.com

This amusement park consistently wins awards for its roller coasters; the park currently has 17. Other diversions include a variety of rides, live shows, restaurants, Soak City Water Park, Challenge Golf miniature golf course and the Cedar Point Grand Prix go-cart race track (additional fee). Price includes unlimited rides and attractions, except Challenge Park.

May-August, daily; September-October, Saturday-Sunday.

WHERE TO STAY
★★BEST WESTERN CEDAR POINT AREA

1530 Cleveland Road, Sandusky, 419-625-9234, 800-528-1234; www.bestwestern.com

103 rooms. Restaurant. Pool. $61-150

★FAIRFIELD INN
6220 Milan Road, Sandusky, 419-621-9500, 800-228-2800; www.fairfieldinn.com
88 rooms. Complimentary breakfast. Pool. $61-150

★★RIVERS EDGE INN
132 N. Main St., Huron, 419-433-8000, 800-947-3400;
65 rooms. Restaurant, bar. Complimentary breakfast. Fitness center. Pool.
Pets accepted. $61-150

WHERE TO EAT
★★BAY HARBOR INN
1 Cedar Point Drive, Sandusky, 419-625-6373; www.cedarpoint.com
Seafood. Dinner. October-April, closed Sunday. Children's menu. Bar.

SPRINGFIELD
See also Columbus, Dayton
Indian Scout Simon Kenton, an early settler, set up a gristmill and sawmill
on the present site of the Navistar International plant. His wife gave the village its name. When the National Pike came in 1839, Springfield came to be
known as the "town at the end of the National Pike."

Agricultural machinery gave Springfield its next boost. A farm journal,
Farm and Fireside, published in the 1880s by P. P. Mast, a cultivator-manu-
facturer, was the start of the Crowell-Collier Publishing Company. The 4-H
movement started here in 1902 by A. B. Graham and hybrid corn grown by
George H. Shull had its beginning in Springfield. A center for some 200
diversified industries, Springfield is in the rich agricultural valley of west
central Ohio.

WHERE TO STAY
★★COURTYARD SPRINGFIELD DOWNTOWN
100 S. Fountain Ave., Springfield, 937-322-3600, 800-321-2211; www.courtyard.com
120 rooms. Restaurant, bar. $61-150

WHERE TO EAT
★★CASEY'S
2205 Park Road, Springfield, 937-322-0397
American. Dinner. Closed Sunday. Bar. $16-35

STEUBENVILLE
See also New Philadelphia
In 1786, the fledgling U.S. government established a fort here and named it
for the Prussian Baron Friedrich von Steuben, who helped the colonies in the
Revolutionary War. It later became Steubenville.

Although its early industries were pottery, coal, wool, glass and ship-
building, the mills of Wheeling-Pittsburgh Steel and Weirton Steel started
Steubenville's economic growth. The town's most famous resident was Dean
Martin, who was born here as Dino Crocetti in 1917.

WHERE TO STAY
★★HOLIDAY INN
1401 University Blvd., Steubenville, 740-282-0901, 800-465-4329;
www.holiday-inn.com
100 rooms. Restaurant, bar. Pool. $61-150

TOLEDO
See also Lima, Port Clinton
The French first explored the Toledo area, at the mouth of the Maumee River
on Lake Erie, in 1615. Likely named after Toledo, Spain, the present city began as a group of small villages along the river. During the Toledo War in the
1830s, it was claimed by both Michigan and Ohio, which resulted in Toledo
becoming part of Ohio and the Northern Peninsula going to Michigan.

Toledo's large, natural harbor makes it an important port. Railroads move
coal and ore to the South, East and North through the city; grain from the
Southwest; steel from Cleveland and Pittsburgh and automobile parts and
accessories to and from Detroit.

Edward Libbey introduced the glass industry to Toledo in 1888, with high-
grade crystal and lamp globes. Michael Owens, a glassblower, joined him
and invented a machine that turned molten glass into bottles by the thousands. Today, Owens-Illinois, Libbey-Owens-Ford, Owens-Corning Fiber-
glas and Johns Manville Fiber Glass manufacture a variety of glass products.
Metropolitan Toledo has more than 1,000 manufacturing plants producing
Jeeps, spark plugs, chemicals and other products.

WHAT TO SEE
TOLEDO BOTANICAL GARDEN
5403 Elmer Drive, Toledo, 419-936-2986; www.toledogarden.org
This garden has seasonal floral displays; herb, rhododendron and azalea gardens, perennial garden, rose garden, fragrance garden for the visually and
physically impaired. Pioneer homestead 1837; art galleries, glassblowing
studios. Gift shops. Special musical and crafts programs throughout year.
Daily.

TOLEDO MUSEUM OF ART
2445 Monroe St., Toledo, 419-255-8000; www.toledomuseum.com
Considered to be one of the finest art museums in the country, this museum
has collections from ancient Egypt, Greece and Rome through the Middle
Ages and the Renaissance to European and American arts of the present.
Included are glass collections, paintings, sculptures, decorative and graphic
arts; Egyptian mummy, medieval cloister, French chateau room and African
sculpture. Art reference library; café; museum store are also present.
Tuesday-Sunday.

TOLEDO SYMPHONY
1838 Parkwood Ave., Toledo, 419-246-8000, 800-348-1253; www.toledosymphony.com
This symphony presents classical, pop, casual, chamber and all-Mozart concerts. Performances at different locations.
Mid-September-May.

TOLEDO ZOO
2700 Broadway, Toledo, 419-385-5721; www.toledozoo.org
On display are nearly 2,000 specimens of 400 species. The zoo has fresh and
saltwater aquariums, a large mammal collection, reptiles, birds, a children's
zoo, botanical gardens and a greenhouse.
Daily.

WHERE TO STAY
★★CLARION HOTEL WESTGATE
3536 Secor Road, Toledo, 419-535-7070, 800-424-6423; www.clarionhotel.com
305 rooms. Restaurant, bar. Business center. Fitness center. Pool. $61-150

★★COURTYARD TOLEDO AIRPORT HOLLAND
1435 E. Mall Drive, Holland, 419-866-1001, 800-228-9290; www.courtyard.com
149 rooms. Restaurant, bar. Fitness center. Pool. $61-150

★★★HILTON TOLEDO
3100 Glendale Ave., Toledo, 419-381-6800, 800-445-8667; www.hilton.com
Situated on the campus of the Medical College of Ohio, this hotel offers easy
access to nearby attractions. A fitness center, tennis courts, pool and a jogging track are available.
212 rooms. Restaurant, bar. Business center. Fitness center. Pool. Tennis.
$61-150

WHERE TO EAT
★★★FIFI'S
1423 Bernath Parkway, Toledo, 419-866-6777; www.fifisrestaurant.com
Fifi's offers a wide array of regional and traditional dishes prepared with a
creative flair. House specialties are soups, such as traditional vichyssoise or
gourmet fruit soups served as dessert.
French. Dinner. Closed Sunday. Bar. $36-85

★★MANCY'S
953 Phillips Ave., Toledo, 419-476-4154; www.mancys.com
Seafood, steak. Lunch, dinner. Closed Sunday. Bar. $16-35

★TONY PACKO'S CAFE
1902 Front St., Toledo, 419-691-6054; www.tonypackos.com
Hungarian. Lunch, dinner. Children's menu. Bar. $16-35

VERMILION
See also Oberlin, Sandusky
Perched on the shore of Lake Erie between Cleveland and Toledo, this small
town is popular with summer boaters and vacationers alike.

WHERE TO EAT
★★★CHEZ FRANÇOIS
555 Main St., Vermilion, 440-967-0630; www.chezfrancois.com
Located in a small, Lake Erie harbor town, this French restaurant has a for-

mal dining room and a more casual, outdoor dining area with a view of the Vermilion River.

French. Dinner. Closed Monday; also January-mid-March. Outdoor seating. Jacket required. $36-85

WAPAKONETA

See also Lima

This small northwest Ohio town is the birthplace of astronaut Neil Armstrong, the first man to set foot on the moon. A museum dedicated to space exploration and named in his honor is located here.

WHAT TO SEE
NEIL ARMSTRONG AIR AND SPACE MUSEUM

500 S. Apollo Drive, Wapakoneta, 419-738-8811;
www.ohsweb.ohiohistory.org/places/nw01/index.shtml

This museum displays everything from early planes to spacecraft, showing aerospace accomplishments; audiovisual presentation; and other exhibits. Tuesday-Sunday.

WHERE TO STAY
★★COMFORT INN SUITES

1510 Saturn Drive, Wapakoneta, 419-738-8181, 800-528-1234

94 rooms. Restaurant, bar. Complimentary breakfast. Fitness center. Pool. Pets accepted. $61-150

WARREN

See also Aurora, Kent

In 1800, Warren became the seat of the Western Reserve and then the seat of newly formed Trumbull County. At one of its stagecoach inns, the Austin house, Stephen Collins Foster is said to have begun writing *Jeannie with the Light Brown Hair*. According to local lore, while walking along the Mahoning River, Foster found the inspiration for *My Old Kentucky home*.

WHERE TO STAY
★COMFORT INN

136 N. Park Ave., Warren, 330-393-1200, 800-424-6423; www.comfortinn.com

54 rooms. Complimentary breakfast. Fitness center. Pets accepted. $61-150

★★★AVALON INN RESORT AND CONFERENCE CENTER

9519 E. Market St., Warren, 330-856-1900, 800-828-2566; www.avaloninn.com

Rooms at this inn are decorated in a colonial style. The resort offers 36 holes of golf, an Olympic-sized pool, and tennis, raquetball and volleyball courts. 136 rooms. Restaurant, bar. Complimentary breakfast. Fitness center. Pool. Pets accepted. $61-150

WOOSTER

See also Akron, Canton

Wooster claims to have had one of the first Christmas trees in America, introduced in 1847 by August Imgard, a young German immigrant. Disappointed with American Christmas, he cut down and decorated a spruce tree, which so pleased his neighbors that the custom spread throughout Ohio and the nation.

The town is located in farm country and near Amish communities. The College of Wooster, a small liberal arts school, is located here.

WHERE TO STAY
★★★WOOSTER INN

801 E. Wayne Ave., Wooster, 330-263-2660; woosterinn.wooster.edu

It seems impossible, but it's true: This college-owned hotel offers more than dorm-style service. The Wooster Inn is a quaint country inn with comfortable rooms and Colonial décor.

15 rooms. Closed early January. Restaurant. Pets accepted. Golf. $151-250

WHERE TO EAT
★★TJ'S

359 W. Liberty St., Wooster, 330-264-6263; www.tjsrestaurants.com

American. Lunch, dinner. Closed Sunday. Children's menu. $16-35

★★★WOOSTER INN

801 E. Wayne Ave., Wooster, 330-263-2660; woosterinn.wooster.edu

Dinner at this inn is served in the main dining room, which overlooks a nine-hole golf course and driving range. In the fall, there is a guest chef series.
American. Lunch, dinner, Sunday brunch. Closed Monday; also early January. $16-35

YOUNGSTOWN

See also Kent, Akron

Youngstown, located five miles from the Pennsylvania line, is the largest city in Ohio's southwestern coal mining and steel manufacturing region. This is not an area known for its tourism, but it is prominent for its role in the production of goods from clothing to lightbulbs.

Youngstown's steel history started in 1803, with a crude-iron smelter. The first coal mine began operating in the valley in 1826; in 1892, the first valley steel plant, Union Iron and Steel Company, opened.

WHAT TO SEE
MILL CREEK PARK

7574 Columbiana-Canfield Road, Canfield, 330-702-3000;

www.millcreekmetroparks.com

This park has more than 3,200 acres of gorges, ravines and rolling hills from the Mahoning River to south of highway 224. A Western Reserve pioneer woolen mill is now the Pioneer Pavilion used for picnics and dancing.
May-October, Tuesday-Sunday; April and November, Saturday-Sunday.

WHERE TO STAY
★★BEST WESTERN MEANDER INN
870 N. Canfield Niles Road, Youngstown, 330-544-2378, 800-937-8376;
www.bestwestern.com
57 rooms. Restaurant, bar. Complimentary breakfast. Pool. Pets accepted.
$61-150

★QUALITY INN
4055 Belmont Ave., Youngstown, 330-759-3180, 800-221-2222; www.qualityinn.com
149 rooms. Restaurant, bar. Complimentary breakfast. Pool. $61-150

ZANESVILLE
See also Cambridge, Newark
Ebenezer Zane, surveyor of Zane's Trace through the dense Ohio forests
and great-great-grandfather of Zane Grey, writer of Western novels, selected
Zanesville's site at the junction of the Muskingum and Licking Rivers. First
called Westbourne, it was the state capital from 1810 to 1812.

Today, beautiful pottery is made here, as well as transformers and automobile components. The "Y" Bridge, which a person can cross and still remain
on the same side of the river from which he started, divides the city into three
parts.

WHERE TO STAY
★COMFORT INN
500 Monroe St., Zanesville, 740-454-4144, 800-424-6423; www.comfortinn.com
93 rooms. Complimentary breakfast. Fitness center. Pool. Pets accepted.
$61-150

★★HOLIDAY INN
4645 E. Pike, Zanesville, 740-453-0771, 800-465-4329; www.holiday-inn.com
130 rooms. Restaurant, bar. Fitness center. Pool. Pets accepted. $61-150

INDEX

CHICAGO O'HARE AIRPORT, IL, 75

★★★★★ INDEX

189

G

GALENA, IL, *82*
Backstreet Steak & Chophouse, *83*
Belvedere Mansion, *82*
Best Western Quiet House & Suites, *83*
Country Inn & Suites, *83*
Desoto House Hotel, *83*
Dowling House, *82*
Eagle Ridge Resort and Spa, *83*
Grace Episcopal Church, *83*
Log Cabin, *83*
Ramada Galena, *83*
Ulysses S. Grant Home State Historic Site, *83*
Woodlands Restaurant, *84*

GALESBURG, IL, *84*
Best Western Prairie Inn, *84*
Carl Sandburg State Historic Site, *84*
Lake Storey Recreational Area, *84*
Landmark Cafe & Creperie, *84*
Packinghouse, *84*
Ramada Inn, *84*

GARY, IN, *123*
Courtyard Goshen, *123*
Miller Bakery Cafe, *123*

GENEVA, IL, *84*
Atwater's, *85*
Festival of the Vine, *85*
Garfield Farm and Inn Museum, *85*
Herrington Inn, *85*
Mill Race Inn, *86*
Swedish Days, *85*
Wheeler Park, *85*

GLENVIEW, IL, *86*
Civil War Living History Days, *86*

Grove National Historic Landmark, *86*
Periyali Greek Taverna, *86*
Summer Festival, *86*

GOSHEN, IN, *123*
Essenhaus Inn and Conference Center, *123*

GRANVILLE, OH, *167*
Buxton Inn Dining Room, *167*

GREENCASTLE, IN, *124*
Different Drummer, *124*
Walden Inn, *124*

H

HAMMOND, IN, *124*
Best Western Northwest Indiana Inn, *124*
Cafe Elise, *124*

HIGHLAND PARK, IL, *86*
Cafe Central, *87*
Carlos, *87*
Del Rio, *87*
Francis Stupey Log Cabin, *87*
Froggy's, *87*
Gabriel's, *88*
Highwood, *87*
Ravinia Festival, *87*

HOMEWOOD, IL, *88*
Aurelio's Pizza, *88*

I

INDIANAPOLIS, IN, *124*
Aristocrat Pub, *129*
Cafe Patachou, *129*
Canterbury Hotel, *127*
Chanteclair, *129*
Children's Museum of Indianapolis, *125*

Wolf Park, *132*

M

★
★
★ INDEX
★
★

199

ILLINOIS

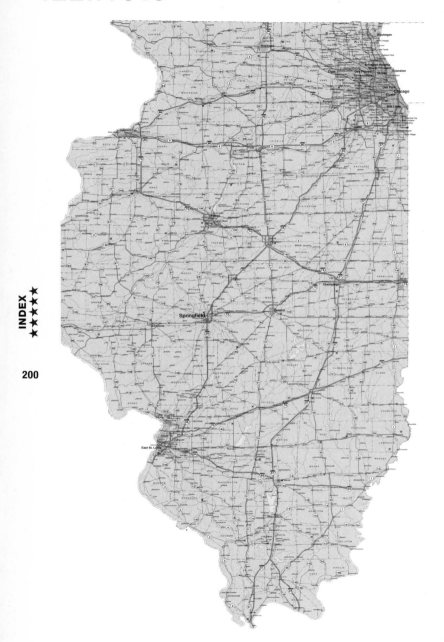

CHICAGO

INDIANA

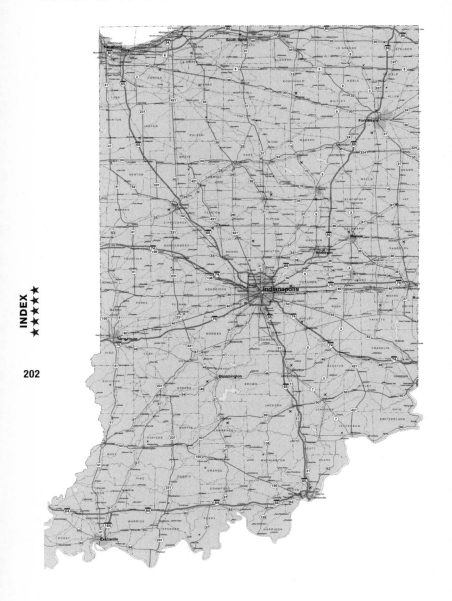

INDIANAPOLIS

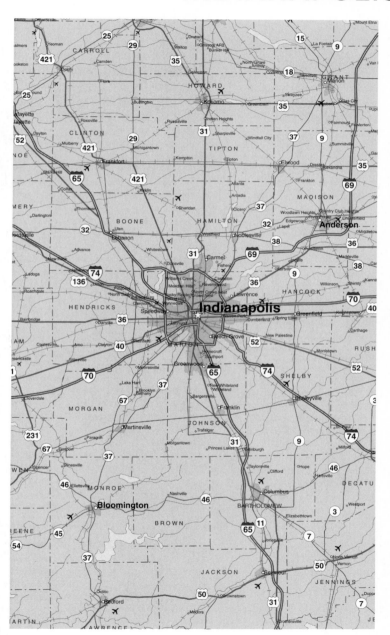

OHIO

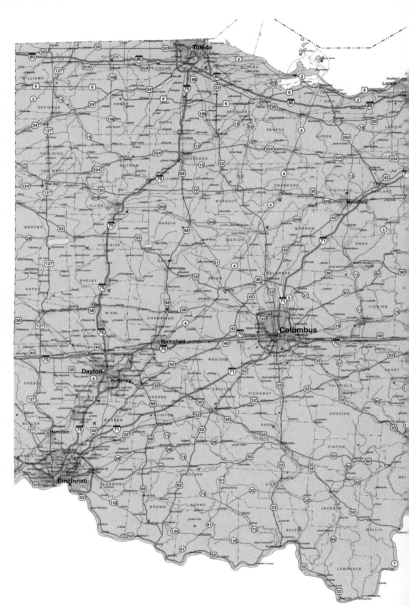

CINCINNATI AND DAYTON

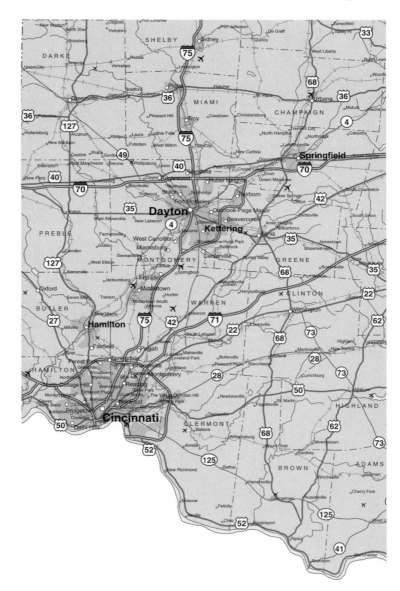

COLUMBUS

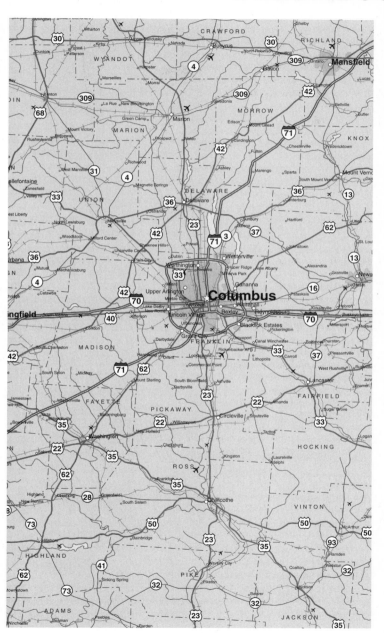

NOTES